Struggle for Freedom

Struggle for Freedom

HISTORY OF THE
PHILIPPINE INDEPENDENT CHURCH

BY *Lewis Bliss Whittemore*

GREENWICH · CONNECTICUT

First published in 1961
by Seabury Press, Greenwich, Connecticut
and
S.P.C.K., London, England

TO MY WIFE
Helen Crawford Whittemore
WITHOUT WHOSE VALIANT SUPPORT
AND CONSTANT ENCOURAGEMENT
THIS BOOK WOULD NEVER
HAVE BEEN WRITTEN

Preface

The General Convention of 1961 will be asked to consider a Concordat with the Philippine Independent Church which will provide for full intercommunion of this large body of Christians with the Episcopal Church in the United States. In order to approach the study of a Concordat intelligently, it seemed wise to make available to our clergy and lay people materials necessary to an understanding of the religious revolution which has been taking place in the Philippine Islands for over sixty years.

The first aim of this book, then, is to inform our own Church about our brethren in the Far East with whom we have been working so closely. The second purpose of this study is to give to the Philippine Independent Church itself a better perspective of its own function as a national Church, both Catholic and Reformed, in a land where an indigenous Church is of such vital importance to the welfare of the country.

The Philippine Independent Church emerged out of a welter of political and religious change. Therefore, much of the material is inevitably controversial. It is my hope that, in dealing with this material, I have acted in Christian charity and that I have kept always before me the greater good of the gallant people of the Philippines. However, it has been necessary to set the record straight in several matters and flatly to contradict some prevailing opinions. If in so doing, I appear to be entering the lists in argument or debate, I ask that the reader remember that truth is not always found in pleasant paths, and that one must sometimes risk greatly in order that God's greater glory may be served.

Lewis Bliss Whittemore

Acknowledgments

I am deeply indebted to many people for their help in preparing this book. The Rt. Rev. Lyman C. Ogilby D.D., Bishop of the Philippine Episcopal Church, Mrs. Ogilby and the entire staff of clergy and co-workers extended the most gracious hospitality to me and Mrs. Whittemore when we were in the Philippines during the winter of 1959-1960. Bishop Ogilby gave me the benefit of his advice and counsel and also aided in a very practical way by putting the diocesan car with Romuldo as the expert driver, at my disposal. I was grateful that he allowed his Suffragan, Bishop Benito Cabanban D.D. to accompany me in all of my journeys by car and airplane. This proved to be of the utmost assistance. The Very Rev. Wayland S. Mandell S.T.D., Dean of St. Andrew's Theological Seminary, advised with me as did the Rev. Conrad W. Myrick and the Rev. Walter R. Foster of the faculty. These men were also good enough to read and criticize the manuscript. The Rev. Richard L. Rising, until recently Dean of the Cathedral in Queson City, also read the manuscript and made helpful suggestions.

A number of bishops of the Episcopal Church have encouraged me with their sympathy and understanding. These include the Rt. Rev. Stephen F. Bayne Jr., S.T.D., the Executive Officer of the Anglican Communion; the Rt. Rev. Robert F. Gibson, D.D., Bishop of Virginia; the Rt. Rev. Harry S. Kennedy, D.D., Bishop of Honolulu; the Rt. Rev. Thomas F. Wright, D.D., Bishop of East Carolina; the Rt. Rev. Malcolm E. Peabody, D.D., Retired Bishop of Central New York; the Rt. Rev. John B. Bentley, D.D. Vice-President of the National Council and Director of its Overseas Department; and also the late Rt. Rev. Norman S. Binsted, D.D., formerly Bishop of the Philippine Episcopal Church. I am also greatly indebted to Dr. Albert C. Jacobs, President of Trinity College, and to Mr. Donald B. Engley, Librarian, for placing the resources of the excellent Trinity

College Library at my disposal. The Rt. Rev. Walter M. Higley, S.T.D., graciously allowed me to use the library of his diocesan house in Syracuse while completing the manuscript, and I thank him and all of his staff for many acts of kindness. Last, but by no means least, I have had the important and constant support of the Rt. Rev. Arthur C. Lichtenberger, D.D., the Presiding Bishop of the Episcopal Church.

My debt of gratitude to the Philippine Independent Church is great indeed. I cannot adequately thank its Supreme Bishop, the Rt. Rev. Isabelo de los Reyes, Jr., for his hospitality and for that of the bishops of the Church whose dioceses I visited. Bishop de los Reyes has given constant cooperation and has furnished invaluable resource material. In addition he has been good enough to read and criticize the completed manuscript. The Rt. Rev. Manuel L. Legasca, Secretary General of the Philippine Independent Church, accompanied Bishop Cabanban and me on many of our journeys and added greatly to their value. His writings, also, have given me needed resource material.

I have made several attempts to locate Francis H. Wise from whose Master's thesis I have quoted liberally. In each case my letters have been returned. I wish it were possible to express my indebtedness to him personally.

To all of these, and to many others whom I might mention, I give my heartfelt thanks.

LEWIS BLISS WHITTEMORE

St. James' Church
Greenfield, Massachusetts
March, 1961

Contents

	Preface	vii
	Acknowledgments	ix
I	A General Perspective	1
II	The Philippines before the Arrival of the Spaniards	13
III	Friar Rule	23
IV	A Going in the Tops of the Mulberry Trees	33
V	The Great Martyr	41
VI	Revolution	52
VII	Vicario General Castrense	63
VIII	The Birth of the Philippine Independent Church	79
IX	Aglipay Makes a Decision	92
X	Religious Reformation in the Philippines	105
XI	Popular Success and Legal Failure	125
XII	Theological Pains	136
XIII	The End of an Era	152
XIV	Port after the Storm	166
XV	The Roman Catholic Church in The Philippines Today	182
XVI	Struggle for Religious Freedom	199
	Appendix	217
	Notes	219
	Index	225

Chapter 1

A General Perspective

It is said that distance lends enchantment. It is also true that sometimes interest in an area decreases in exact proportion to its remoteness. The fate of South America appears of vital concern because that continent is nearby, but what transpires in southeast Asia does not stir our imagination to a similar extent. The happenings ten thousand miles away seem of small importance compared with an approaching local election. Actually there is no near or far, and we are slowly learning that the events in this part of the world affect us vitally indeed, and that in it the Republic of the Philippines occupies a strategic position.

The United States, therefore, has more than a sentimental interest in the fate of the new Philippine Republic. The sentimental interest, however, is very strong. For nearly half a century we gave the best we had to a people who had emerged from three centuries of feudalism. The roll of American governors, administrators, teachers, and engineers is a distinguished one. One of our presidents was the first Governor General. The caliber of these men was a revelation to the Filipinos. Our army won the war, but these men won the hearts of the Filipino people. Some day there will come a recognition of the devoted service of American men and women who loved the Philippines and believed in its destiny. In the war with Japan American and Filipino soldiers fought and died side by side, experiencing that wonderful comradeship which comes to men who share peril and suffering. The Filipinos are truly our friends.

But our interest in this new nation rests on more than senti-ment. We do not fully realize the power of this country, both actual and potential. Hayden, in his authoritative book *The Philippines,* writes as follows:

"The national stature of the Philippines is more evident where the population of the Commonwealth is compared with that of other countries. In Europe only the "great powers" (Great Britain, France, Germany, Italy, Russia and Spain) and Poland have more inhabitants. The Philippines is more than twice as populous as Sweden, Belgium, The Netherlands or Greece. More people live in Spain's former Asiatic colony than in any country in the Western Hemisphere ex-cept the United States, Brazil and Mexico; more than three times as many as reside in any Latin-American State save the two mentioned and the Argentine Republic. . . . The combined population of the British Commonwealths in the South Pacific, Australia and New Zealand is only slightly greater than one half of the Philippines." [1]

Hayden goes on to state that this country with huge unde-veloped resources could support as many as 51,000,000 people. That it will do so is indicated by its rate of growth up to the pres-ent time. When the Spaniards arrived in 1521 there were less than one million inhabitants. When the United States occupied the Islands the population had grown to over 7,000,000. In the less than half century of American control the population more than trebled. At this writing it numbers about 22,000,000. [2]

In 1946 the Philippines became an independent Republic with democratic institutions like our own. We have more than a nos-talgic interest in seeing it survive because what happens there will affect not only its own fortunes but will influence the whole of Southeast Asia. There, too, small nations are struggling to stand before the menace of Communist China. Australia and New Zealand are in the path of this threatened inundation. If the Phil-ippines topples, other nations striving to achieve a viable economy on a democratic basis will fall as well. The fall of the Philippines would be a tremendous victory for Communism and a corres-ponding defeat for the United States of America.

In estimating the political capacity of the Filipino people, one should note the leadership which is already being exercised by able representatives of this nation. It was the great speech by Romulo at the Bandung Conference which turned the tide against Communist China at that meeting. Its repercussions echoed around the world. Everyone should read his *Crusade in Asia* where he tells the story of Magsaysay's fight against the Communist Huks on the Island of Luzon. A country which can produce men like Rizal, Queson, Osmena Magsaysay, and Romulo—to mention but a few—is fully capable of speaking in world councils, and is already doing so.

So it is not only a superficial feeling which binds us to the Philippines. This nation is a Christian and democratic outpost in a vital sector of the battle line. Putting it baldly, we cannot afford to see the Philippines fail. Our national interests to no slight degree are bound together.

The issues affecting the outcome in the Philippines are not limited to naval protection, favorable trade arrangements, and government loans. There is a spiritual element involved. Toynbee says somewhere that the ultimate issues confronting mankind are religious. The final divisions are in the sphere of men's deepest convictions about the meaning of life. That is why we cannot help another country until we understand, insofar as possible, its deepest culture and innermost motivations. We must, therefore, speak of the religious side of the picture in the Philippine Islands, if we would understand its deepest problem.

Religiously, the situation in the Philippines is unique. Here we find the only nation in the Far East which is nominally Christian. With the exception of the Igorots of northern Luzon and the Mohammedans along the south coast of Mindanao, the Spanish friars won the great mass of the Filipino people to the Christian faith. This is a matter of world-wide significance, for alone among the peoples of that great area the Filipinos have a natural disposition to the West. No one will deny the contribution which Spain and the Spanish Church made to the Islands. In the long perspective of history a much fairer estimate of the total Spanish occupation is being given. But the other side of the picture is

dark indeed, because the great orders of friars sent from Spain
became a state within a state. For a hundred years these men
worked with selfless zeal and, to the end, there were many
good men among them. As the great orders gained wealth and
land, their power increased so that they were in a position to defy
the Spanish king, the governors general, the secular archbishops,
and even the pope. They dominated the civil authorities in each
municipality and province; and under the system as it developed
there were incredible abuses which are not exaggerated in the
novels of Rizal and the writings of many others.

The Filipinos who for centuries had been given a bad press in
the world court of public opinion, with but little chance to present their side of the case, decided that decent self respect compelled them to rebel. This will be discussed at greater length in
later chapters; yet it can truly be said that if our own Revolution
was justified, that of the Philippines had a ten-fold justification.
If George the Third was stupid, Spain had been incredibly more
stupid and over a much greater length of time.

Because the motives of the Filipino leaders were both political
and religious, the results were twofold. One result was the even-
tual acquirement of political freedom. The second was the appearance of a reformation Church the success of which is essential to the well-being of the democracy of which it is a part. Born
three hundred years after the Reformation in Western Europe
the Philippine Independent Church was the product of essentially the same causes. Its history is most similar to that of the
English Church in that, while breaking with the pope, it
still retained the substance and many of the old forms of the ancient faith. Its present membership is estimated to be between
1,500,000 and 2,000,000 people; thus it is an important part of the
body politic.

Hence, in studying the religious situation in the Philippines
we are confronted not by the problem of a Christian Church in
the midst of an alien culture, but by divisions within the Christian
Church itself. All the Reformation problems come to a focus
here and we must consider afresh the claims of the Reformation

and the attitude of Rome as both strive to witness to the Gospel of Christ.

We of the Reformation heritage have no quarrel with the great religious emphases of the Roman Church. This Church has been, and is, one of the great bulwarks of the Christian faith. It is a part of the world picture. All the non-Roman Churches of the West have their roots in this "church of the ages," and they owe much to its sturdy witness to the great verities. Paul Tillich, one of the greatest of the non-Roman theologian-philosophers, writes of it as follows:

"The (Roman) Catholic Church . . . has manifestly been able to preserve a genuine substance that continues to exist, although it is encased in an ever-hardening crust. But whenever the hardness and the crust are broken through and substance becomes visible, it exercises a peculiar fascination; then we see what was once the life substance of us all and what we have now lost, and a deep yearning awakens in us for the departed youth of our culture." [3]

Within the "hard crust" of which Tillich speaks there does exist a genuine piety. The Church has produced, and is still producing, saints and martyrs. The catalog of its various contributions to human life would be endless. In spite of this the Roman Church is a "riddle" as it has been aptly called by Pelikan.[4] It is still the Roman Church which boasts that it is "semper eadem"—always the same. To know its real attitude one must not listen to the utterances of individual bishops, no matter how distinguished; one must study the official doctrines of the Church. The ideal of this Church is the Roman Catholic state as embodied in a one-sided interpretation of Augustine's "City of God." [5] In this state the hierarchy rules; and while there are the "two swords," the spiritual sword dominates the civil. This Church has never rescinded the *Syllabus Errorum* published in 1864 during the pontificate of Pope Pius IX. In this syllabus "the Church was defending the traditional doctrine against the progress of what were called modern ideas of liberty—that is the independence of religious authority shown by secular societies, liberty of conscience, the equality of all religious confessions before the State, etc." [6] It was under this same pope, who had made his belief in Church domination so plain and who condemned the separation of Church and State, that the Vatican Council met in 1870. In addition to proclaiming the infallibility of the pope, this Council made many of the condemnations of the Syllabus of Errors its own in its dogmatic constitution *De Fide Catholica.* Thus it ranged itself squarely on the side of reaction. Here we have the real position of the Roman Church in its attitude toward the fundamental tenets of democracy.

The fact of the matter is that Roman Catholicism, in throwing up bulwarks against all phases of modernity, whether legitimate or not, is losing its universal appeal to the minds of men. In striving so desperately to maintain its identity it is losing its catholicity. By and large it is losing ground as many are coming to consider it an anachronism not relevant to modern needs. As Pelikan says, "Separated from Protestantism and isolated from modern culture, Rome still claims to be universal though the only way to recover universality is by acknowledging some sort of validity both in Protestantism and in modern culture." [7] Rome is becoming a weaker and weaker defense against the inroads of alien and naturalistic ideologies.

Here and there one can detect stirrings of heart and conscience within this great body, and nowhere is this more evident than in the United States. In this country it is still a minority church in a land where there is complete freedom of worship. Roman Catholic laymen, therefore, are in close and intimate contact with great numbers of citizens who are not of the same persuasion. They live on the same streets as neighbors and friends. They do business together and belong to the same clubs. The spirit of the religious liberty of free men has penetrated through the great body of intelligent laity. There is some evidence that this spirit is not entirely absent from some sections of the clergy. When the pope orders that Roman Catholics shall not belong to certain luncheon clubs, Catholic laymen rise in rebellion. In presidential elections prominent Roman Catholic laymen and laywomen assert principles which are not in accord with the official position of the hierarchy. They declare that they believe in the separation of Church and State; they want religious freedom with equal spiritual rights for all. When the Roman Catholic candidate for President declares that he will not be controlled by Rome, we believe him. If the "hard crust" of which Tillich speaks is to be broken, this will happen when the great mass of the Roman Catholic laity in the United States assert their influence. Already the big drums of the hierarchy are muffled on this side of the Atlantic. Eminent bishops and leading theologians speak softly about the official claims of Rome. This may mean much or little. At least it is a portent, and the reason is that American Catholics are beginning to realize that their church is caught in an official position which is out of touch with the realities of the modern world. Strangely enough the Roman Church is prospering here more than in most countries because the ancient drums have been muffled and it is bearing true witness to the verities of the Christian faith.

Take the Roman Church out of the American context and things are different. Even during the election of 1960 the American bishops in Puerto Rico spoke with a very different voice. In that country the Roman Church has a nominal majority, and it takes the position that the people must be told what to do and that it is a sin if they disobey. In later chapters we shall see how reminiscent this is of the attitude of the Spanish friars before the American advent in the Philippines. They too, after three hundred years in which the education of the people was in their hands, claimed that the Filipinos were too ignorant to make up their minds about public questions.

The Roman Catholic Church in the Philippines was granted a new lease on life with the coming of America. Separation of Church and State gave it a legal status and restored its properties. In the presence of competition, however distasteful, it awoke from its lethargy of the centuries. It has improved its educational work, modernized its seminaries to a certain extent, appointed native bishops, and in other ways has shown new life. If this were all, there could be no quarrel. Everyone recognizes that the Roman Church is in the Philippines to stay. It should stay. But, unfortunately, the leaders, dominated by the powerful religious orders, take their cue from the Vatican Council of 1870. They want a Roman Catholic State. If they cannot get that, they want to dominate legislation as much as possible. Freedom of worship, now guaranteed by the Constitution, gives them real distress and they see no place for non-Roman communions in the Philippines. Their antagonism is directed with especial venom against the Philippine Independent Church which is by far the largest reformed Catholic body in the Philippines. As an ally of this communion the Episcopal Church is also in the direct line of fire. The fact that a full dress attack is being made upon both Churches at the present time is evidence of their deep concern and fear.

In its religious life the Philippine Republic needs the witness of a powerful Reformation Church which will offer to a catholic minded people an alternative to Roman Catholicism and thus redress the balance which is lacking. The need for this redress has been felt for a long time. José Rizal once said to Gregorio Aglipay that he hoped that the latter would do for the Philippines religiously what he, Rizal, hoped to do politically. The Philippine Independent Church which looks upon the great martyr as a saint, is the embodiment of that aspiration. One can catch something of the spirit of this movement by reading a part of an utterance of this same Gregorio Aglipay who became its first bishop. This is to be found in the sixth of a series of "Fundamental Epistles" which were sent to the clergy and people of this Church in the very early days. It reads, in part, as follows:

"It (the Independent Church) has not been formed solely because of the human question of curates and bishops,[8] but for the imperious necessity of re-establishing in all its splendor the worship of the one true God and the purity of the sacred doctrines of Jesus Christ contained in the New Testament, redeeming consciences from all error, from the oppressive nets of simony and from all exaggeration and anti-scientific scruple against the laws of nature and against sane, free judgment.

Man has come forth perfect from the omnipotent and generous hands of God like all of his admirable work, and consequently with all his rights. He was born free like the bird that sings in the boughs of the trees, like the plant which sweetens the valleys with the perfume of its flowers, like the stars and all other creatures. Liberty! One only knows its value when it is lost; one can only love it in the sad obscurity of the prison.

A free man is the complete man, respected, of advanced sentiments, dignified, honored, accompanied by all his rights and his unavoidable duties as well; but a man, who by his own will makes himself a slave, is of a vile heart, one who fawns, (is) deceitful, slow—an object of pity.

We were born with the right to think freely and to express our sentiments according to the light of the reason which God has given us; we are born with the right to associate ourselves with those whom we choose in order to achieve our perfection and to obtain our necessities; we are born with the right to govern our person, our family, home and native town; we are born with the right to do freely what we please provided that we do not usurp the liberty or the rights of others . . .

Liberty is one of the most precious gifts with which God has favored us, and we can give it no more limits than those imposed by that most pure and right conscience (which God) has placed in all things."

No one can read this pronouncement without being impressed by its sincerity and its genuine religious feeling. Our ancestors would have understood it perfectly. We understand it because it breathes a universal aspiraton of the human heart; it expresses the desire for freedom—personal, religious and political—freedom in the fear of God. Understanding this we understand something at the very heart of the Philippine Independent Church.

This book attempts to give the general reader an idea of the background and history of this remarkable Christian movement, and to place it, in so far as possible, in its religious and national setting. However, something of its state and attitude may be gathered at the outset from a recent article by its present Supreme Bishop, the devoted and brilliant Isabelo de los Reyes. After saying that the young nations of Asia had discovered that their newly acquired freedom was not the key to Utopia, he writes:

"The people of the Philippines, and particularly the religious leaders of the Philippine Independent Church, had long before learned that political independence can easily be the liberty to starve and that full nationhood can only be enjoyed by virile peoples through democratic institutions, education, increased purchasing power and higher standards of living, of knowing and of worshipping.

The Philippine Independent Church is today the poor Filipino Church and will always cherish and maintain its integrity and independence. Its estimated two million faithful take pride in the record of their fathers in laying the foundation of the largest non-Roman Christian Church in Asia, and are fully persuaded that their church's mission—the salvation of souls—is not only theirs or belonging to Americans, Romans or Spaniards, but Christ's. With such conviction the *Iglesia Filipina Independiente* is not reluctant to receive—but welcomes—the generous help of the American Episcopal Church in training our divinity students at St. Andrew's Seminary near Manila where, today, something like fifty of our best young men are undertaking excellent training for the priesthood.

The demand from all parts of the Philippines for St. Andrew's graduates is so great that one of the main sorrows of our bishops is that it so much exceeds the available supply. Such demand is no surprise when the record of accomplishments by the new priests is examined. Wherever one of these new priests is assigned, in a matter of short months a new cement parish church replaces the former dilapidated wooden structure; the congregation becomes aglow with religious fervor, and the local intelligentsia soon join the church with religious enthusiasm springing not only from religious nationalism but from a deeper appreciation of Christ's Gospel . . .

In one way or another each generation has its fight for truth and progress in the conditions of its time. Not everything has been easy sailing for the Filipino Church in its search for better trained priests, better methods of organization, and better ways for effective pastoral work and action. We agree with I.S.S. Malelu of India that foreign subsidies flowing in too freely may foster a sense of irresponsibility, but we also know that our meager resources are the main stumbling block to our earnest endeavors . . .

In the Philippines where today almost a million pagans and Muslims have never heard of the Lord Jesus, the Filipino Church has taken determined steps to convert to Christianity the Negritos of Zambales, the Moros of Mindanao, the Tinguianes of Isabela, the Mangyans of Mindoro and the Itas of Palawan. So far several congregations of Moros, Negritos, and Itas have been organized with patience, constant preaching, and the aid of God.

Not long ago the Rev. Timoteo P. Quintero, a graduate of St. Andrew's Seminary, left the Philippines to plant the Filipino Church among the Filipino communities of Hawaii. He went under the auspices of the American Episcopal Church and the Rt. Rev. Harry S. Kennedy, Bishop of Honolulu . . . (all this giving) a perfect inter-communion, between Anglicanism and Filipinism, with Christ.

The Philippine Independent Church today has about 550 parishes in the towns and cities of the Philippines; 2,000 chapels in the barrios and rural areas, and is served by a clergy composed of 580 priests, 20 diocesan bishops, 18 suffragan bishops; two apostolic prefectures, and the dedicated cooperation of about 20,000 members of the Woman's Auxiliary, approximately the same number of laymen organized in laymen's committees, and countless youth organizations of both sexes . . . As the true expression of Christ's Holy Catholic Church in the Philippines, the Iglesia Filipina Independiente looks confidently toward the future, praying for the blessings of God which have brought it through hardships in the past as it strives to do His will in our beloved country."

The Philippine Independent Church has endured through the years because it has had a God-given sense of mission. It carries in its heart the message of the great patriots and saints of the past. It has been a lonely Church as it wandered through the wilderness. It has been sustained because, within it, dwells the soul of the Philippines. The cry of Aglipay was for Liberty—liberty under law, liberty with due regard for the rights of others, but *liberty*. For three hundred years the greatest hardship the Philippines had to endure was the deprivation of liberty to think, to initiate, to follow one's own life's bent. For three hundred years every evidence of original thought, every sign of individual initiative was deliberately smothered. The only thing allowed was the liberty to obey the friars, and that was called "Christian" liberty. C. S. Lewis has expressed it well in an essay entitled *Lilies that Fester*. Lilies that fester, he says, smell far worse than weeds. "The higher the pretensions of our rulers are, the more meddle-

some and impertinent their rule is likely to be and the more the
things in whose name they rule will be defiled. The highest
things have the most precarious hold in our nature. By making
sanctity or culture a *moyen de parvenir* you help to drive them
out of the world. Let our masters leave these two, at least, alone;
let them leave us some regions where the spontaneous, the un-
marketable, the utterly private can still exist." [9]

Whenever the Roman Church, or any other Church for that
matter, seeks monopoly and strives to rule, "the lilies fester."

Chapter II

The Philippines before
the Arrival of the Spaniards

For three hundred years the Filipinos were given a bad press both by the Spanish friars and by the Spanish Government. It was a settled policy to depict these people as semi-savages without culture, refinement, or any religion worthy of the name. Even though the friars pictured the Philippines as an Eden when under their control, they never ceased to give the world the impression that the Filipinos were a pretty poor lot.

It is not strange, therefore, that some of the great Filipino writers during the last stages of the Spanish rule, may have gone overboard a bit on the other side. In connection with this wholly natural development a curious bit of Filipino history may be recounted. The Spanish friars had founded Santo Tomás University in 1619. The instruction followed the scholastic method long after it had been abandoned in the Universities of Europe, except in Spain. The courses for young Filipinos were limited so as to bar any influx of new and dangerous ideas. It was felt, however, that it was quite safe to allow these young men to study paleontology. In the dictionary this discipline is described as "The branch of biology that treats of the ancient life of the globe, of fossil organisms either of plants or animals." This, it seemed to the friars, was safe enough. However, it transpired that the Devil can use paleontology as well as the Bible for his purpose. A hidden danger lurks within. Brilliant young men like Isabelo de los Reyes Sr. (the father of the present Supreme Bishop of the Philippine Independent Church) plunged into this domain with enthusiasm as they discovered that quite properly it could include the study of the pre-history of the Filipino people. Men like José Rizal followed suit, and they discovered that these people decidedly were not savages before the arrival of the friars. They did have a culture; they could read and write; they engaged in commerce with foreign nations. These scholars, in their reaction against "the religion of the friars," even discovered that their forefathers had a religion of their own which was better.

Somewhere there must be a middle ground between the low estimate of the Spaniards and the idealism of men like Isabelo de los Reyes—and this we shall try to find. To do this we must go far back in pre-history.

Dr. David P. Barrows in his book *The History of the Philippines* says that in all probability the Malayan race, to which the Filipinos belong, came from southeastern Asia. Through many generations, these people spread from the mainland through the islands of the East Indies, and then curved upward in massive waves. Some think that they got as far as Formosa and even to Japan, though the Japanese are predominantly Mongol. In the Philippines they pushed back the aboriginal Itas, or Negritos, into the mountains where they survive as an ethnological remnant of a once wide-spread race, traces of which are to be found even in far away Africa. The inhabitants of the Mountain Province of northern Luzon, among whom the Episcopal Church has done such invaluable work, represent the first early Malay invasion. These sturdy, independent people long resisted Spanish power. Isolated in their mountain fastnesses and therefore without touch with later cultures, they have preserved the habits of life of their earliest Malay ancestors. As a result, a description of this extraordinarily interesting group made soon after the American occupation is also a description of their culture perhaps as much as fifteen hundred years ago. They present a fascinating field for the ethnologist. In 1908, as a teacher in the Government schools, I attended a teachers' conference held in Baguio, the capital of the Mountain Province. The school authorities had brought over some professors from American colleges to compose the faculty. One night, for our entertainment, the Igorots of the neighborhood were asked to give one of their native dances. As the men danced with their *ganzas* in their hands, an Igorot minstrel sang in quavering notes, as a sort of recitative, the story of Igorot experiences with the Americans. He related how they had been called from their towns to work on the roads, how they were treated, and so on. The professor of English was greatly excited by this performance. "This," he exclaimed, "is the beginning of literature. Literature starts with oral or sung stories which preserve in this manner the racial memory. It is constantly being added to as very recent events are chronicled in the same manner." I do not doubt but what the minstrel was improvising as he went along in this present instance, but doubtless his account was stylized by repeated renderings.

Dr. Barrows writes of these people whose manner of life had not changed for many centuries: "In northern Luzon in the great Cordillera Central, there are many of these primitive tribes. These people are pre-eminently mountaineers. They prefer the high cold and semi-crests and valleys of the loftiest ranges. Here, with great industry, they have made gardens by building stone-walled terraces on the slopes of the hills. Sometimes hundreds of these slopes can be counted in one valley; and they rise one above the other from the bottom of a canyon for several miles almost to the summit of a ridge. These terraced gardens are all under most careful irrigation. Water is carried for many miles by log flumes and ditches to be distributed over these little fields. The soil is carefully fertilized with the refuse of the villages. Two, and frequently three crops are produced each year. Here we find undoubtedly the most developed and most nearly scientific agriculture in the Philippines. They raise rice, cotton, tobacco, the taro, maize, and especially the *camote*, or sweet potato, which is their principal food. These people live in compact, well-built villages, frequently of several hundred houses.

Some of these tribes, like the Igorots of Benguet and the Tingians of Abra, are peaceable as well as industrious. In Benguet there are fine herds of cattle, much excellent coffee, and from time immemorial the Igorots have mined gold." [1]

Other facts about this mountain people seem to indicate that the original Malays came from much farther inland in Asia than had been supposed. The institution of trial marriage has been found to be similar to a like practice discovered deep within the Continent. There seems to have been a primitive currency, based on *palay*, the unthreshed rice. LeRoy says that this had all the essentials of modern money.[2] The Igorot also appeared to have been a metal worker, without going through the stone age and without benefit of China or Japan. From the above description of the Igorots we can at least deal with the canard that the Malay is essentially lazy. Given the proper stimulus he can be as industrious as the next man.

Other waves of Malay peoples followed these first arrivals. These people were of a more advanced culture and they took over the rich, agricultural fields of the lowlands. They are the ancestors of the present Christianized Filipinos who constitute the great body of the nation's inhabitants. Although these people were ethnically homogeneous (and this is important from a national point of view), their geographic grouping produced certain differences. This was bound to happen because of the difficulty of travel in an archipelago. So the Visayans were and are to be found in the central islands of Cebu, Panay, Negros, Leyte, Samar, Bohol, and northern Mindanao. At the southern end of Luzon are the Bikols, while in the central provinces of that great island are the Tagalogs. The great plain of northern Luzon is occupied by the Pampangos and the Pangasinans. The northwest coast is inhabited by the spirited Ilocanos. There are smaller groupings as well, but these are the most important ones. There has never been a large-scale war between these groups and one might say that the difference in outlook is not much greater than that between a Texan and a Californian. The traveller notices particularly the differences of dialect; but it is remarkable how quickly a Filipino going from one region to another can pick up the language.

The ancestors of the present Christianized Filipino people were profoundly influenced by the civilization of India. Kroeber[3] says that the Hindu influence upon the early Filipinos did not come from an invasion from India, as no ruins are in evidence. Nor did this influence show itself in the establishment of a crystallized religious cult—or, if so, it disappeared. Rather it came by way of that chain of islands, of which Sumatra and Java are links, over which the ancestors of the Filipinos passed as on a bridge. Sumatra was Buddhist by the sixth century, and there was a Brahmin empire in Java which lasted until the Mohammedans destroyed it in the middle of the fifteenth century.

There were more than a thousand years in which Indian culture infiltrated. It was not a single influence focused on a single objective: it was a set of influences in the form of religious ideas, practices, words (many Filipino words are from the Sanscrit), and an alphabet. As a result the Filipinos had a system of writing and could correspond with each other before the Spaniards arrived. A literature either did not exist, or it was destroyed by the friars as of the Evil One. From India came both mechanical and industrial knowledge. We know that international trade had developed. Pigafetta, the chronicler of Magellan's historic voyage, reported that when the latter's fleet reached Cebu harbor, a junk from Siam was anchored there. Barrows comments that this, "together with the knowledge that the Filipinos showed of the surrounding countries including China on the one hand and the Moluccas on the other, is additional evidence of the extensive trade relations at the time of his discovery." [4]

While the rich Filipinos were clothed in the silks of Asia, the Indian influence along one line had not been helpful. It had not communicated the idea of an ordered or structured society. Kroeber writes in this regard, "With all this first step the lowland Filipino of three or four centuries ago had, however, reached only the germ of a political constitution of society. He never succeeded in welding the local *barangays* (villages) into larger units . . . The head of each barangay acted for himself and his people with him; each was intent on his own interests even though they might be brothers." [5]

It cannot be concealed that between the local units there was continually "a feudin and a fightin." Magellan found this out immediately, and to his own cost, after his arrival in Cebu. There he formed a compact with the local chief who was at war with the people on the island of Mactan just off the coast—indeed this island serves to form the harbor of Cebu. Magellan, attempting to aid his new ally, proceeded to Mactan with fifty men. In the engagement that followed this master mariner of all history was wounded in the arm and then killed by spear thrusts in his breast.

Before the Spanish advent the Philippines were affected by another great force. The Mohammedan conquests had penetrated to the East as well as along the northern coast of Africa and into Spain. The extreme tip of this eastern advance was the Philippines. When the Spanish arrived they found that the followers of the Prophet had made inroads on the southern coasts of Mindanao and had even gained a foothold in Manila. Spain expelled them from Manila and confined them to certain sections of the great southern island. Thus the Moro advance was stopped. While their cultural influence on the rest of the Philippines has been small, their negative influence has been powerful indeed. Unlike their neighbors to the north, the Moros had the idea of kingship through Sultan and Dato, and therefore possessed something of the concept of a state. As a close knit fighting force they were a thorn in the flesh to the rest of the Philippines. They felt that they were doing Allah acceptable service and, at the same time, enriching themselves by their constant raids on the coastal towns in which they both plundered and murdered. The Spaniards had no trouble in conquering the rest of the Philippines (except for the Igorots in the north), but they never conquered the Moros and for centuries did not even contain them within their own borders. It was not until the advent of the steamship that they could do anything effective; the Moro war canoes had been too fast for them. To this day the problem of assimilation is a difficult one, but real progress is being made. The fact to remember is that numerically the Moro population is only a tiny faction of the Republic.

The primitive religion of the ancient Filipinos, like that of many other countries, was a form of animism. The dominant belief was in the existence of a class of supernatural beings called *anitos*. These were gods or divinities proper, good and evil spirits of a lower rank, and the souls of dead human beings. Any being without a body, who possessed intelligence, whether well or evil disposed, was an anito.

This included the idea of ancestor worship which was common and has endured in some places until the present day. The Romans had the same belief, and so did the American Indians who believed that in crisis the spirits of their forebears should be consulted. The word "worship," however, is probably too strong in describing the relgion of the Filipino. At least it can be said that these people believed that these "ancestor" anitos had to be taken into account in the conduct of their lives. The relationship had to be kept on a satisfactory footing by some means of propitiation. Ancestors resented neglect and they could make their resentment felt.

There was also the belief that these spirits had dealings among themselves. There were creditor and debtor spirits. And when the debtor could not pay, the creditor plagued his descendants in the flesh. Therefore the descendant had to make sacrifices to extinguish the debt of the dead.

There were innumerable classes of spirits—spirits of the mountains, the forests, the streams. Once, when the writer was being taken in a banca from Dumaguete at the southern point of Negros up the Strait of Tanon, the native boatman gave the credit for the favoring wind to the god of the mountain to the south of us. I forget the name of this particular deity but, with the boatman who said this in all seriousness, I was willing to give thanks to whatever gods there be, for our quick and safe passage. Some of the spirits were demons who hurt human beings. Others, if not benevolent, were at least neutral and could be propitiated.

The approach to the spiritual world was two-fold—through sacrifice and prayer. The meat of the animal sacrificed could be eaten as the god had use only for the soul. Hence, every sacrifice meant a feast with much eating and drinking. I would guess that we find here the origin of the present day religious fiestas which are so much a part of the life of the people. This combination of religion and general entertainment did much to give the Filipino religion a pleasant flavor and to efface the element of dread.

But true prayers to the anito were said at the time of the sacrifice and these were believed to draw the gods to the place of worship. The appeal was for immediate succor—"not then, but now, not there but here."

On the outward side of their religion the apparatus was simple: there were no great temples, no official priests with distinctive vestments, no pageantry. There were mediums who could converse with the spirits, but only tiny bamboo and nipa houses were used as places of sacrifice and prayer. The many myths which, as with other peoples, told of the origin of heaven and earth and included heroic romances which exalted the virtues they admired, as well as revealing a sense of the tragedy of life. There were as well all sorts of local superstitions which, childish as they were, showed that at the heart of the people was the sense of encompassing mystery. When I lived in Cebu I was told that on the island of Mactan, near by, was a magical tree. It was not really what it seemed, for in some way it was the entrance to a sort of terrestrial paradise whence sorrow and pain had fled.

Hocking in his *Types of Philosophy* says that we must not disregard primitive belief because there may be a germ of truth in it. Later systems may be much more sophisticated, but if that primitive insight has disappeared something has gone astray somewhere. One can therefore trace many fundamental religious attitudes in the religion of the ancient Filipinos. We find here, as well as elsewhere, the belief that there is another world beside this present one and that it cannot be disregarded. In the belief that their ancestors still lived, though in disembodied form, we can see that the thought of immortality was present. In the belief that there could be continued touch with those who had gone before we have a dim foreshadowing of the doctrine of the Communion of Saints. The thought that we can even be of assistance to the departed is akin to the belief in the Roman Catholic Church that masses for the dead can speed their departure from Purgatory.

Sacrifice is fundamental in the primitive religion of the Filipinos and it is fundamental in the Christian faith today. Our Lord's was that "full, perfect, and sufficient sacrifice, oblation, and satisfaction, for the sins of the whole world." We, too, connect the idea of sacrifice with the great ascetic Christian feast at which we eat and drink in anticipation of the heavenly banquet. And we, too, connect that sacrifice with prayer, feeling that God is present—"not then, but now, not there but here."

In estimating the validity of the old religion of the Filipinos we must recognize that the outstanding fact about it was that before the arrival of the Spaniards, and even amidst a welter of belief and of superstition, there had emerged at long last a belief in monotheism. There was one supreme God, Creator of heaven and earth. The Tagalogs called him *Bathala*, the Visayans *Laon*, and the Ilocanos *Kabunian*. Christianity could not have secured so great a hold on the Filipino people had there not been an antecedent preparation. As in Israel their prophets were crying, "Hear, O Philippines: the Lord our God is one Lord."

This was an intellectual as well as a spiritual advance. It meant that there had come to these people the apprehension that since God is Creator his creation is a universe, not a multiverse. There is that which binds together its most diverse phenomena—the dropping of the rain, the wind in the trees, the motion of the stars, and man himself who is a part of a great order. All science rests on this conception. All thought seeks to pierce through to the hidden unity which hides itself under infinite variety.

It was true enough that the essential character of this One was not fully realized. But the Filipino world was ready for the revelation that God was Father as well as Creator. It was ready to believe that the infinitely great was also the infinitely near. It was prepared to learn that God is love and that he had so loved the world that he had given his only begotten Son, that through him even the humblest man might not perish, but have eternal life.

It is evident, therefore, that José Rizal, Isabelo de los Reyes, and other Filipino writers struck "pay dirt" in their studies in paleontology. It certainly showed that the Spaniards, upon their arrival, did not find a barbarous if not savage people only slightly above the level of the *carabaos* with which they worked the fields. They had admirable human qualities, an advanced culture, and a religious nature which was showing itself responsive to the leading of the Holy Spirit. Above all, they had shown one essential of greatness in any people—the capacity, while maintaining their own identity, to assimilate the best of the cultures with which they came into contact. In so doing they had grown in stature intellectually and spiritually. This consciousness of personal dignity, plus openness of mind and eagerness of heart, characterize the Filipino people today.

If the Filipino writers here and there painted a brighter picture of ancient times than was warranted, they were laboring in a good cause. They have served us well in helping to restore a truer image of the Filipino people in the eyes of the world.

Chapter III

Friar Rule

Upon the Luneta in Manila stands a monument erected during the Spanish regime in honor of Miguel Lopez de Legaspi and of Andrés de Urdeneta. The figures of these men, standing side by side, represent the military and religious power with which Spain conquered the Philippine Islands. Legaspi was one of the greatest of the Spanish Conquistadores; Urdeneta was an Augustinian friar. Spain under Philip II had a twofold object in sending out expeditions in that age of exploration and conquest. One object was to obtain wealth for the Crown and to reward military leaders in a manner impossible at home. The other object was to convert the natives of conquered countries to the Christian faith. Legaspi's expedition was ordered to reach and colonize the Philippines, to trade for spices, and to discover a return sailing route across the Pacific to Mexico; it was also to convert the natives. The friars who accompanied the expedition were to be sent as "holy guides to unfold and wave the banner of Christ even to the remotest portion of the Islands and to drive the Devil from the tyrannical possession which he had had for so many ages, usurping to himself the adoration of those peoples." [1]

Philip II was a religious man at the head of a Roman Catholic State. His wars in the low countries against the Protestants and his ill-fated Armada against England were not simply undertaken because of the lust for power. Philip sincerely believed that law and order in human affairs presupposed Christian unity. His father, Charles the Fifth, had been at the head of the Holy Roman

Empire and he had taught his son to believe that there should be one great Catholic Church overriding and minimizing national boundaries. The thought of a divided Church was intolerable. Philip wanted to overcome England in order to save its own soul, as well as to extend his political power. Of course, the pope and the Roman hierarchy gave him their blessing in his warlike ventures. So it was with the Philippines.

The expedition of Legaspi and of Urdeneta arrived in the archipelago in 1565, twenty years before Philip's supreme effort against England. Thinking that the northern countries, where Protestantism was rife, offered but a barren field for missionary work, the King of Spain and the Church turned their attention to the lands discovered by their intrepid navigators in the Far East. They thought that in these regions, at least, the Christian Gospel would have easy access. There the Church would redress the balance lost in northern Europe.

Motives are always mixed, but we make a mistake in not recognizing that the Crown's desire to gain riches was mingled with a sincere desire to render God acceptable service. In passing, one cannot refrain from contrasting this double motive with the purely commercial spirit of other nations in their colonizing efforts in Asia and elsewhere. In criticizing the colonial policy of Spain we must not be guided by modern standards, and the record of Spain in the Philippines will bear comparison with that of Holland, France, and England in tropical countries.[2]

The limits of this book do not allow a study of the very rapid subjugation of the Philippines by the redoubtable Legaspi aided by such brilliant men as the young Salcedo. We are more concerned with the spiritual conquest effected by Urdeneta, the Augustinian friar, his companions and successors. Urdeneta was a great and sincere man and like his counterpart in Mexico, Las Casas, with whom he has been compared, he felt for the natives and did much to mitigate the severity of military rule. To Urdeneta, more than to any other man, is due the selfless zeal of many of the friars during the first century of the Spanish occupation—a period which has been called "The Golden Age."

Friars from the great orders—Augustinians, Dominicans, Franciscans—and Jesuits followed in increasing numbers and settled in the extensive areas which had been conquered by Spanish arms. Spanish soldiers might be far away, but these men took up their habitation in towns and villages near and far in the midst of an alien people. One can easily imagine the difference between their former life in Spain and this tropical land in which they found themselves. With the best intent in the world they might easily have made mistakes which would have turned the people against them. It was an astounding and hazardous spiritual adventure, and one cannot but admire their missionary zeal and faith. They learned the native dialects, they preached the Gospel, they identified themselves with the needs and the sorrows of their parishioners by their pastoral work—and they protected them from the Spanish army. At the same time they helped to establish their ascendancy by erecting large church buildings which took the place of the nipa and bamboo "spirit houses," and by exciting the imagination of the populace with gorgeous vestments, a colorful ritual, and dazzling pageantry.

During this golden age of the first century the country enjoyed more internal peace than at any time in its history, and that, too, was appreciated by the people. In the capital city something was done for education by the establishment of Santo Tomás University, the first of a number of educational institutions. Founded in 1610 it has always boasted that it was well on its way by the time that Harvard was established. "Santo Tomás was old Santo Tomás when Harvard was a pup," to paraphrase the classic battle cry of that American institution. In the towns and villages the friars established elementary catechetical schools.

But human nature is frail, and power never ceases to corrupt. The Devil found his way into this Eden as the friars described it. The Serpent varies his methods only to achieve the same objectives; and in this case the temptation was in the form of wealth. Large grants of land were made by the Governors General not only to their military chieftains, but also to the orders. Thus they became great landlords corresponding to the *Encommenderos* in

South America, with much power over the inhabitants of hundreds of thousands of acres. The orders were granted a number of profitable trade monopolies, and they proved to be excellent business men. Not content with these large grants they added parcel to parcel after the manner of some of the kings of Israel. By devious methods in many cases they deprived Filipino landowners of their property and there seemed to be no redress at law. The story of Cabesang Tales in *El Filibusterismo* by Rizal was no exaggeration. This hard-working man, with the help of his wife, had cleared the forest and planted his crops. He was doing well. However, the friars, after letting him do all the work, coveted these fields even as Ahab did the vineyard of Naboth. Ahab, at least, offered to buy, but these men just claimed it. In vain Cabesang made appeal after appeal to the law. The friars had complete political control. At last, after trying to defend his fields, his weapons were taken from him and he took to the hills where he joined the Tulisanes. Like many others he "fled the bells," as the saying goes. In telling this story Rizal was basing it on a somewhat similar instance which had actually befallen his own family. So a new spirit had entered into the garden of the Lord, and it was a spirit which gradually turned the people against the men who at the beginning had won their confidence. Respect and affection gave way to hate.

Friars are supposed to stick to their community life. The work among the people in parishes belongs to the so-called "secular" clergy, that is, to those who are not under monastic rule. Previous to the Spanish arrival in the Philippines, the Council of Trent had affirmed this principle; but in view of the conditions prevailing, the orders were given a special dispensation. The fact of the matter was that there were no Spanish secular clergy available. This continued to be a difficulty. There was too much work for the seculars to do nearer home, and in addition they were not much attracted to the Philippines anyway. The result was that the friars who were sent out from Manila became firmly established in the towns and villages. They liked being "little Kings" with all the comforts, privileges, and perquisites involved. They were not going to give all this up without a struggle.

As time went on, a certain number of Filipinos were given some training (they said it was purposely poor), and after being ordained to the priesthood they were allowed to serve the friars as coadjutors. They were simply the lackeys of their masters. The pretext for not raising up a large body of Filipino "seculars" who might take over was simply that the Filipinos, in general, were of a low moral and intellectual order. They were just not up to it. All this led to increasing tension as the years sped to their inevitable climax. The friars were not impressed by the decrees of the Tridentine Council.

The Spanish archbishops in general were grievously handicapped. Some did not find it so; they were friars themselves and therefore in sympathy with the orders. There were, however, archbishops who believed in Filipino capacity, but any attempt to put Filipinos in charge of parishes met with the stone-wall opposition of the friars. They strove in vain to exercise even a supervisory authority over the work in the Islands. The friars, even though they were acting as secular priests, said that they took their orders only from the monastic heads of their orders in Manila or Spain. The friars defied both the archbishops and the King of Spain (Anda's report, summarized, appears later in this chapter).

The "secularization issue," as it has been called, had large implications for the people as a whole. The controversy was about a narrow issue but it served to point up a larger problem. If the Filipinos had the innate capacity to become priests competent to bear the whole weight of a parish, other Filipinos might become good lawyers, doctors, business men, scientists, and educators. Any lowly *tao* or peasant might have within him the power to rise to high position, and the great majority of this class might develop into self-reliant citizens capable of doing their own thinking. Of what quality of human stuff were the Filipinos? The future of the Philippines was wrapped up in that question.

History is full of surprises, and at a very dark period two great Spaniards did much to set new forces at work in the Islands—forces favorable to the Filipinos. The first of these two was Don

Simón de Anda y Salazar. He emerged into prominence at a time of crisis. On September 2, 1762 during the Seven Year's War (the French and Indian War to Americans) an English fleet entered Manila Bay. Its forces captured the city after a bloody engagement. At the time, Anda was an *oidor*, or judge, who had attained a good deal of influence. Before the capture of Manila, the Spanish authorities appointed him Lieutenant Governor and Judge-at-Large, ordering him to leave the capital and to organize resistance.

His first task was to organize a temporary government which he did in his capacity as Lieutenant Governor. The next obligation was to create an army with which to free Manila from the English. In this effort he reports that only the Franciscans and the *Recoletos* helped him. The other orders, which apparently hated Anda whom they could not control, even tried to have him removed for treason. After the "war" was over, it was charged that the Jesuits had had suspicious intercourse with the English.[3] It is certainly true that the claim that the friars as a whole gave their support to Anda is wide of the mark.

The army was formed under Anda's direction, but it never took the field. The war ended in 1763 with the Treaty of Paris, which, among other things, returned the Philippines to Spain.

Anda returned home to be received as a national hero by a grateful monarch. Emboldened by this he wrote a report to King Carlos III in which he said exactly what he thought about conditions in the Philippines. It reveals what manner of man he was, and it throws a flood of light on conditions in that country. Anda said that abuses and disorders had been fostered in the Philippines under the cloak of religion. While the King should be the real owner of the Islands, he is only so to the extent that he pays the bills. The people of the archipelago are really vassals of the friars and they live in virtual slavery.

He goes on to attack both the University of Santo Tomás and the Jesuit University, saying that Manila cannot support two such institutions. There are only eighty or ninety students in both "universities" and the instruction is poor, a "mere ceremony."

While the Jesuit institution had been closed through the expulsion of the Order, Santo Tomás should also close its doors. Governor Bustamente had established a secular university, but the orders did not rest until they had destroyed it.

The friars assert that the King is not the master of the Islands, in that the friars are the ones who have really conquered the country. They even discourage the people from paying the government tax while, on the other hand, they charge high fees for all the sacraments.

The orders of the archbishop are disregarded, while in the provinces the Spanish governors (alcaldes) and the local Filipino municipal authorities are under the control of the friars. If a Filipino obeys the Spanish Governor or the local judge against the wishes of the friars, he is given a hundred lashes.

The friars ought to sell their great estates even though they have a clear title, as such business is inconsistent with their profession. It is a fact, however, that in many cases the friars have usurped their titles from the *Indios*, as Filipinos were then called.

The friars do not want Spaniards in the provinces, and they apply the laws against bad Spaniards to the good ones as well who may wish to venture into their territories to earn an honest living. They drive all Spaniards out. This means that the natives do not come to know and love Spain and the population becomes hostile. To keep control the friars will not allow the natives to learn Spanish and even punish them if they attempt to learn the language.

The *dalagas*, or young women and girls, are made to work in the houses of the friars without pay, and if they neglect to do so they are punished with the lash. The local Filipino officials are treated with contempt as if they were servants.

During the recent war against England the provincial Franciscans and the Augustinian Recoletos were the only friars who helped Anda raise his army. All the rest were declared enemies who even accused him of treason and tried to depose him.[4]

That Anda's report had had a powerful effect upon the King was proved by the fact that at the first opportunity, he appointed

Santa Justa Archbishop of Manila. Santa Justa had already proved his mettle against the friars as he had helped the King expel the Jesuits from Spain. He was not afraid of them when he arrived in Manila. He began to appoint Filipino priests to fill the vacant curacies in his cathedral, his diocese, and elsewhere. He also inaugurated the policy of giving native candidates for the priesthood adequate training for their future duties. They were to become more than office boys. Later he insisted on supervising the friars who were doing parochial work. All this angered the friars; it also scared them.

The King also showed his faith in Anda, who had been accused of treason by the friars, by appointing him Governor General of the Islands in 1770. He arrived not long after Santa Justa and plunged into the herculean task of reforming the administration. Handicapped by the lack of capable assistants he accomplished as much as was humanly possible. Naturally, he assisted the Archbishop by every means in his power. These two men should always be remembered in Philippine annals because they did something for the Filipino soul. And the King, too, should receive his meed of praise.

From the earliest times there had been sporadic revolts by the Filipinos against friar domination, though not against Spain itself. Cornish says that the estimates on the number of these rebellions range from thirty to two hundred and twenty-seven, depending on what is meant by the word "rebellion." [5] One of the first of these, on a purely religious basis, occurred in the middle of the nineteenth century and this leads to the story of Apolinario.

Apolinario de la Cruz was born on July 31, 1815 in Pandok, a barrio of Lukban, Queson Province. The parents, Pablo de la Cruz and Juana Andrea, were devout Catholics and they had dedicated their son to the priesthood. The young man's inclinations ran strongly in that direction and he desired not only to be a priest but to join a religious order. With this objective he went to Manila where he soon learned that a Filipino could not become a "regular" and that a secular priest was looked upon as an inferior.

Though baffled by this repulse, the desire to become a priest remained strong and Apolinario found a job in the Hospicio de San Juan de Dios where, during his spare time, he studied Catholic theology and familiarized himself with the practices of the Church. Unable, however, to enter the priesthood he made up his mind to found a lay religious brotherhood. As he had great capacity as a leader and, in addition, possessed the gifts of oratory, he soon gathered a group around him which he called the "Cofradía de San José." The lay brotherhood, without rules to guide, worshipped God in its own way; and soon, influenced by Apolinario's zeal and eloquence, thousands joined. Apolinario had no desire to leave the Catholic Church and now applied for the recognition of his Cofradía as a lay organization. In the eyes of the hierarchy this was a startling and unwelcome development, and the appeal was refused. More than this, the government was informed that this was a dangerous organization. Now both the hierarchy and the government were determined to stamp out the movement. Apolinario, forced into rebellion, armed his followers as best he could, but he was defeated by the government forces and he, himself, was captured.

He was executed on November 4, 1841 in the town of Tayabas. His body was quartered and the pieces were exhibited in the regions where his followers had been most numerous. So died the first martyr to liberty and religious equality.[6]

This tragic story shows how the friars looked with alarm upon the emergence of any Filipino leadership. They believed that their dominant position could be maintained only by suppressing initiative which might manifest itself among the masses of the population. If Apolinario became heretical after being so roundly repulsed, it was only because his religious zeal had to be expressed somehow. The natural result of oppression is to create violent reaction, mentally as well as physically. With his sincerity, devotion, and oratorical talents he could have done much to purify and strengthen Roman Catholicism in his native land.

This chapter takes us about to the middle of the nineteenth

century and has necessarily been episodic. While the friars did much for the Philippines, especially during the first century of their occupation, James A. LeRoy, the great Philippine authority, has this to say as a final judgment: "The Church which was opposed to liberalism was represented in the Philippines by ministers (the friars) who were probably the most reactionary and medieval in the world, the most backward monastic products of the most backward of the old nations of Europe." [7]

Chapter IV

A Going in the Tops
of the Mulberry Trees

The Philippines could not be unaffected by world currents forever. The wonder is that it was isolated for so long a period.
Rumors of the American and French Revolutions reached it at
the end of the eighteenth century. It was as though a very light
wind were blowing from a new direction. The revolt of the
South American nations in the early part of the nineteenth century made more of an impact, for these nations had been under
Spain. The news spread, though no one knew exactly how, and
it caused a stirring of unaccustomed ideas. This same new wind
blew slightly harder. There was a "going in the tops of the mulberry trees" and the Filipinos began to bestir themselves—a little.

But it was in the last half of the nineteenth century that the
Islands gradually emerged from their tropical paradise into the
modern world. From time to time liberal governments in Spain
alternated with periods of reaction and all this was reflected in
the archipelago. As early as 1814 permission was given to foreigners to establish trading houses in Manila, and this privilege
was later extended to other cities as well. By 1858 there were fifteen such houses, some of which were American. Trade monopolies and other government abuses were stopped though much
corruption remained. In 1863 the Spanish authorities decreed
that there should be a system of public primary instruction established in each pueblo. Very significantly it was ordered that

the instruction was to be given in Spanish. Up until this time the friars had refused to teach Spanish in order to keep the people divided and to protect them from access to liberal ideas. The friars were still to be in charge of all education, and the curriculum was made up of the catechism and related religious subjects. Even at that, however, the movement was a step forward. More Filipinos learned Spanish and this meant a broadening of mental horizons.

In 1869 the Suez Canal was opened, shortening the distance to Europe; and the advent of steamships made the journey shorter still. The oceanic cable meant that the news of the outer world could reach the Philippines instantly. Moro piracy was subdued by gunboats which could overtake the swift war canoes, even though they fled into the eye of the wind. Spaniards of liberal ideas, who had been influenced by the constitutional struggles in Spain, made their way to the Islands. These men began to agitate against the iron rule of the friars. The press, though under heavy censorship, achieved a wide influence. The horizons were further broadened by the fact that the sons of wealthy Filipinos went to Europe and Spain to complete their education, and came back full of new ideas.

By this time, the friars were thoroughly frightened. Isolated throughout the country, and surrounded by a disillusioned populace, they were not only in danger of losing their sinecures—they also feared for their own safety. They had had their first real shock at the time of Archbishop Santa Justa and Governor Anda who had begun the battle for the secular Filipino clergy. While, at that time, the friars had started their systematic depreciation of the Filipino clergy, now their fury knew no bounds. They hated not only the secular Filipino priests, but all Filipinos and Spaniards who they suspected were harboring liberal sentiments. Rizal, in his novel *Noli Me Tangere* was not exaggerating when he tells how the hero, Ibarra, just returned from abroad, tried to build a good school in the town of San Diego with the result that the friars attempted to kill him. Failing in this, they finally accomplished his ruin.

Wise writes that after 1863 there was no longer any reticence about the attack on Filipino character and capacity. It was made publicly with no regard for truth or consequence. A Spanish official, distinguished for his defence of the friars, recited verses in the presence of two thousand students at Santo Tomás University, in which the Filipinos were represented as mere animals, building their houses like birds in the air and living like lowest beasts. The Dominican newspaper in Manila not infrequently referred to the people as "monkeys." [1]

The secularization question, however, seemed to embody in itself all other issues. Here, one particular class of Filipinos was definitely endeavoring to assert its dignity; here, in a special sense, the soul of the Filipino people was at stake. It was for this reason that the first martyrs in the cause of equality and liberty were Filipino priests. Nor did the friars confine themselves to vituperation. An incident connected with the return of the Jesuits in 1861 showed to what lengths they would go. Two duties were assigned to the returned Jesuits. The first was to devote themselves to higher education in Manila—and in all fairness it must be said that in this they did very well. It helped because they had recently been in touch with educational progress in Europe. Secondly, replacing the Recollects, they were sent to Mindanao to do missionary work. The latter were sent north to replace Filipino seculars with the deliberate intent to reduce them to subordinate positions. This transparent attack provoked a storm of protest and no one was more indignant than a Filipino priest named Pedro Pablo Pelaez, a brilliant young man connected with the Cathedral. Pelaez began a vigorous campaign for Filipino equality both at home and abroad. Had he not been killed by the great earthquake of 1863, while preaching in the Cathedral, he would doubtless have shared the fate of his contemporary, Apolinario. The "thing" was building up, and the tops of the mulberry trees were in commotion.

Conditions at this time of the century are revealed by a letter of Archbishop Martínez, an honest and brave man, to the King of Spain. It is dated December 31, 1870. In this letter it is made plain that conditions have become worse rather than better. He says that his archdiocese has been disturbed by the fact that curacies occupied by Filipinos, as a result of Santa Justa's reforms, have been returned to the friars. Antagonism between the two orders of the clergy has become marked and he fears that sentiment will turn against Spain itself. If, at the very beginning, Spanish seculars had been sent out, conditions might have been different; but such was not the case. It is too late to do that now, even if such men could be obtained. In addition, the expense would be more than the royal treasury could bear. The native seculars have a real case and the archbishop agrees with them that the government itself is assisting the friars in their "immoderate aspirations." There seems to be a settled policy of reducing the Filipino clergy to "insignificance." It is necessary for the sake of Spain that this "small fire" should be extinguished before it grows into a formidable conflagration. Archbishop Martínez concludes by "imploring" the King to take action. Unlike that of Governor Anda, the appeal of the good archbishop met with no response.[2]

From the time of Santa Justa the archbishops of Manila had kept the most brilliant Filipino priests at the Cathedral. Among these men was Father Burgos, and associated with him were two other priests whose names will also be cherished so long as there is a Philippines. Their names are Zamora and Gómez. Father Burgos, the son of a Spanish Lieutenant and a Filipino woman, was born in Vigan, Ilocos Province, in 1837. He therefore came from an area which has produced so many great Filipinos. Sent to the Dominican College of San Juan de Letrán to study law, he changed his vocation to that of the ministry despite the objections of his parents. While there he was easily the leader among the students and was chosen "head of the house." When his term had expired, a successor was appointed whose only qualification was that he was a favorite of the vice-rector. Doubtless this was due to the fact that the vice-rector wanted a man whom he could control. The students protested, and in the riot that ensued the faculty who had made the mistake of entering the lists were badly worsted. Burgos with his four friends transferred to Santo Tomás University where again he became the student head. He was brilliant in his studies and finally achieved the degree of Bachelor of Theology *summa cum laude*, and later he became Doctor in Theology. After leaving Santo Tomás he became parish priest at the Cathedral and master of ceremonies at the University. Immediately he began to show his interest in larger affairs. He was active in the fight to secularize the school system which gave the Philippines the so-called "public" schools in 1863. With him were associated laymen of various professions. When Queen Isabella was deposed in 1870 and a constitutional Republic was in the offing, he eagerly entered into the struggle for still wider reforms. Liberalism was in the air. Men thought that the Islands might become "assimilated" with Spain and so be under the same laws as the Peninsula. Gone, they thought, would be the special and unjust laws under which they had been living. The friars, too, in accordance with the Tridentine decrees, would be out. There was great excitement among the students and as we read about this period, we come across the names of young men who later became famous. There were such men as Panciano Rizal who lived with Father Burgos; José Rizal, his brother, who was studying under that same brilliant priest, and Marcelo del Pilar who later lived in Spain and published a paper, *La Solidaridad*, devoted to Philippine affairs. These young men and many others were swept into the current of rejoicing. Fathers Burgos, Zamora, Gómez and many laymen established a "Committee of Reform" which was to press for assimilation and for secularization. This all meant open warfare with the friars, but at the moment it seemed that the time had come.

But, alas, all this excitement was short lived. The King of Spain was restored and all the decrees of the Republic of Spain were annulled. On April 4, 1871 General Rafael de Izquierdo, the first Governor to come by way of the Suez Canal, arrived in Manila. He was on vengeance bound and of course the friars were constantly at his elbow. He restored censorship of the press and de-

nied freedom of speech and association. Upon friar insistance he
decreed that any agitation for reform was treason against Spain.
On the religious side he banned the Filipinization of the parishes
and, over-ruling the Archbishop, he placed the training of Filipino seminarians entirely in the hands of the orders. This meant
that they could not only limit the number but could also ordain
only men who were "safe."

Then the Governor and the friars looked about for means to
quell all Filipino initiative and leadership. All he needed was an
incident which would allow him to give the Filipinos an object
lesson they would never forget.

Among other decrees, he had ordered that the army should
pay tribute. This led to an uprising among the soldiers in Cavite
who were angered by this unusual tax. Wise states that the uprising was secretly instigated by the "supporters of the old Catholic State." [3] This sort of thing is described by Rizal in *Noli Me
Tangere* where the hero, Ibarra, is finally ruined by being falsely
connected with a local uprising instigated by the friars. As Rizal
bases his novels on actual occurances, we may be sure that the
technique was not unusual. At any rate, the uprising which was
easily quelled, gave Izquierdo the opportunity he wanted.

The revolt, therefore, was followed by the arrest of a large number of Filipinos who had been conspicuous advocates of reform.
A hasty council of war condemned to death forty-one of the par-
ticipants in the Cavite riot, and these were shot on the morning
of January 27, 1872 on the field of Bagumbayan. A great many
others, both priests and laymen, were exiled.

Fathers Burgos, Zamora, and Gómez were considered too brilliant and dangerous to be left alive. It was charged that they were
implicated in the Cavite plot. The full proceedings of the trial
were never reported as they would have been had there been clear
evidence. Their real guilt was that they were leaders of their
people, and the condemnation was a matter of course. The sentence was that they were to die upon the *garrote*.[4]

Appeals were made to Archbishop Martínez to degrade these
men by stripping them of their priestly habits. One can imagine

the feelings of this good man who had fought so hard for secularization. Because of the implacable hatred of the friars, he had been unable to secure a fair and open trial for these priests of his. But one thing he could do and that was to show his faith in their integrity by refusing to unfrock them. He refused the appeal and Burgos, Gómez, and Zamora died upon the garrote clad in their priestly garments. Their bodies were not cut in pieces like that of Apolinario, but no one knows where they were buried.

José Rizal dedicates his second novel *El Filibusterismo* as follows:

"To the memory of the priests, Don Mariano Gómez (85 years old) Don José Burgos (30 years old) and Don Jacinto Zamora (35 years old). Executed in Bagumbayan Field on the 28th of February, 1872.

The Church, by refusing to degrade you, has placed in doubt the crime that has been imputed to you; the Government, by surrounding your trials with mystery and shadows, causes the belief that there was some error, committed in fatal moments; and all the Philippines, by worshipping your memory and calling you martyrs, in no sense recognizes your culpability. Insofar, therefore as your complicity in the Cavite mutiny is not clearly proved, as you may or may not have been patriots, and as you may or may not have cherished sentiments for justice and for liberty, I have the right to dedicate my work to you as victims of the evil which I undertake to combat. And while we await expectantly upon Spain some day to restore your good name and cease to be answerable for your death, let these pages serve as a tardy wreath of dried leaves over your unknown tombs, and let it be understood that every one who, without clear proofs, attacks your memory, stains his hands in your blood!"

The judicial murder of these priests, the execution of many laymen, and the exile of men both clerical and lay whose only crime had been to demand reasonable reform, shocked the entire country. The Governor and the friars thought that they could terrify a people into submission. What they actually accomplished was to arouse an opposition which finally culminated in the uprising of the Katipunan in 1896, the Revolution of 1898, the end forever of Spanish control and the founding of the Philippine Independent Church. Burgos, Zamora and Gómez are now on the roster of national heroes, and in the Independent Church they are revered as saints.

From 1872 on the "going in the tops of the mulberry trees" was very loud indeed. The King, the Governor, and the friars were not only wicked—they were stupid.

Chapter V

The Great Martyr

After the Cavite Mutiny and the execution of Burgos, Zamora and Gómez, events marched to the climax of 1896 and the arrival of the Americans in 1898. One does not kill the spirit of a people by creating martyrs, and from this time on new leaders arose who carried on the fight for Filipino equality and dignity. At the same time the attitude of the monastic "corporations" hardened. The monks began a last desperate fight against modernity in all of its forms. They relied on the Syllabus of Errors, published during the pontificate of Pius IX, and the decisions of the Vatican Council of 1870 which confirmed most of the principles of the Syllabus. The Roman Catholic "crust" of which Tillich speaks, became harder than ever leaving not the smallest opening for accommodation. While focussed on the secular clergy, the hatred of the friars ranged far and wide, extending to all, of whatever class, who were not in sympathy with them. Of course there were exceptions. The wealthy Captain Tiago in Rizal's *Noli Me Tangere* is an example of the prosperous Filipino who flattered and toadied to the friars. But many well-to-do and influential Filipinos had been inoculated with new ideas, even though their wealth made them conservative. While these men had nothing to do with the Katipunan uprising of Andrés Bonifacio in 1896, many were suspect and suffered grievously from friar wrath.

The new leaders in the cause of liberty were men who had been boys at the time of the Cavite uprising—old enough, however, for this event with its tragic aftermath to make a deep impression on them. Such an impression was made on young José Rizal who was born on June 19, 1861 in the town of Calamba, Laguna Province. By the time that he was a student in Manila he had seen his mother imprisoned on a false charge; he had seen how the Dominican monks had harrassed his father; he had, himself, suffered physical violence from an *alferez*, or head of the Civil Guard, because he had not saluted him when they passed on the street. The events which he narrates in his novels were not only founded on similar occurences but to a large degree upon the misfortunes of his own family.

Rizal, pure Malay, had inherited a profound sense of dignity, self-respect, seriousness, and self possession from his father and the temperament of the poet, dreamer, and bravery for sacrifice from his mother.[1] In his early days in school he showed himself strong and brave enough to subdue the local bully. In school and college in Manila he found that he could more than hold his own intellectually with the students of purely Spanish origin. All this made him wonder. Able from an early age to think in large terms, he had been impressed not only by the way his own family had been treated but also by the plight of all his people. He rebelled at the thought that they were considered an inferior race. In college his thought carried him still farther. He began to conceive that he belonged to a *nation* and that the Philippines was his motherland, not Spain. He saw it whole and he saw it free, and began to wish that he might vindicate his people in a national as well as an individual sense. With his head he conceived all the millions of the Philippines as one self-conscious, self-respecting people; with his heart he loved the Philippines with a singular devotion. His heroine, Maria Clara in the novel *Noli Me Tangere* was to him, like Dante's Beatrice, a symbol of something beyond himself. In his case it was his country, his Philippines.

He must find out for himself whether these intimations of the greatness of his people were true. And so, upon the completion of his college course, he decided to go abroad and compare his people with the other peoples of the earth. He did this in 1882 at the age of twenty-two.

We cannot trace his pilgrimages up and down the face of the earth during the next five years. All this can be found recorded in Palma's book to which reference has been made. It was in Germany that he wrote his first great novel mentioned above which, smuggled in and passed from hand to hand, created such a sensation in the Islands. He had an extraordinary linguistic talent; and he learned much and made many friends, some of them well-known scholars and scientists. But he loved his family as well as his country, and against the advice of friends he returned in 1887. He endeavored to live quietly at home with his own people in Calamba. A physician and an eye specialist, he restored his mother's sight by removing a cataract; and soon people began to come to him for treatment from far and wide. But his novel had raised too much of a storm, and while the Governor General found nothing subversive in it, the friars at Santo Tomás University took a very different view. In a letter to the Governor the friars summed up their reaction by saying, "The whole narration, absolutely the whole in its entirety and in the details, goes against the dogma, against the Church, against the religious orders and against the institutions, military, civil and political which the government of Spain has implanted in these Islands; wherefore, the undersigned, supported by the opinion of the examining committee, has the honor to inform your Most Illustrious Excellency, that the narration of *Noli Me Tangere* of J. Rizal, printed in Berlin, if it should circulate in the Philippines, would cause very grave damage to the faith and to the morals, would lessen or extinguish the love of the natives for Spain, and perturbing the heart and passions of the inhabitants of the country, might occasion more unhappy days for the Mother Country . . . Fr. Gregario Echavarría, Most Excellent and Illustrious Archbishop of Manila.[2]

The Governor still was not satisfied and sent the book to the Censorship Commission composed of friars and laymen. The Augustinian friar Salvador Font, parish priest of Tondo, sent back a long report concluding by saying "that the importation, reproduction, and circulation of this pernicious book (should) be absolutely prohibited."[3]

Governor Terrero did not let himself by intimidated by the

friars who wanted him to take repressive measures, with the result that no disorders or executions took place. He gives us an example of the type of liberal Governor sent from Spain from time to time. But it began to be so hot for Rizal, who was peacefully treating people in his native town of Calamba, that for the protection of his family, if not for his own, he decided again to leave the Philippines. One of his former teachers, the Jesuit father Faura, said to him on his departure, "You have not written a novel. You have described the sad conditions of our time." The Jesuits, whom he had placed in a favorable light in this novel, agreed with him in the bottom of their hearts, but in public, had to condemn him. They had been too long in Europe, they had too many scientific men among them, not to have a sneaking sympathy for this young man.

In connection with the scientific accomplishments of the Jesuits the writer is reminded of an incident told him by Dr. Ogilby the late President of Trinity College, and at the time the Headmaster of Brent School in Baguio. He said that he had come down on the train from Dagupan to Manila in company with the head of the Jesuit Observatory in Baguio. The Jesuit was a delightful travelling companion, and during the conversation they fell to talking about a recent destructive typhoon. The Father discussed its origin and behavior at great length. "He talked about it," Ogilby said, "as if he owned it!" But when Rizal was reminded of the scientific prowess of the Jesuits, he replied that science, in itself, is not progress but only an accessary to it.

In London, as well as elsewhere, he still kept in touch with the Philippines. Upon receiving a telegram from Manila stating that there were arrests and imprisonments of people who possessed anti-friar writings, he wrote: "All these persecutions and intrigues help to open the eyes of all who are asleep and diminish the prestige of the hypocrites who disguise themselves as harmless lambs and victimize the unwary with their sharp claws and venomous fangs. All these imprisonments and abuses are a necessary evil in a corrupt society, like a medicine or surgical operation for one enjoying good health. If the Filipinos, in this cruel and unequal struggle, prove their fortitude and valor in spite of everything and everybody, then they will be worthy of liberty and then we can say *Dumating na angtadhana*—the deadline has been reached. If they do not, if they are cowardly and weak, then let the tree mature first, because if it is cut prematurely, it will soon be eaten through by mites and will be good for nothing." [4]

During this second period of exile he wrote his novel *El Filibusterismo*.[5] In this book Rizal's thought had matured. It is really more of a sociological treatise than a novel. Its fundamental teaching is that a nation gets the kind of government it deserves, and that the Filipinos must progress through their own labors. Simoun, who is in reality the Ibarra of the first novel, says on his deathbed, "I do not mean to say that our liberty will be secured at the sword's point, for the sword plays but little part in modern affairs, but that we must secure it by making ourselves worthy of it, by exalting the intelligence and the dignity of the individual, by loving justice, right and greatness, even to the extent of dying for them—and when a people reaches that height, God will provide a weapon, the idols will be shattered, the tyranny will crumble like a house of cards and liberty will shine out like a first dawn."[6]

Rizal, as we have said, was eager to rectify the world's opinion of the Filipino people. He wanted to reveal that, even before the arrival of the Spaniards, they had made great advances. He was delighted to discover in the British Museum a rare copy of Judge Antonio de Morga's history *Sucesos de las Islas Filipinas* which was written in 1609, only a few years after the Spanish occupation. De Morga, on an early voyage, had the opportunity to observe the manners and customs of the natives while still untouched by Spanish influence. Unlike so many Spanish writers of subsequent days, he did not endeavor to prove something, least of all to glorify Spain. He was an accurate and impartial observer, and for this reason Rizal felt that he could prove from this book that the Filipinos of earlier days, far from being uncultured savages, were of an advanced civilization. He published a new edition of De Morga and his careful annotations were as long as the book itself. Rizal was determined to do what he could to make the world revise its opinion of Filipino character and capacity.

He kept in touch with other Filipinos wherever he could find them in the constant endeavor to stimulate their love for and their pride in their country. They must raise their sights. He wrote articles for *La Solidaridad,* which was being published in Madrid by Marcelo H. del Pilar, in order to influence Spanish public opinion. He even made a trip around the world, during which he visited the United States, to observe conditions in every country possible and to compare them with those in his native land. But always he yearned to return home. Like St. Paul he was impressed that he must return to "Jerusalem," even though bonds and imprisonment awaited him. This was, therefore, more than a natural nostalgia; he believed that he could fight best on the field of battle, and various events in Spain and the Philippines made him think that the time was propitious. Among other things, the new Governor General, Don Eulogio Despujol, was reported to be of a liberal disposition.

His family, however, was opposed to his return as they knew what danger he would be in from the friars. They proposed that they meet him in Hong Kong, and so he went there to have a joyful reunion with them. He learned from them how the Dominicans had evicted the tenants from their holdings in the town of Calamba. Sick persons had been dragged from their homes. Entire families had to spend the nights in the open air because the Dominicans had prohibited the rest of the neighborhood from affording hospitality to those who had been ejected. The residents had seen with their own eyes how their houses had been destroyed and burned by the soldiers after the local laborers had refused to do so. He also learned that his own mother had been the victim of another act of vengeance by the Civil Guard. It seems that she who was properly named Teodora Realonda de Rizal, preferred to be called Teodora Alanzo. For this "nefarious crime" the Civil Guard had sent her to Santa Cruz, the capital of the province, and had insisted that she make the hard trip over the mountain. She had asked that she be permitted to travel by boat, offering to pay her fare and even the fare of the soldiers, but she was not permitted to do so. Fortunately, when the mother and sister arrived at Santa Cruz, the Governor of the Province, deeply moved, paid no attention to the accusation and ordered them back home.[7] Harrassed by persecution as members of Rizal's family, his father declared that he never wanted to return.

So they lived in Hong Kong. As a physician, Rizal had no difficulty in making provision for himself and his family. Patients came from near and far. But his mind was in the Philippines. He conceived the grand idea of a *Liga Filipina*. This Philippine League, without Government aid, was to unite the whole archipelago into a compact body—vigorous and homogeneous. The basic thought was that reform must come from within through the efforts of the people themselves. For too long had the Filipinos assumed that salvation must come through some kind of paternalistic government action. Rizal thought that help must not come from the top but from below through the cooperative efforts of countless individuals.

Other objectives of the League were to stimulate instruction, agriculture, and commerce and to carry on the study and application of reforms on every level. The most lowly Filipino *tao* must play his part in this. Not a word hinted separation from Spain.

Recognizing that life for him in the Philippines would be difficult if not impossible, he conceived the project of establishing a Filipino colony in north Borneo where, at least, he would be near by. The project was not as impractical as it sounds, because the British authorities wanted colonists and gave him a good deal of encouragement. However, he needed the sanction of Governor Despujol and was disappointed when he received no reply to his letters. The fact was that Governor Despujol, however well-inclined, was not at all eager to have Rizal either in the Philippines or near by. He had enough troubles of his own.

With the Borneo project in mind, as well as the desire to get the Liga Filipina started, Rizal made up his mind to go to Manila even though the Governor had offered him no security. Rizal wrote to the Governor as follows: "This is to inform Your Excellency that on board this same mail-boat I am going to my country to place myself at your disposal first, and later to arrange some private affairs of mine. Friends and outsiders have tried to dissuade me from taking this step, reminding me of the hidden risks to which I am exposing myself, but I confide in the justice of Your Excellency which protects all the Spanish subjects in the Philippines, in my just cause, and in the tranquility of my conscience. God and the laws will guard me against all hidden dangers." [8] He arrived in Manila in June, 1892.

Despujol, at his request, pardoned his father and mother and they returned to the Islands. The Governor, however, discouraged the Borneo project saying that the Philippines could not spare laborers. He offered, however, to give him lands on any island two leagues distant from Calamba. That was the end of Borneo. Rizal's friends greeted him with enthusiasm wherever he went. It was a sort of triumphal progress from place to place and house to house. In the home of a friend in Tondo he met Andrés Bonifacio who was to be the leader of the Katipunan uprising. Everywhere he spoke, not of Spain, not of the friars, but of the Liga Filipina. He was distressed to learn that every house he visited was immediately searched for guns, ammunition, and seditious literature. No guns were found, but it was proclaimed that in each house were found incendiary proclamations, copies of *El Filibusterismo*, and incriminating letters. As a matter of fact nothing seditious, nothing contrary to the laws of Spain was discovered. But the Dominicans were out for the kill, and Despujol who was disliked by the friars because his sympathies were not with them, finally gave in, feeling himself defeated. At his orders Rizal was arrested on July 7, 1892 and without due trial was banished to Dapitan on the north coast of Mindanao. Another well-meaning Governor had found the orders too much for him!

Indignation ran high in the Philippines excepting in the Spanish press. Newspapers throughout the world shared this indignation. Rizal had become an international figure and symbol. Andrés Bonifacio prepared for action.

In Dapitan Rizal practised his profession and had a little farm. In no way did he mingle in Filipino politics; although Bonifacio, claiming his support, used the Liga Filipina for his own purposes. At last, when he could stand inaction no longer, he wrote to Governor Blanco who had succeeded Despujol, requesting that he be allowed to serve as a physician in the Spanish army in Cuba. The Governor acted humanely in giving him permission, and he set sail from Manila. When his ship left Port Said the Captain received a telegram ordering him to arrest Rizal and to confine him to his cabin. At Barcelona he was imprisoned in the Castle of Montjuich of which we shall hear later, and then sent back to Manila for trial. He was condemned by a military council; but the case had been prejudged by the friars and the trial was only a matter of form.

In prison, just before his death, he wrote *My Last Farewell*, a poem which has been translated into many languages. I quote a few stanzas of this thrilling and touching poem. Of course, something is lost in translation.

Fare thee well, motherland I adore, region the sun holds dear,
Pearl of the seas oriental, our paradise come to grief:
I go with gladness to give thee my life all withered and drear.
Though it were more brilliant, more fresh with flowery cheer,
Even then would I give it, would give it for thy relief.
My dreams while merely a child, or when nearing maturity,
My dreams when a youth full of vigor at length I became,
Were to see Thee one happier day, O jewel of the orient sea,
Thine ebon eyes dried of their tears, thine uplifted brow clear
    and free
From the frowns and the furrows, the stains and the stigma of
    shame.
My idolized motherland, whose grieving makes me grieve,
Dearest Filipinas, hear my last farewell again!
I leave to thee my parents, my loved ones I leave.
I go where there are no slaves, a brute's lash to receive,
Where faith does not kill, and where it is God who doth reign.[9]

On December 30, 1896 he was shot on Bagumbayan field in the presence of a vast multitude. His request to face the firing squad was denied; but he refused to kneel. All wondered at his composure. The last shot, Palma says, was lost in a vast sigh of the multitude. A few Spaniards shouted "Long Live Spain. Death to traitors." Rizal was just in his thirty-sixth year.

Thus perished one of the world's great men. He was like Lincoln in that, with the passage of time, his figure looms ever larger. His life and works provide an inexhaustible field for study, and the literature about him continues to grow. He was, in himself, the answer to the calumnies heaped upon his people during the centuries. Anxious to prove that human greatness can be found in the rich soil of the Malay race, he, a pure Malay, demonstrated the fact beyond a doubt. His life has universal human significance and contributes to our belief in the dignity of Man.

It is no wonder that the Philippine Independent Church has canonized him as one of its saints.

Author's Note

The Jesuits claimed that in his last hours Rizal had recanted and had been received back into the Church as a forgiven penitent. This was published in the newspapers of Manila. However, reports began to circulate that this was not the truth, and a year after the execution the Jesuits found it necessary to encourage the publication of booklets purporting to give the details of what happened during the short period when they had access to him before his death. Palma, in his biography, examines these statements and finds them almost puerile in their inaccuracies. It is significant that the Jesuits did not authorize or sign these publications officially. They used the third person. Not only was this supposed retraction completely out of character, but events following the execution furnish the most conclusive evidence that Rizal did not retract. The document of retraction was kept secret for thirty years, though copies were given to the newspapers. When the family asked to see the original, the request was denied. The family asked for the disposal of the body; this request should have been granted if Rizal died in communion with the Church. They asked in vain. The body was delivered to an association friendly to the friars and the burial was kept secret. The family had to search diligently to find the unmarked spot. There were no masses said for his soul, nor was there a Roman Catholic funeral. He was buried in unconsecrated ground, not in Paco cemetery. His name does not appear in the record of those buried on December 30, 1896, but only on a separate page where appear the names of those buried by special order of the authorities. Here the name appears between the record of a man burned to death, and thus not to be identified, and that of another who was a suicide. This means that he died impenitent. Rizal had no motives to impel him to retract, least of all his fear of death. He welcomed death as a sacrifice for his country, and this accounts for his composure and even radiance on the way to Bagumbayan. The Jesuits and the friars, on the other hand, had every motive to attempt to destroy his influence after he died. It was, as Palma says, a "pious fraud." I would strike out the word "pious."

Chapter VI

Revolution

With the execution of Burgos, Zamora and Gómez in 1872 new leaders arose to take the place of the older ones who had been killed or deported. Of these Rizal was the greatest, but there were others as well. Marcelo H. del Pilar, who had watched his brother Father del Pilar and his tutor Father Sevilla taken aboard ship for the Marianas, felt a deep desire to avenge his people. Ten years later he was publishing his paper *Plaridol* in Tagalog in which he carried on a campaign against the friars. His work in the Philippines culminated in 1888 with a parade and a petition to the government to remove the Spanish friars. This time there were no garrotings, but many were deported and Marcelo himself sought safety in Spain. Here he purchased the pro-Filipino paper *La Solidaridad* from Jaena and continued its publication. Rizal, also in Spain, wrote articles for it. By 1895 Marcelo gave up hope for the success of peaceful measures and planned, with Ponce, on direct action. They were to meet in Hong Kong and direct the revolution from there, but Marcelo fell sick and died in Hong Kong on July 4th, 1896.

Another man, of whom we shall hear much in these pages in connection with the Philippine Independent Church, was Isabelo de los Reyes, father of the present Supreme Bishop. Isabelo (or "Don Belong," as he was called) was one of the most remarkable men ever to appear in the Philippines. He was born in Vigan, Ilocos Sur, on July 7th, 1864, the son of Elias de los Reyes and Leona Florentino. His grandfather had been a member of the Spanish Cortes. The father, Elias, was a man of substance engaged in trade and shipping. Leona Florentino was a famous Ilocano poetess. One can see a certain resemblance in this parentage to that of Rizal. From Isabelo's father he inherited good solid qualities. From his mother he inherited the capacity to dream great dreams. From both came his intellectual quality. But Isabelo would take nothing for granted, and even in the grammar school of the Vigan Seminary he showed his independent nature. Gregorio Aglipay said of him at that time:

"He was avid at the Bible but he found that the keepers of the souls at the Villa Fernandina were not in accord with it in practice nor with the behaviour of the laymen of that tiny feudal-like city of fanatics. Don Belong, even at that time, began manifesting his hatred of hoaxes. He showed inclinations for the clergy and should have proved to be a great clergyman, but although he is not, he has turned out to be a priest just the same of a religion embedded not in Roman hoaxes but in the human heart." [1]

Isabelo met Aglipay at San Juan de Letrán in Manila in 1880 and there began a friendship which endured through life. The two had tremendous arguments but the bond between them was never broken. At San Juan de Letrán he developed his gift of writing at which he showed extraordinary facility. At Santo Tomás University he studied the Civil Code, Penal Code, Mercantile Code, the art of judicial proceedings, and drafting of public documents, paleography, and anthropology. He became a notary public at twenty-two, but was too young to practise. As a result he became absorbed in journalism; and it is as a journalist that his son Isabelo Jr. always speaks of him. He contributed to Spanish periodicals, although in those days indios were not permitted to write articles. At eighteen he wrote the history of the Chinese invasion under Limahong in 1574. This was published in the *Diario de Manila*, the oldest and most important publication in the city, and as a result Isabelo became one of its regular staff writers. He founded the first Filipino newspaper, *El Ilocano*, published in Spanish, Tagalog and Ilocano. It was full of humorous sallies and satire about "matrons and extravagant friars." In Manila he even dared to attack the activities of "arrogant friars and jingoistic Iberians." This almost cost him his life. His son and biographer, José, says that while Rizal, Marcelo del Pilar and Jaena wrote in free Spain, Isabelo wrote in the Philippines in the midst of his enemies. His books included such titles as *Historia de Ilocos, Philippine Folklore, Memorial on the Commercial Products of the Philippines, The Visayan Islands, Pre-history of the Philippines*, various articles on the *Ethnology, History, and Customs of the Filipinos*. At the request of the Bible Society of England he translated the Gospels of St. John and St. Luke and the Acts of the Apostles into Tagalog and Ilocano. He was a member of the Academic Societies of Paris, Indo-China, Vienna, and Madrid; the Folk-lore Society of Spain; the Geographic Societies of Madrid, Vienna, and Lisbon. His weapon, like that of Rizal, was his pen. His biographer says that "some thought him a fanatic demagogue; others thought him a great leader."

In the midst of all this activity he was an active business man selling rice, tobacco, maguey, and indigo. There was not much income from his literary work which is, alas, the experience of many authors. No one was more surprised than he when the Katipunan revolt, led by Andrés Bonifacio, suddenly broke out. This changed the whole picture.

Fighting began in August, 1896 and it inaugurated a veritable reign of terror in the Philippines. The middle and upper-class Filipinos, together with the intelligentsia, had nothing to do with it. Rizal thought the whole thing immature. These men were conservative, most of them still hoping that Spain would inaugurate reforms; but the hatred of the friars extended to every class of men whom they suspected of harboring modern ideas or against whom they had a grudge. The result was that, at friar instigation, a great many innocent people were tortured and killed for alleged complicity in the rebellion. This drove many to the side of Bonifacio for they were caught between two fires. If the friars had left the Governor General and the authorities alone, the insurgents, ill-equipped and armed for the most part with bolos and machetes, could have been overcome without too much trouble. But in their death throes the friars were to blow up the Katipunan uprising into a major effort which finally swept Spain out of the Islands.

Isabelo had narrowly escaped friar wrath thus far, perhaps because of his popularity, his humor, his cleverness, and his disarming personality. Now he was thrown into Bilibid prison along with thousands of true Katipuneros, and others of every class who were only suspect. In prison he wrote his *Sensacional Memoria* addressed to Governor General Primo de Rivera. He wrote it at a time when he could hear the shots executing his fellow prisoners, not knowing but what his turn would come next. Primo de Rivera had the reputation of being a humane man, and for this reason Isabelo hoped that his appeal would strike a responsive chord. He wanted the Governor to "know the truth." Kalaw[2] states that this Memorial is one of the most important documents of the Revolution. It is quoted here in part. He states:

(1) That the friars from year to year increased the rate of the land rent despite the serious commercial and agricultural crises through which the country had been passing for a decade, the rice crops having been destroyed by locusts, the coffee plants by an insect much more terrible, and the decreased price of abaca, sugar and other products of the Philippines;

(2) That the friars, instead of using the legal measure when receiving the tax in kind, computed the rice in sacks of 30 to 33 *gantas* instead of 25 which is the legal content of a *cavan,* or sack, of rice;

(3) That the friars arbitrarily fixed the prices of products when accepted by them in lieu of specie;

(4) That, in addition to these abuses, the friars would often confiscate lands which the Filipinos had inherited from their forefathers; all that is needed to do this being the inclusion of such lands in the drawings or maps of the friars, or else, they would despotically order a tenant to vacate a farm which he had improved after years of hard labor and heavy investments;

(5) That the friars mercilessly persecuted those who dared to resort to legal means, even going to such lengths as to have the government deport tenants and protestants thus causing the ruin of many families;

(6) That the friars would not bury the poor free of charge as is their duty and that they charged excessive rates for the performance of religious rites, enforcing excommunication to punish the erring and intimidating the poor to force them (to) give to the Church what little they possess in payment for the funeral services over their relatives;

(7) That the friars meddle in family affairs and in the welfare of the community in order to create dissensions and to wreak vengeance on those who oppose them;

(8) That the friars flout in the most scandalous manner the laws and decrees of the government and of the Church, disregarding everything with impunity as they have disregarded the absolute prohibition to appoint friars as provisors and fiscals which the government of His Majesty instituted in 1896, and notwithstanding such officers continue to be friars;

(9) That instead of being examples of Christian conduct to their flocks in the towns over which they rule, they are the embodiment of scandal because of their vices and incontinence, sacrificing to their carnal appetites the peace of happy homes;

(10) That they are opposed to the progress of the country, even impeding Spanish immigration because they believe the Spaniards would fiscalize and curtail their abuses; they oppose the enforcement of laws and all kinds of government and administrative reforms and unblushingly apply such terms as exploiters and filibusters to former Secretaries of Foreign Affairs, Balaguer, Maura, Moret, Romero-Robledo, Becerra and others to whom the country owed some beneficent reforms.[8]

Included in the Memorial is a resumé of the atrocities committed by the friars, or at their instigation. It is a truly terrifying account of tortures, of false confessions in which priests implicated priests, relatives implicated relatives and friends, friends. It was a time for paying off scores, and the friars whispered in the ears of subservient government officials. Isabelo took pains, however, to distinguish between the "corporations" or religious orders as such and individual friars, many of whom were good men—but helpless to remedy conditions.

In the Memorial Isabelo states that he is not anti-Spanish in the sense that he is against the Spanish Government, in fact he is looking to the Spanish authorities for redress. What he wants is reform and in the Memorial he outlines what should be done:

(1) The Dominican, Augustinian, Recoletos, and Franciscan friars should be expelled from the Philippines and their property confiscated. For this they should be indemnified.

(2) The same political, administrative, and economic consessions made to the Antilles should be granted to the Philippines, including a Constitution, with liberty of the Press, liberty of association, unification of the laws, administrative and economic autonomy. Only the friars oppose this.

(3) The army should be half Filipino and half Spanish. High public offices should be given to the Filipinos.

(4) The return of lands usurped by friars to their owners. Legitimate friar lands, once confiscated, to be sold in small lots by the State like the Royal lands.

(5) Stop injuries, immoralities, illegal exactions; forbid insults to the people from the pulpit and press. Stop deportations.

(6) Stop useless expenditures in order to have railroads and public works.

(7) A general amnesty.

The Governor General paid no attention to the Memorial. He would not even allow Isabelo to visit his dying wife, Josefa. Shortly afterward, in June, 1897, he was deported to Spain and imprisoned in Montjuich where Rizal had been confined. While de Rivera was not devoid of humane instincts, he was a weak man. Some say that he deported Isabelo to save him from execution; this may be the case. However, when the Governor returned to Spain, he attempted to show how severe he had been. He did advocate some mild reforms, perhaps influenced by Isabelo's appeal, but he said that Filipinos should be shielded from modern thought which only led to revolutions. He desired to do good "feebly," to paraphrase a remark by Theodore Roosevelt.

Achútegui and Bernad [4] quote a letter from Isabelo written to the Spanish author Retana from the prison of Montjuich in which the former seems to retract all that he had said in the *Sensacional Memoria* sent to General de Rivera. If genuine, it can only be explained as a momentary and irresponsible reaction of a sick and abused man. On the long voyage from the Philippines he had, according to his biographer, been treated with the greatest harshness. In Montjuich he was held incommunicado for a long period. He was concerned for his family whom he had left behind. Even so, this letter seems completely out of character because most of the facts narrated in the Memorial were well known in the Islands. He could not have denied them "in their entirety" unless he was out of his mind. The letter does not hold together because in the latter part he says "the blind confidence that General Primo de Rivera had inspired in me to address the Memorial to him *perhaps caused me to use phrases a little too violent.*" This is a far cry from saying that he repudiates the entire Memorial. Isabelo's subsequent history reveals that he had not changed his convictions. The whole matter will bear further investigation. These convenient "retractions" are suspicious.

The Katipunan uprising ended with the peace of Biak-na-bato which was concluded in December, 1897. In the general amnesty Isabelo was freed. By that time war with the United States was imminent and Spain wanted the Filipinos to fight on its side. Isabelo was made consultant to the Minister of Foreign Affairs in the hope that his influence would help. He married a Spanish woman and Isabelo de los Reyes Jr. was born of this marriage.

We shall hear of Isabelo de los Reyes in following chapters, as he had much to do with the emergence of the Philippine Independent Church. In attempting to analyze his character, we must remember that he had long been a radical. While still in his younger days he had been influenced by the free thought of Europe. In Spain he made the acquaintance of many men who would have been called heretical by the Roman Church. After the stuffy and stultifying atmosphere of the Philippines, the new air of freedom to think was intoxicating to de los Reyes. He absorbed everything from every imaginable source—philosophical, political, and religious. Granting that he had the ability, he never had the time to sort out all his knowledge. But he had deep and continuing convictions. Essentially he was religious. His passion was for the weak and the oppressed. He founded the first Filipino labor union. He loved his country with sincere devotion—and he was a very brave man.

In 1947, when his biography written by his son José was printed, Justice Gregorio Perfecto of the Supreme Court, wrote a prefatory word. In this he says in part:

A genuine pioneer in several cultural and patriotic fields of activity, the figure of Isabelo de los Reyes stands in bold relief within the space of half a century of our national life. Courageous writer and newspaper man, indefatigable crusader, founder of a religion, initiator of organized labor movements in the Philippines, his biography is worth reading, not only for its intrinsic dramatic interest, but also for the wealth of information and lessons to be profited by present and future generations.

Appearances are not a sure guide to the stature and power of a person. This cannot be truer than in the case of Don Belong. I had the privilege of his personal acquaintance. His air of apparent childishness, his tilting talk verging on stammering, his unusual mannerisms were not the most favorable means of inducing an attitude to take him in earnest and seem paradoxical in a man of his greatness, whose outstanding achievements can hardly be equalled. A complete and conclusive appraisal of said achievements is yet to be made, but their author's name is secure in a prominent place in our national history. I hope that scholars in the future will undertake the writing of a thorough study of his life and work.

Justice Gregorio Perfecto
Supreme Court
Manila, May 15, 1947

It is regrettable that brilliant writers like Achútegui and Bernad will explore every library and look into every corner in the relentless effort to find details in the private life of such a man which may reflect upon his character. His true greatness escapes them entirely. With all his judgments it is not necessary to agree, but he remains forever a symbol of man's quest for intellectual liberty. He will be long remembered in the Philippines as one of the great men in a critical period of her history.

In this short history it is not possible to enlarge upon the careers of many other great Filipinos. Some of them had much to do with the formation of the Philippine Independent Church. In the crippled body of Don Apolinario Mabini dwelt one of the finest minds and spirits the Philippines ever produced. He was Secretary of State during the brief existence of the first Republic of the Philippines. Nor can we speak of men like the youthful and heroic General Gregorio del Pilar who might be compared with Salcedo of earlier days. We must hurry on to the climax of 1898.

When Rizal was banished to Dapitan, Mindanao, in 1892 there were immediate repercussions throughout the Philippines. Upon no one did this act have more of an effect than upon young Andrés Bonifacio. Bonifacio was not one of the intelligentsia like Rizal and Marcelo del Pilar, nor did he belong to the more wealthy middle class. According to de los Reyes he was a simple employee of a small foreign firm and could hardly speak Spanish. But he was a natural leader, and no one more than he felt the wrongs which the poor people had suffered. When Rizal was exiled to Dapitan, Bonifacio gave up all hope of gradual reform and immediately began to organize what was called the Katipunan. This was a secret society with its own discipline, educational program, and rites of initiation to various degrees of membership. Its objectives were definitely "separatist"—that is, to get rid of Spain by direct military action. For some years the secret was kept and the membership grew into the thousands. The intelligentsia, the wealthy and prominent Filipinos, and the priests had nothing to do with it. Bonifacio tried to use Rizal's name through a revival of the Liga Filipina which had collapsed when the latter was exiled; but this was without his permission or connivance. The time for the uprising was set for the end of December 1896, but there was a leak through the confessional and the secret was out. Bonifacio raised the "Cry of Balintawak," and the first fighting began at Pinaglabanan in August. The fighting spread. Emilio Aguinaldo of Cavite (where he lives to this day, a very old man) joined Bonifacio's forces and seized command. On the 23rd of March 1897 he was proclaimed head of the Revolutionary Government. The bloody conflict resolved itself into a stalemate, though most of the Philippines was under the control of the insurgents. In December of 1897 at Biak-na-bato, to which town Aguinaldo had transferred his headquarters, he signed a treaty of peace. There was to be a general amnesty and the Spanish authorities agreed to pay the *insurrectos* about 1,500,000 pesos, under certain conditions. Aguinaldo was actually given 400,000 pesos and he and his party agreed to go to Hong Kong. No other money was ever paid. Political reforms were promised, but this amounted to nothing. The friars remained as strong as ever. Nothing was done to improve the lot of the Filipino clergy.

This was a truce, not a peace. General Macabulos, who had refused to go with Aguinaldo to Hong Kong, did not disband his army until January 14, 1898. Soon after, this general was at the head of a new revolutionary committee. With Isabelo Abaya, and others as far away as Cebu, he organized municipal councils in many towns. Railroad tracks between Manila and Dagupan were torn up. At the same time Spain, recognizing that war with the United States was inevitable, began to make desperate efforts to win the Filipinos to her side. Calderon, of whom we shall hear later, was asked what reforms would induce them to side with Spain. In Manila, Archbishop Nozaleda issued a proclamation on May 8 attacking Americans as barbarians, heretics, and infidels. Hearing about all this General Macabulos organized the Republic of Central Luzon as a precursor to a Republic of the Philippines.

In the midst of all the turmoil Dewey's fleet arrived in Manila Bay on May 1st, 1898. Corregidor had only a few useless guns and the Spanish fleet off Cavite was an easy prey.

With Dewey's victory the smouldering insurrection took on new vigor. Macabulos drove all Spanish troops outside Manila into the capital city and placed it in a state of siege. Friars were captured in large numbers and some were killed. All the archipelago, with the exception of Manila and a few outposts, were in

Filipino hands. The insurrection was all but victorious. Aguinaldo upon his arrival from Hong Kong took charge of the Filipino forces. A verbal promise from Admiral Dewey that the United States would grant independence made him decide to cooperate with the great American democracy. Spain was through forever.

Chapter VII

Vicario General Castrense

Gregorio Aglipay was born in the town of Batac, Ilocos Norte on May 5th, 1860. He, therefore, was an Ilocano and grew up in that high-spirited region which has produced so many great Filipino leaders. Independence runs in the blood of its people. His father was Pedro Aglipay Cruz and his mother Victoriana Labayan Hilario. His mother died when he was only a year and seven months old and he was brought up by his grandparents who sent him to the Seminary school in Vigan. His people were humble folk, tillers of the soil. Accounts of his boyhood state that he was industrious and lively. He liked to ride spirited horses and to swim in swollen streams. He did his share of fighting with other boys.

At the age of six he was taken back "clandestinely" by his father, and for a year they lived at Aparri. The next we hear of him, he and his father (or some other relative) were arrested for not having planted the tobacco quota demanded by the government. It has been explained that they were really not at fault as the lowland had not become sufficiently dry to permit farming operations. Whatever the facts, it was a kind of petty persecution and fortunately they were let off without a beating. Aglipay was then about sixteen and this incident combined with the fact that his father had arranged a marriage which was not to his liking made him resolve to go to Manila. Here he stayed with his grandfather Francisco del Amor who was a steward at Santa Catalina College. The grandfather had him tutored for two years before entering San Juan de Letrán. He was accepted as a *capista*, in other words a working student. He did well and in time was made a tutor in logic, although it was said that his independent observations in class savored of "liberal" tendencies. He transferred to Santo Tomás where he continued his studies. At first he thought of the law, but finally made up his mind to enter the priesthood. Some biographers tell us that he was influenced in this decision by José Rizal who was also a student at Santo Tomás. They became friends and doubtless Rizal heard the story of Aglipay's early poverty and imprisonment. Impressed with his personality and lively spirit Rizal thought that his friend might be the one to carry on the tradition of Burgos, Zamora and Gómez. They were both fond of fencing, the great student sport in those days, and one time while resting between bouts José said to Gregorio:

"Why don't you study for the priesthood?" Gregorio replied, "Are you forgetting what happened to three Filipino priests?" Rizal is reported to have answered, "Aglipay, in all parts of the world where an honest man lifts his thoughts for reform he encounters a Golgotha. Do not let that frighten you. Christ had nowhere to lay his head while Herod and Pilate governed. The same thing will happen in the Philippines. Popular ignorance will exalt the power of false idols who ruin instead of promote the public welfare. On the other hand it is probable that they will not execute us, but will try to bring our moral death by covering our memory with slander. But do not let that frighten you, we will be oriental Quixotes of the minds." [1]

This conversation has been challenged by Achútegui[2] on psychological grounds. In the account given by Wise, which we have no reason to doubt, these men were speaking of reform, not of independence as Achútegui states. Reform was in the air and both of these young men were in touch with other students who were highly critical of prevailing conditions. In addition, the fact that Rizal himself had decided against the priesthood would not mean that he saw no hope for reform from within that body. A recent letter from the Supreme Bishop of the Independent Church to the writer furnishes additional corroboration.

Bishop de los Reyes reports that one day when he was out driving with Bishop Aglipay, the conversation turned to Dr. Rizal as they passed some of Rizal's old haunts. Bishop Aglipay said, "It was one afternoon during one of our fencing sessions that Rizal asked me, 'What are you planning to be?' I told him that I was eager to become a lawyer. But Rizal attempted to discourage me from that saying, 'What our country needs, Aglipay, is priests like Father José Apolonio Burgos. You had better take the priesthood and follow in his footsteps.'" This story does not "fall of its own weight." At any rate Aglipay decided to study for orders, and, after receiving his degree of B.A., he entered the Seminary of Vigan under the Bishop of Nueva Segovia in 1883.

His stay there was not a happy one. There seemed to be continual tension between him and the faculty. Fellow priests who were students at the same time, have, in later years, attempted to show that this was all Aglipay's fault. He read "forbidden books, and when he was reprimanded he asked, "Is there no liberty left?" He escaped from his room at night and serenaded the girls of the town. They did allow that he had a "kind and generous heart."

The fundamental reason for his departure is contained in a statement by Achútegui and Bernad that "the (faculty) priests of the diocese were not well fortified against the onslaughts of the schismatic spirit that came in the guise of nationalism."[3] Now as well as then the Roman Church looks upon a valid national spirit with suspicion and fear. It is quite evident that Aglipay's real crime was the forthright way in which he expressed his convictions. He found himself at odds with the closed and inflexible friar mentality which in former years had crushed the young and eager Apolinario.

It is evident that others did not share the opinion of the Seminary faculty nor did they listen to the gossip of fellow students. The Vical General of the Diocese of Nueva Segovia granted him his dimissory letter to the Archdiocese of Manila on the recommendation of the parish priest in Batac. Again Achútegui asserts that this was mysterious and regrettable.[4] If we believe, as we well may, that he was recommended to Manila because there was no real reason why he should not be, the mystery disappears. If this was "regrettable," we may regard it as a matter of personal opinion.

In Manila he was ordained sub-deacon in 1887, deacon in 1888 and priest in 1889. His first mass was said at Santa Cruz, Manila on January 1st, 1890.

It is quite evident that even at this stage in his career Aglipay had marked characteristics and the power of making influential friends. One of them was the Rector of Santo Tomás University, Father Gregorio Echevarría, who had doubtless singled him out when he was a student at that institution. The fact that he be-friended him upon his arrival in Manila would argue that he was well acquainted with the young man's character and believed in him. The second friend was Father Eugenio Leyte of the Cathedral Chapter. When he and Aglipay became acquainted the writer does not know; probably it was when the latter was at San Juan de Letrán or at Santo Tomás. He, too, had confidence in Gregorio Aglipay.

During the period 1890-1898 Aglipay was assigned to a number of parishes. The first one was the parish at Indang, Cavite, where he may have got to know Aguinaldo. Then followed parishes in San Antonio, Nueva Ecija, San Pablo in Laguna and Victoria, Tarlac where we find him in 1898. Achútegui, in his relentless search for any detail which might reflect upon Aglipay, has even scanned the record of his periodic examinations during this period. It seems quite evident from the reports that Aglipay only did passably well, though this might stem from lack of time for preparation in those troublous days as much as from lack of ability. Not able to do too much with this, Achútegui concludes with the general observation that such frequent changes of parish did not look too well. Other less sinister interpretations are equally plausible. It might be that Archbishop Nozaleda found him very useful. Or, perhaps, Aglipay was shifted about, according to the good old Roman custom, because he began to build up a following wherever he went, even though he was only a lowly assistant. Jealousy might have played its part especially if he began to press for reforms in the local parish.[5]

However, various friars sent in word to Nozaleda that Aglipay was associating with the revolutionaries and had been in communication with General Macabulos. Like the General, he was not satisfied with the Pact of Biak-na-bato which was concluded in December of 1897. At this period Aglipay's sympathies were with Catholic Spain—provided that the friars could be expelled, their properties confiscated, and Filipino priests and bishops put in place of the Spaniards. About America he knew little except that it was a Protestant and heretical country. He was aware that in the United States Church and State were separated, so that with American domination, if it should come, the friars would remain. What he wanted was a national Filipino State Church and he believed that only a Philippines which was independent politically could bring this to pass.

On August 13, when Manila was captured, the question was no longer an academic one. Spain was definitely out of the Philippines forever as a political power, and this marked a new stage in Philippine history. From May, 1898 to February 1899 there was an uneasy period of uncertainty. The Americans held Manila; but the Filipino Army, over which Aguinaldo had taken charge, lay around the edges. The Filipinos, relying on Dewey's pledge of immediate independence, were waiting to see what President McKinley and the American Congress would do. As months went by reports from the United States began to be disconcerting. There was much anxiety about the terms of the settlement with Spain. They learned that their representative in Paris was not even allowed to state the case for the Philippines. By November the terms of the treaty became general knowledge and it was learned that the United States was to acquire sovereignty, at the same time paying Spain the sum of $20,000,000, the amount of the national Philippine debt. This made them feel that their country was being sold "like a sack of potatoes." They also knew that not a word was to be said in the treaty about the friars and the friar lands. The Treaty of Paris was signed on the 10th of December. It was evident, or so they thought, that Dewey's promise meant nothing. Nothing that was said about the benevolent intentions of America could alter the belief that the Philippines had been betrayed. It is quite easy to understand the growing bitterness. By January, 1899, all that was needed was a spark to set off the explosion.

On February 4, 1899, an American sentry was guarding a bridge into Manila. A Filipino approached and the sentry signalled him to stop. The Filipino kept on coming and the American soldier shot him; it was another shot that rang around the world. Why did the Filipino keep on with his advance after the signal? The writer is quite convinced that it was due to a misunderstanding of the American gesture. In America the universal signal to "halt" is to throw the right hand up and forward with the palm open. In the Philippines, at least in some regions, the signal to "come on" is the same gesture with the fingers closing as the gesture is made. The Filipino naturally misunderstood and advanced to his death. On such slight things do great events turn. If the spark had not ignited in this way, it would have come in some other; at any rate, this is the way it happened and the war was on.

The thing to keep in mind in trying to trace the confused events of this period is that from Dewey's victory in May, 1898 until the following February there was an interval of suspense. Would America grant the independence for which the Filipinos had been shedding their blood for two years and which had been promised by Dewey, or would there be a clash between the two armies? The United States held Manila. The Filipino forces circled the city and were consolidating their gains over the entire archipelago. The Filipinos believed that they had won their war and were entitled to the fruits of victory. But here was a strange and unexpected factor in the situation. America.

Each of the leaders in the drama acted in accordance with his own predilictions and from his own point of vantage. Gregorio Aglipay was still a priest in the Roman Catholic Church. He was actually in Manila at the time of Dewey's victory. He had played no part in the revolution, but the insurgent leaders knew that he was sympathetic to the cause of Philippine independence. Aglipay, however, was thinking mostly of the religious situation in the Islands. This was natural for he was a sincerely religious man in addition to being a priest. Perhaps in these days, he remembered his conversation with Rizal; in any case, he had a special sense of mission. There was much more to it than a simple desire to replace the friars with Filipino priests and bishops. He believed that the Church should be the very soul of the Islands and that the dignity of its Filipino priesthood should both symbolize and energize that soul. This could not be achieved, he was convinced, without complete independence. His picture, therefore, did not wholly coincide with that of Aguinaldo. Unlike the latter he believed in the union of Church and State with the State occupying the same position in relation to the Church that it had in Spain. The pope would be forced to deal with an independent nation in which Church and State were united, and therefore could not help but recognize the Filipino Church as an integral part of the national structure.

During this whole interlude of six months Aglipay remained a priest under Bishop Nozaleda, even though the latter was well aware of his increasing identification with the revolutionary cause. Word even got around that Aglipay was pro-Spanish, a possibility which did not displease Nozaleda who thought for a while that Aglipay might be useful in persuading Aguinaldo to switch to the Spanish side. This, of course, the Archbishop was desperately eager to do. He even sent Aglipay on a mission to the great northern Diocese of Nueva Segovia hoping that he could encourage his many friends among the leaders to fight the American enemy. General Tinio of the revolutionary army had pushed north and was in control of the entire country. He had captured Bishop Hevia Campomanes and confined him in Cagayan. Church affairs were in the utmost confusion. On this mission, which he undertook with Aguinaldo's as well as the Archbishop's blessing, Aglipay did a good job for the Church.

He succeeded in securing the release of two Jesuits. On his return he reported first of all to Aguinaldo who was still at Bacoor near Cavite, the latter deciding to make him a military chaplain in spite of his anti-Americanism. Passes through the lines enabled him to report to the Archbishop that the Bishop of Nueva Segovia was indeed a prisoner and that the parishes were supplied with secular clergy, as the Spaniards had either escaped or had been taken prisoner. He also said that the Filipino clergy were confused not knowing but what they might be subject to ecclesiastical censure for aiding the independent movement. He also reported that he had been appointed military chaplain.

Nozaleda saw the advantage of this military appointment as it gave Aglipay freedom of movement in the territory controlled by the Filipino army. It was early in September that Aglipay, in his new capacity, made a decision which led to grave consequences. In his character as military chaplain he appointed Father Eustaquio Gallardo as Provisional Vicar General of the Diocese of Nueva Segovia. In view of the importance of this appointment and its consequences, the pertinent portion is given in full.

In view of the circumstances through which the country is passing, and having been named Military Chaplain of the Revolutionary Army by the President of the Philippine Revolution, Don Emilio Aguinaldo, with full powers to effect an understanding with the Filipino clergy, seeing that no delegate has been appointed to represent the Most Illustrious and the Most Reverend Bishop of this Diocese who has absented himself, it has seemed to me necessary to appoint a Provisional Vicar General for the good order of all, and in consequence I have appointed the secular priest D. Eustaquio Gallardo, parish priest of Santo Domingo, to whom you shall address yourselves in everything concerning your ministry until such time as some other arrangement should be made.[6]

This appointment, however unwise canonically, was done to rescue this great region from ecclesiastical chaos. It was not challenged until many months later. Aglipay was in a difficult position, but his objective was plain enough and he never swerved from it. He was anxious to establish and keep his hold on all of the Filipino clergy, many of whom had not shared in the Revolution and were uncertain about the issues. All wanted the friars out, but they did not want to see Church and State divided. Doubtless they had heard rumors that Aguinaldo and Mabini were in favor of such a separation, and that disturbed them. With a State Church they would be assured of an adequate income, possession of all the Church properties, Filipino priests in charge of the parishes and Filipino bishops in charge of dioceses, a place of importance in State affairs and protection against the Protestants. Their influence among the people was great, and so not only Aglipay but also Aguinaldo and Mabini felt that the success of the Revolution depended in no small measure upon their cooperation.

Archbishop Nozaleda had his problems as well. Even though during this six months period he saw that Aglipay was identifying himself more and more completely with the Revolutionaries, he still could use him. Not only was the latter helpful in Nueva Segovia, but he served as the sole means of communication with Aguinaldo whom, at first, he had hoped to win to the Spanish side. If independence should be achieved either by negotiation or by a Filipino victory in war (should it come to that) he would have in Aglipay a man high up in the counsels of the government. If the Filipinos did not succeed in their objective, he would have Aglipay at his mercy. He would regret the separation of Church and State, but at least the Roman Church would have a legal status. Though much would be taken much would abide. He had nothing to lose.

Aguinaldo, as has been indicated, wanted the separation of Church and State from the beginning. He had seen only too clearly that the Church in the Philippines had reduced the State to a shadow. The Church *was* the State. While still at Cavite his government, urged by Mabini, had ordered that a civil marriage must precede a Church ceremony in order to be valid. This was separation of Church and State by anticipation. But in the months succeeding Dewey's victory, Aguinaldo required time. His army needed reorganization, training, discipline, and supplies. He had to consolidate his own power as he was dealing with some prima donnas, though they were men of great ability. He had to play for time no matter what the outcome might be, and so for a while he did not turn a deaf ear to the pleading of Nozaleda and others. In other words, he stalled.

Aguinaldo's government was moved to the town of Malolos on September 15. Up until now there had been government by decree, but the leaders felt that a firmer base than this was needed, and so official representatives of the various provinces were summoned to formulate a constitution and elect a president in due form. One of its first acts was to confirm Aguinaldo's Declaration of Independence made at Cavite on the 12th of June. Aguinaldo, as was inevitable, was elected President.

Aglipay was the only priest who was a member of the Congress. Nozaleda looked to him as the means whereby he could communicate with it. The debate was of a high order and showed a thorough knowledge of governmental systems elsewhere in the world. The Constitution, as it took form, followed the United States model except that the chief executive was given more power, a precedent which was followed in the present Constitution. One of the high points was the debate about the relationship between Church and State. For some reason, probably because of his heavy duties, Aglipay was not present at all sessions and did not appear to have taken part in the public argument. It is probable that he believed that the conservatives under Calderon would win the day without difficulty. The opposition, however, showed surprising strength and at the end the proposal to separate Church and State was successful—by one vote! The wise Mabini pleaded that this provision should not be put into effect until later; he knew that it would shock many of the clergy. The new government, as has been stated, desperately needed their support because of their influence among the masses of the people. The government could not even assure the people that the burning question of the friars and the friar lands would be settled at the peace table.

It was in a further effort to gain clergy support that Mabini at

Malolos suggested to General Aguinaldo that he promote Aglipay from simple military chaplain to the more exalted office of *Vicario General Castrense* which would make him religious leader of the whole people at arms and this, of course, included the clergy. Aguinaldo agreed and the appointment was made on October 20, 1898. It read as follows:

Don Emilio Aguinaldo y Famy, President of the revolutionary government of the Philippines and General-in-Chief of the Army:

Whereas, attending to the merit and circumstances vested in Father Gregorio Aglipay because of the great spiritual services he has rendered to the Revolution, I come to bestow upon him by my resolution of today the office of Military Vicar General.

Therefore I direct all authorities, military as well as civil, to acknowledge him as such Military Vicar General rendering to him the prominence he is entitled to by virtue of his office.

Given in the Presidencia on the 20th day of October eighteen hundred and ninety eight.

The President
(Sgd) Emilio Aguinaldo

The Secretary of War
Baldomero Aguinaldo[7]

Aglipay was now the head of the Catholic Church in the Philippines so far as the Filipino government was concerned. He immediately sent out a series of Manifestos to the clergy in order to organize them into a national Church which would ultimately appeal to the pope for recognition. The first Manifesto, dated October 21st reads as follows:

My beloved brethren: Inasmuch as the Revolution tends to liberate the Filipino people from Spain, it is also necessary that we also work to throw off the yoke with which the Spanish clergy pretends to subjugate us so that we may be worthy successors of the Filipino priests who sacrificed themselves in defense of our unquestionable rights which were usurped with the greatest arrogance by the friars who made themselves Lords of our beloved country.

The Revolutionary Government of the Philippines is supporting us in our aims because it cannot recognize as head of the Filipino clergy any Spanish bishop, for the powerful political influence of the clergy in the Spanish government is proverbial.

If it is true that because of our sacred ministry we are called to defend in these Islands the immaculate purity of the Catholic religion, it is very necessary that we take advantage against the avalanche of impiety which always takes politico-social disturbances to infect the purest tradition with its filthy breath.

If we continue recognizing the ecclesiastical headship of the Spanish prelate, the Revolutionary Government, by political necessity, will withdraw its support from us without which we shall not be able to consolidate our moral influence in the minds of the people, or to check later, the influence of pernicious doctrines.

And inasmuch as all of the country is in a state of war until such time as we may obtain from the nations the recognition of our independence, I have thought it best to propose to you the promulgation of the following rules:

(1) All Filipino priests, who actually exercise the office of parish priests in every province, shall gather in order to designate by plurality vote the priest whom they consider the most capable for the office of Lieutenant Military Vicar. (*Teniente Vicario Castrense*)

Said priests shall form by a common accord a list of all those who attend the meeting, specifying the town of residence of everyone; and they shall send it to me together with their candidate to the office mentioned in the previous paragraph, in order for me to obtain from the Revolutionary Government the appointment of the *Capellanos Castrenses* in favor of those who appear in the list, and the appointment of *Teniente Vicario* in favor of the one who is appointed for that office.

(2) Said priests shall appoint from among themselves an ecclesiastical delegate who shall be a member of the *Cabildo* (Council) to be presided by the Vicar General, and shall advise and aid him in the performance of his duties.

(3) The Capellanos Castrenses shall recognize as their immediate chief the Teniente Vicario Castrense of their respective province, and as their superior chief, the Military Vicar General.

(4) In the first meeting of the Cabildo there shall be appointed a special delegation entrusted with the duty to present the Holy See, in the name of the Filipino clergy, its most inviolable adhesion and to obtain the canonical appointment of the priests whom the same Cabildo shall designate for the office of Filipino Bishop and Archbishop.[8]

Aglipay's anxious desire to win the clergy as well as to command them is shown by the fact that he sent out two more Manifestos in rapid succession, one on October 22nd and the other on

October 28. The second Manifesto which is really a circular letter sent out the day after the first, has a pastoral tone and is designed to quiet the consciences of any priests who might feel that their canonical vows of obedience could not be set aside on the score of patriotism. The endeavor is made to show that this is justified as the Filipino Government is not anti-Catholic.

The Third Manifesto was written to show that Aglipay's action does not mean that the Church should be subservient to the State. The Church is supreme in its own sphere but must live in harmony with the State. The pope, however, is able to reward friendly governments, and so it is to be expected that the Philippine Government would grant the clergy the necessary rights.

All of this, of course, presupposed that in the Philippines there would be the union of Church and State, a question which had not been decided by the Congress at the time of the publication of the Manifestos. It should be remembered, too, that when the separation of Church and State was decided upon, it was also voted to make that provision inoperative for the time being. This hesitation by the Congress may have made Aglipay feel that there might come a reversal later on.

And now, immediately after Aglipay's appointment as Vicar General of the whole nation, and so in command of its clergy, an extraordinary incident occured. In November he visited the imprisoned Bishop Campomanes in Cagayan and from him he secured the appointment as Ecclesiastical Governor of the huge Diocese of Nueva Segovia which covered a large part of northern Luzon. Before we charge him with inconsistency (having just declared that the Spanish Bishops were without authority) let us remember that St. Paul said that he was all things to all men if only he could win some. With the Jews he boasted that he was a Hebrew of the Hebrews, blameless in every point of the law; with the Gentiles he claimed that the law had been superseded. So Aglipay was Catholic of the Catholics and had no hesitation in claiming that lineage if only he could hold together his uncertain followers among the clergy. So, in his new and exalted office, with all the authority of the nation behind him, he went to visit the imprisoned Spanish Bishop. While there he did a good deal for him. His authority was sufficient to secure the Bishop liberty to celebrate masses and he even made it possible for him to ordain some candidates. The Bishop was much impressed and he naturally shared Aglipay's genuine anxiety about his diocese. As a result Bishop Campomanes appointed Aglipay Ecclesiastical Governor of Nueva Segovia on November 15th.

So in his double role as Vicar General and as the canonically appointed Ecclesiastical Governor of the Diocese, he proceeded to the See City of Vigan arriving on December 16th, 1898. It was one of his great moments. There were thunder clouds in the background, but of these Aglipay and the town where he was so well known and loved took little account. The Philippine Army, yet to be pitted against the American forces, was in full control. The Treaty of Paris which had transferred sovereignty to the United States had been signed, but there was still hope of American recognition. Aglipay's relations with Archbishop Nozaleda were fast approaching the breaking point, but in the meantime the people in the former's home country rejoiced. The whole story of Aglipay's installation as Ecclesiastical Governor reveals so clearly the spirit of the time that the newspaper account given in both *La Independencia* and *La Republica* is given in full. Anyone can get the feel of it; those who have lived among the Filipino people, can reconstruct the scene vividly in their imaginations. The newspaper article is entitled "Echoes of Vigan."

"Father Gregorio Aglipay arrived at the city of Vigan at the night of 16th of December, 1898. In view of the influence of the said father and the popularity that he enjoyed in the Ilocos, he was received with great enthusiasm. In his trip through the different towns of the province he was greeted and given all the considerations due to his high position in the hierarchy of the ecclesiastic government of Nueva Segovia and the chief chaplain of the Revolutionary movement. Fr. Aglipay held mass on the 18th in the Cathedral of Vigan. He himself singing the *Te Deum* as a thanksgiving to the Almighty for his appointment as Governor, which appointment was celebrated with

grand solemnity and with the attendance of military, civil, and ecclesiastical elements. After the Gospel, the parish priest of Sta.
Catalina, Fr. José Evangelista, ascended the pulpit. After the exordium
the priest recalled those days of suffering of our military prisoners and
those who shed their blood at Bagumbayan. He urged the audience of
the necessity of contributing whatever they can give for the need of
the Republic.

After the *Te Deum*, the provisor, Mr. E. Gallego, ascended the
pulpit and read the appointment of Fr. G. Aglipay as ecclesiastical
governor of the diocese made by Bishop Hevia (Campomanes), who
(i.e. Aglipay) was in charge of the spiritual need not only of the
dioceses but also of the whole Catholic Church in the Philippines, over-
looking all political and human considerations. He did not hesitate
to appoint Father Aglipay to this position.

After the religious ceremony Father Aglipay went up to the balcony
of the Cathedral, formerly the Episcopal Palace, and reviewed a
military parade which was given in his honor. The Battalion, headed
by Captain Pedro Carmen. The great celebration ended with break-
fast enjoyed by all who were present.

On the night of the 26th a solemn event took place. We are referring here to the inauguration of the restored Seminary of Vigan.
This ceased to be such during the Revolution; it was converted into
military quarters by the soldiers.

Before 6.00 P.M. of the said afternoon the town was in a gala mood
owing to the different bands of musicians that were parading inside
the town and the many vehicles that were trying to push their way to
the direction of the Seminary. At exactly 6.00 P.M., the hour appointed for the inauguration, the people invaded the building and
Father Aglipay took his place before a table that was prepared for the
occasion. On his right was the military chief and also the Rector and
Secretary of the Seminary. As soon as silence was established the
secretary stood up and read the communication of November 1st of
the Department of Protection, ordering the opening of centers of instruction in Ilocos. Then he read the names of the faculty of the
Seminary . . .

When the reading of the minutes was finished, Father Aglipay stood
up and made a speech . . . When the speech was finished a thunderous
applause resounded in the sala, and immediately the provincial chief,
Mr. Acosta, stood up and shouted "Long Live the Philippines, long
live the President of the Revolutionary Government and long
live the Revolutionary Army" which was respectively answered by
the immense crowd who were present. After that the Rector stood
up and made a short speech.

The audience was also served with sweets, wine, and cigars, ending the solemn act by sending a wire to the President of the Revolutionary Government with the following message:

Aglipay to Mr. President of the Republic-Malolos.

Father Aglipay, the Rector and Professors of the Seminary College which inauguration we are celebrating at 6.00 P.M. today, with pomp and solemnity, have the pleasure of greeting you with enthusiasm and gratitude in the name of all Ilocanos for your kindness in organizing decent educational centers in these parts of the islands.

Present at this inauguration are the provincial military chiefs and army officials, municipal mayors, parish priests of the different towns, the youth of the province and a big crowd acclaiming with madness the President of the Republic, shouting enthusiastically "Long live liberty and the independence of the Philippines."

The Philippines as a Catholic nation can wait (expect) much from Father Aglipay as long as he is backed by his brothers and protected by the government, knowing how active he is when it comes to the activities in favor of the Roman Apostolic and Catholic Church.

Also, because of his strong initiative, pretty soon we shall have in Vigan a bi-lingual newspaper, or review, which publication will contribute very much to the cultural advancement of the Ilocano people."

Vigan, December 30, 1898

The triumphal moment for Gregorio Aglipay soon passed. In Manila Archbishop Nozaleda was already taking steps leading to his excommunication from the Roman Catholic Church.

Chapter VIII

The Birth of the
Philippine Independent Church

The Treaty of Paris was a grievous disappointment to the Philippines. The Islands had simply been transferred from one foreign sovereignty to another. Informal promises of independence had been made, but they were not confirmed by the treaty. The Filipino representative at Paris had not been allowed to testify and no issue had been raised about the friars and the friar lands. American rule meant the separation of State and Church and so Archbishop Nozaleda was back in business.

During the uneasy interval between May 1898 and February 1899 the American forces had been built up so that Nozaleda was able to see that if war should break out the Filipinos would have little chance of success. He did not believe in the separation of Church and State, but if it had to come he would rather have it under American than Filipino sovereignty. At one time he had hoped that the Philippines would win the war and had endeavored to inflame passion against the barbarous and materialistic Americans. His idea then was that the Philippines might emerge, like the South American Republics, with the Church supreme. The Malolos Congress with its vote to separate the civil and ecclesiastical power had shown the way the wind was blowing. So, with the Paris Treaty ratified, he switched to the side of the United States. It is no wonder that the Filipinos now regarded him as a traitor and an enemy. He was scathingly denounced by

Aglipay who recalled to mind his proclamation of May 8, 1898.[1]

By December, therefore, Nozaleda, now counting on an American victory, felt that he no longer had any use for Aglipay. Even while the latter was having his moment of triumph at Vigan, he began to summon him to an accounting. By May, the superior American forces had made such progress that there was no longer the slightest doubt about the outcome. Nozaleda took the final step against his enemy.

Some major offense had to be found. Aglipay's appointment as Ecclesiastical Governor of Neuva Segovia could not be challenged because that had been made by Bishop Campomanes the preceding November. But Nozaleda thought he had him because Aglipay had appointed Fr. Gallardo as Vicar General of that same area on September 4th earlier in the year. This he had done in his capacity as Military Chaplain, and the authority for it came not from the Church but from Aguinaldo's government. While this was undoubtedly invalid from the ecclesiastical point of view, Aglipay had made the appointment while Bishop Campomanes was a prisoner in Cagayan in the far north, and Bishop Nozaleda was confined to Manila with no way of exercising his authority beyond the encircling Filipino lines. The great diocese was in a chaotic condition. The Spanish friars had fled or were imprisoned. The bewildered and uncertain Filipino clergy were carrying on as best they could. Some kind of authority had to be re-established, and the only one who could do it was Aglipay who was in the good graces of, or at least being tolerated by, Archbishop Nozaleda. Aglipay was influenced by a sincere concern for the Church and it is well to stress this point in view of the charges that his motives were entirely political. It would be still truer to say that his political motives had, as their final objective, the salvation of the Church.

Archbishop Nozaleda, who must have known about this appointment of Gallardo in early September, did nothing about its irregularity until December when he had become convinced that the Filipino Revolution was doomed to failure. Even then, he did not proceed to the final step of excommunication until the following May when he was sure that the American forces had the upper hand.

On May 5th Aglipay was formally excommunicated from the Roman Catholic Church. The charges may be summarized as follows:

(1) Employing the Title of Military Vicar General;

(2) Claiming plenary powers to confer with the Filipino clergy;

(3) Appointing a provisional Vicar General for the Diocese of Neuva Segovia in the absence of the Bishop;

(4) Distributing two circulars advising the Filipino clergy no longer to recognize the Spanish prelates;

(5) Usurpation of ecclesiastical power.

The excommunication was, of course, a direct blow against the Revolutionary Government and people. It stunned the Philippines. But Nozaleda knew that many of the Filipino priests were with him. It did not weigh with these timid spirits that Aglipay was making a distinction between the Spanish hierarchy and Rome, and that he had no idea of schism. One can, perhaps, understand the motives of these men; but they played far from a heroic part. Had they had the spirit which animated Aglipay and the brave priests who stood by him, Philippine history might have been different. Their passivity only makes to shine out more clearly the courage and patriotism of those priests who were in the true tradition of Burgos, Zamora and Gómez. Because of their lack of courage the great majority of Roman Catholic parishes today are ruled by foreign monastics dominated by the idea of the Roman Catholic State.

Aguinaldo met this challenge to his Vicar General immediately. In June he issued a decree directing the Vicario General Castrense to inspect all the parishes of northern Luzon and to order that all moneys possible be invested in national bonds and *that the forwarding of funds by native priests to Archbishop Nozaleda would be considered a highly unpatriotic act.*[2] (Italics mine)

While in May the regular Filipino Army was being everywhere repulsed by the greatly augmented American forces, an event occurred in June which led to almost complete demoralization. Aguinaldo had summoned the brilliant General Luna to a conference, but upon arriving at the house the latter was killed by a group of soldiers. Aguinaldo was not present and there have been various versions of the incident. It was a disheartening blow to the spirit of resistance. Aguinaldo sent Aglipay, his staunch supporter, to conduct the funeral services and the latter stoutly defended his commanding officer at this critical juncture. The Filipino Government was confused and uncertain about its proper course. However, in August it decided to carry on the war. This may have seemed like a strategy of despair, but through it all Aguinaldo was hoping against hope for United States recognition of Philippine independence. He wanted to show Filipino capacity and determination. He knew also that the war was unpopular with the Democratic party in the United States. There was still hope, and Aglipay concurred wholeheartedly with the decision to continue fighting.

Aglipay did not reply to Nozaleda's excommunication until August when it had definitely been decided to carry on the war. This he did on August 19 in what has been called the Fourth Manifesto to the Philippine People and Clergy. It is long, but it may be summarized in the following main points.

(1) Archbishop Nozaleda, in excommunicating me, has disregarded the new order of things caused by the Revolution. The Revolutionary Government is the only power having authority and it has recognized me as Military General Vicar.

(2) Nozaleda has no jurisdiction because of the Revolution and because of the will of divine Providence which cares for the oppressed people and clergy.

(3) When the Revolution is successful and the nation has secured recognition, Nozaleda would have no power, because an independent nation is entitled to have one of its sons in the supreme ecclesiastical seat. For this reason he has gone over to the enemy.

(4) Fortunately the Filipino people have opened their eyes to the real motives of Nozaleda, and they will look with contempt upon this extravagant excommunication.

(5) As a Filipino and a Catholic priest I am working for the right relation with the Catholic Church. I am striving to see that the people in the different towns shall not be without spiritual ministrations. In order that this may be accomplished the Philippine Government has made me Vicar General of the Army, which includes all the people of the Philippines, in order that I may perform this spiritual service.

(6) The Philippine Government has not *appointed* me to this office but has *recognized* me in it, so that the Pope's authority has not been denied. I exercize this authority for the good of the Church and the Pope cannot disapprove.

(7) I propose that a Commission be appointed to present to the Pope the adhesion and respect of the Filipino Church and to pray for his blessing.

(8) Archbishop Nozaleda does not want the Filipino clergy to address the Pope directly. He wants to remain the one to whom appeals are made; but this is impossible as the Filipinos will not accept an enemy of the people as head of the Church. To do this would make the Filipino clergy the enemy of the people. They must be true to the memory of Burgos, Gómez and Zamora.

(9) Nozaleda is incapacitated because he cannot go beyond the protection of American bayonets. He is impotent.

Aglipay's final paragraph reads as follows:

I did for the Church all that I believe it was my duty to do, or my strength could do, when it was threatened with great perils that the revolution has brought. This deserved a blessing, not a censure, for I do not expect any compensation. I shall not incur in the ridicule of fulminating on my part an excommunication against Nozaleda even though he deserves it, because that would destroy the prestige of the Church. I limit myself to expose the full facts to the intelligent and honest opinion in order that the Filipino people and the universal conscience shall execrate and scorn him who deserves it. I hope confidently that the Roman Pontiff will approve my actions . . .[3]

One cannot read this last paragraph without being moved. Aglipay was hard hit by the excommunication and was sore beset. Apart from the personal blow, he knew that this would make it still harder to command the allegiance of all the clergy. Everything became more difficult. In this crisis he falls back upon his fundamental convictions. He thinks of the clergy martyrs of the past and conceives himself to be in a true succession from them. So, in the day of peril, he decides to rely upon his deepest intuitions and appeals to the universal conscience of mankind.

But it was not enough to reply to Archbishop Nozaleda. By October, 1899, Mabini thought that the time had come to organize a Filipino National Church as called for in the First Manifesto of Aglipay. It was time, in his opinion, to separate the sheep from the goats among the native clergy and to get started with what strength could be mustered. Mabini, therefore, made a proclamation to the people reviewing the issues and calling for such an organization as had been outlined earlier.

In this proclamation he used one novel argument. All Spanish bishops in the Philippines had to be presented to the King for his approval and appointment. Inasmuch as the King paid the salaries of both bishops and parochial monastics, this is easily enough understood. Mabini argued that inasmuch as the King, representing the State, had appointed the bishops, their appointment became null and void with the end of Spanish sovereignty. This same argument, or a variation of it, was used later in the dispute about Church property. Another point, also urged by Mabini, was that if the Pope should in the future appoint Spanish bishops, the native clergy would never accept them—particularly Nozaleda who was declared the enemy of the Filipino people. He concluded with the following paragraph:

Let the Filipino clergy show their zeal and love for the Church; let them show their capacity to govern not only the parishes but also the diocese; let them show that the regular orders are not needed in the Philippines to maintain alive the faith in the Catholic religion, and the Pope who cannot separate from justice as Vicar of Christ who is God, has to recognize the rights and merits of the Filipino priests. This is the most opportune occasion which divine Providence offers them to obtain the reparation of their grievances; those who aspire to be something more than mere coadjutors and pages must not let this occasion pass . . .[4]

The call shows how grievously disappointed the Revolutionary Government was with many of the Filipino clergy. Removed as many were from the scene of the fighting, happily occupying the parishes from which the friars had been driven, they were blind to the real issues upon which their continued occupancy depended; they thought that they were sitting pretty.

Encouraged by Mabini's manifesto, Aglipay, on October 23, 1899, called for an ecclesiastical assembly at Paniqui, Tarlac, to implement the first Manifesto. It was to effect the organization of an independent, all Filipino, Catholic Church which still recognized the authority of the Pope. About 26 clergy, all from the Diocese of Neuva Segovia and the northern regions of the Archdiocese of Manila, responded.[5] Their names constitute a roll of honor as they were taking their ecclesiastical lives in their hands. The secretary was Pio Romero who has been called the ecclesiastical counterpart of Mabini.

Aglipay made a long apologia in his inaugural address. He recounts the difficulties of his position and the doubts which he had felt about his ability to sustain it in the midst of misunderstanding and enmity. He has been urged to carry on, however, by people in high position in the Republican Government. He goes on with a review of the present state of affairs in which no Spanish bishops are exercising jurisdiction and says that he has longed to give an accounting to the Pope in which he could tell him of the suffering and injustices which both people and clergy have endured. In every way he has sought to find a solution, but no help was to be found from many of the most influential clergy. They had even charged him with being ambitious. He had been subjected to excommunication as a result of his manifestos, and had desired to retire to private life. Only reluctantly had he yielded to the importunities of men in high position who had promised him help and protection. For this reason he has summoned this assembly in order that it might see through what abnormal times the country was passing and to take steps to remedy the situation. It is time for the clergy to organize a Council (Cabildo) which would regularize their position and quiet uneasy consciences. It must be made plain that the Council is not separating from the Roman Catholic Church, and therefore its position would not be schismatic. The regular Cabildos in each diocese are not functioning save in Manila, and that one is impotent. Therefore the responsibility for the Church reverts to the clergy who should organize a Cabildo to prevent anarchy. A Commission must be sent to the Pope, but the times are not ripe at present. Right now the Pope would only say, "My children, I do not know you."

The "Temporary Constitution" adopted by the Paniqui Assembly may be briefly summarized as follows:

The Preamble states that the temporary Constitution has been formulated to provide for the spiritual necessities of the people, to preserve and propagate the Catholic faith and must be obeyed until duly appointed bishops shall be in charge of dioceses, at which time all of the sacred canons of the Church must be observed.

Canon 1. The object of the Constitution is the temporary organization of the Filipino clergy which will save the Church from peril and protect the legitimate rights of the clergy. This organization is necessary in order that a lawful body may negotiate with the Pope.

Canon 2. The Constitution establishes a Council to carry on the government of the Church. This body will be composed of two delegates from each diocese.

Canon 3. The Council shall govern the Church, in so far as possible, in the spirit of the sacred canons. It shall impose contributions on the parish priests and ask for an accounting. It shall appoint ecclesiastical governors for each diocese.

Canon 4. This provides for the appointment of various Commissions of the Council.

Canon 5. The Council shall appoint members of the Commission to Rome and provide for their expenses.

Canon 6. This is quoted in full.

> The Council will not recognize any foreign bishop as pastor of any diocese without previous approval of the majority of the Filipino priests in a general plebiscite.

> The Council will only recognize foreign bishops with the rank of Monsignor or Apostolic Legate of His Holiness.

> The Filipino priest who violates provision number 1 of this canon will be incapacitated to occupy any ecclesiastical office in the Philippines.

Canon 7. This describes the duties of the Military Vicar General.

Canon 8. This is quoted in full.

> The Council may have the services of any Spanish bishop that may side with it to provide the necessities with reference to the exercise of the power to ordain, provided that said Council will act in accordance with the Republican Government.

Canon 9. When Filipino priests have been appointed bishops of the dioceses of the Philippines, this Constitution shall cease to be observed and the Church shall come under the sacred canons.

Temporary provisions were added to the above:

(1) The present Vicar General, Gregorio Aglipay, shall be President of the Council, *pro tempore*, and the Council shall consist of two delegates each from the Diocese of Neuva Segovia and the northern part of the Archdiocese of Manila.

(2) When dioceses not represented shall elect their delegates to the Council, a permanent President shall be elected. All this was ratified in due course.

Aglipay was striving to regularize the proceedings of this Council so far as possible in accordance with Roman Canon law. This provides that in the absence or incapacity of the bishop the diocesan cabildo, composed of priests, shall take charge of the diocese. Of course such a cabildo would not have the power to ordain or to confirm, and for this reason Canon 8 provided that a "friendly" Spanish bishop might be used for this purpose, provided that the Government did not object. Canon 6 has been quoted in full as it provides that no foreign bishops can be recognized (as diocesans) without the approval of the majority of all the priests. The only foreign bishops who would be recognized would be direct representatives of the Pope. In this way it was made plain that there would be no dealings with the local Spanish hierarchy. It was a declaration of independence of all save the Holy Father, and the assembly assumed the power to deal with him directly.

Thus we find here the emergence of the Philippine Independent Church in its first incarnation. It was an act of transcendent importance in the religious life of the Philippines.

Achútegui in his "judgment" on Paniqui[6] states that this new national Church, if not schismatic, was schismatic in trend. Admitting the close connection between the Spanish Government and the Church, the fact remains, he says, that spiritual jurisdiction remains with the bishops even though the appointment was made by the King and he was paying the salaries. Only the Church can consecrate bishops, and Nozaleda remained the Archbishop of the Manila Archdiocese and Campomanes the Bishop of Nueva Segovia and so on, no matter under whose sovereignty the nation might happen to be. From a canonical point of view he is quite correct. What he does not take into account is the long history antedating this movement: the hatred which the friars had engendered, the suppression of private opinion and initiative, the insistence that the people should be considered as children, the denial of their capacity, the power which the friars had exercised over the government in the municipalities and provinces and over every liberal-minded Governor who had been sent over from Spain. Equity is a principle of law and this should include canon law. Even at this late date it might have been possible for the Pope to have recognized the causes of the Revolution and to have taken steps to lessen the tension. But the Pope did not listen to the cry of the Filipinos. He listened, instead, to the voice of the powerful Spanish orders. The Pope's voice was that of his delegate Chapelle whom he sent after the Revolution was over, and it was a very harsh voice indeed.

Paniqui was, in truth, a step toward schism; but it was schism from the Roman, not the Holy Catholic Church. The Orthodox Church has been in schism for many centuries, so far as Rome is concerned, but it is still a part of the body mentioned in the great Creeds. Rome was hard and stiff, enveloped then—as it is now—in that "hard crust" of which Tillich speaks.

These were brave men, these men of Paniqui, for ingrained training is strong and Rome is powerful. They obeyed the inner voice which whispered of liberty—although this freedom could only be won at the risk of life, even at the risk of their immortal souls. Something deep within them had whispered that this aspiration within them was the voice of God who stands above canon law. It was the call to assert their essential manhood and to emulate the example of brave men throughout the ages who have carried the torch of human progress. They defied ecclesiastical thunderbolts and in doing so they saved their souls alive.

The Constitution of Panique was never implemented; events had been hurrying on too fast. In November, realizing that open warfare was no longer possible, the Government decided on guerilla tactics. Each General was to act independently in the effort to weary the Americans by harassment.

Aglipay, a fighter to the last, became a guerilla General in the Ilocos region. Towns like Vigan in the north had been captured by the Americans, but Aglipay was immensely popular in his home territory. He had been the Ecclesiastical Governor of the whole area; and while his excommunication had deprived him of this honor, the glamor of his office lingered on. More than that he represented the Revolutionary Government as Vicar General of the Armies. He *was* the government. His powerful personality had a magnetic quality about it and attracted the bold and fearless. Many gathered around him in the hills. Legend credits him with many exploits including the saving of the life of Aguinaldo (which seems to be well substantiated) and that of other leaders. It is a fact that he was in many engagements and at one time he was wounded. He was also charged by his enemies with having committed atrocities. About this one can only say that guerilla warfare is not a gentle affair. Troops are not disciplined and often take matters into their own hands. During the last stages of the war American soldiers desecrated the corpse of the heroic young General Gregorio del Pilar, after his defense of Tirad pass in the north. Achútegui[7] commemorates this in big type. Only in a note at the bottom of the page, in fine print, does he mention the fact that Lt. Dennis Quinlan of the 11th Cavalry gave the body "decent burial." The fact of the matter is that the American officers were filled with admiration for this young man and he was buried with full military honors. In recent years President Magsaysay was criticized for his tactics against the Communist Huks; and his only reply was that this kind of warfare was not nice business. He had been a guerilla leader himself against the Japanese.

Whatever his methods, and whatever his men may have done, Aglipay was a thorn in the flesh of the American army. A price of 50,000 pesos was put upon his head. Finally he was induced to surrender, but he was the very last of the guerilla leaders to do so. The surrender took place outside of Laoag in Ilocos Norte on May 25, 1901. It was a festive affair and the whole region rejoiced in the return of peace. Aglipay said, "All beings need rest."

So ended this dramatic episode in the life of one of the great Filipino heroes. Lest anyone should detract from his stature, because he was a priest of the Church, let us remember that one of our Episcopal bishops became a general in the Confederate Army during the War between the States. Both men were animated by sincere convictions. Aglipay believed that only through complete independence could the Church come to its own in the Philippines; and he was willing to sacrifice his health and, if need be, his life in that cause. Books may be written which seek with meticulous care to discover every frailty in this man. They are written in vain. As the Church with which his name is connected gains in power, as it bears increasing witness to religious freedom, there will come a clearer realization of what Gregorio Aglipay has done for the independence and the spiritual welfare of the Philippine Republic.

Chapter IX

Aglipay Makes a Decision

We must now go back and pick up some threads. By the beginning of 1900 the war was nearly over. A few guerilla leaders were still in the field, but these men were soon to surrender. All was peaceful in Manila, outwardly at least. Filipino priests all over the Islands were still in charge of parishes and enjoying their new authority. In reality nothing was settled except that the Americans were winning. The great question was that of the friar lands and, even more, that of the friars themselves. The Filipino clergy were anxiously asking whether these same men were to return to their parishes. Would they once more become mere "coadjutors?" The old pattern of Filipino life was broken—the new one had not yet emerged. It was a period of mental and emotional disturbance. Charges were followed by counter charges. The friars issued a long defense of their position based on the Vatican Council of 1870 and the Syllabus of Errors. The Masons attacked them vigorously. Many scurrilous pamphlets were printed on both sides of the question. The Press had a field day in reporting this under banner headlines. Newspapers printed questionnaires in which all were invited to express their opinions—a sort of miniature Gallup poll.

The Philippine Commission, a body of Americans who had been appointed early in 1900 to prepare the way for Civil Government, decided, as one of its first acts, to try to get to the bottom of all this furor; and it asked all who would to testify. It was the first time that America had ever tried seriously to learn about the causes of the war. The Philippines had been far away. At Paris, as has been stated, the Filipino envoy was not heard— a tragic error because much trouble it could have saved later on. At any rate, America, in this group of men, sat down at table to find out what this was all about. It might be said that the Commission represented not only America but the whole world and that here, for the first time, the Filipinos were given an impartial hearing. Archbishop Nozaleda, of whom we have heard so much, told his story as did poor Bishop Campomanes who had had such a rough time in the north. He was still in some disgrace with the Roman authorities because he had made Aglipay Ecclesiastical Governor of Nueva Segovia. The friars were called in and made an earnest defense of their career in the Philippines— from their own point of view. Of course, much of the testimony was anti-friar.

Achútegui has this to say about the hearing:

It was in such an atmosphere that the Philippine Commission conducted hearings in 1900 on the question of the friars and the friar lands. The hearings were doubtless well meant. Their purpose was to establish the facts, since the facts could not be determined from the accusations and counter accusations contained in the memorials and in the press. But the holding of the hearings in such an atmosphere was unfortunate, and their publication in the United States even more so. For although some of the testimony was favorable to the friars, including that of the bishops and the friars themselves, yet the bulk of the testimony was bitterly anti-friar, and it was not clear how much was reality and how much was irresponsible accusation. One thing was certain: the hearings established (if there was ever any doubt about it) the fact that considerable animosity existed in the country against the friars, and that this animosity was shared by a sizable proportion of the more influential and better educated citizens.[1]

This Commission consisted of the following men: Judge William Howard Taft, Judge Luke E. Wright, Judge Henry C. Ide, Professor Dean C. Worcester of the University of Michigan, and Professor Bernard Moses. These men were accustomed to sift evidence, even in an emotional atmosphere, and it is hard to agree with Achútegui's implication that circumstances made it difficult for them to make a true judgment. They saw that the friar question was the heart of the whole matter. It was because of this that they decided that Taft should go to Rome to negotiate with the Pope for the purchase of the friar lands and the expulsion of the Spanish friars themselves. Taft, as a matter of fact, after acquainting himself with the whole situation endeavored to get the Spanish friars to leave voluntarily; but in this he was unsuccessful. He made the trip in the early months of 1902.

This was not all that happened during the years 1900-1901, for various appeals were made to the Roman authorities by the Filipino clergy and others. Archbishop Nozaleda was adamant as might have been expected. He was himself a Spanish friar but when Placido Louis Chapelle, Archbishop of New Orleans arrived in the Philippines on January 2, 1900 as Apostolic Delegate, there was great rejoicing. Here at last was the Pope himself in the person of his representative. No longer did the Pope seem like a powerful but remote and shadowy figure, hedged about by impenetrable barriers. They felt that now the cry of his children could reach him. It was not long before they were undeceived: Chapelle, in no uncertain and even angry terms, made it plain that he was on the side of the friars. Once more, as had happened so many times in Philippine history, hope was turned into despair. An incident which happened at a reception given in Chapelle's honor, showed how violently the tide had turned. Achútegui and Bernad describe what occurred.

If the delegate had any doubts about the reality of the anti-friar feeling, they must have been dispelled by an unpleasant experience only three weeks after his arrival. A reception was held in his honor on 23 January 1900 at Calzada 4, San Miguel, attended by prominent persons, including General Otis, the Archbishop of Manila (Nozaleda) and the provincials of the various religious orders. When Chapelle mentioned the need for the press to adopt some reserve in handling certain delicate questions which at the time were under negotiation between the government and the Church (in other words, the friar question), someone shouted *"Afuera los frailes!"*—"Away with the friars! Death to Nozaleda who protects the friars!" In the consternation which followed, Chapelle fell into a seat, his head in his hands. Nozaleda, on his way home in his carriage, was stoned in the streets. Eventually Nozaleda left the country.[2]

Hope dies hard, however, and it was felt that if there could be direct touch with the Pope things might be different. Two Filipino priests, Fathers Araullo and Chanco, left the Philippines for Rome in April 1901. They might have known that their mission would be unsuccessful. It was not likely that the Pope would go over the head of his emissary who was already in the Philippines, and these men were simply looked upon as malcontents. They made the threat, however, that there would be rebellion if the demands of the native clergy were not heeded. Schism was in the air.

Isabelo de los Reyes had been active in Spain after his liberation from Montjuich prison at the end of the year 1897. He had been given a government position in the expectation that, forgetting his treatment by Spain, he would stir up his countrymen against the Americans. However, his pen was as prolific as ever and he became Aguinaldo's only European representative. He published *Filipinas Ante Europe,* a periodical defending the Filipinos, and also *The Religion of the Katipunan* many of the doctrines of which were woven into the theology of the Philippine Independent Church at one stage of its history.

Naturally this remarkable man was eager to help in the effort to obtain a sympathetic hearing from the Pope concerning the grievances of the native clergy. He, in his capacity as a Government official, made two approaches to the Papal Nuncio in Madrid, Nava di Bontife, seeking the latter's aid in the approach to the Pope. He was received graciously but nothing came of it. He knew that his appointment at the Paniqui meeting would not be recognized, and so he asked individual parishes and clergymen in the Philippines to give him an endorsement. This effort again, was unsuccessful. He had just one resource and that was to send a communication to the Pope in the name of a lay commission which was part of "The Republican Filipino Committee" of Madrid. The Memorial reads, in part, as follows:

Most Holy Father:

The undersigned, members of the lay commission of the Nationalist Filipino Clergy, in the name of all Catholic Filipinos, have come with great submissiveness to your Holiness, as sons who have been buffeted by a violent social storm, seeking to find in the immense tenderness and recognized wisdom of Your Holiness the salvation of the interests of religion in their poor country which is now a theatre of war . . .

Most Holy Father: Your illustrious delegate, Monsignor Chapelle, upon his arrival in the Philippines was received with warm affection and acclaimed enthusiastically by the people. But as soon as he showed himself in sympathy with the friars, and as soon as he showed his intention of bringing North American priests to administer the parishes, he was savagely attacked and even ridiculed by the entire Philippine press . . .

Not only the Filipino priests but all Filipinos consider it essential to the national honor that all the ecclesiastical dignities in those Islands should be given to the native clergy, as is the case everywhere.

In granting this Your Holiness would not be doing more than to repair the injustice suffered for centuries by our clergy, of being by-passed, because of the inaccurate and biased reports sent to Rome. You will be demonstrating the undeniable love that Your Holiness has for our clergy, for our Filipino people, for justice and for the constant traditions of the Church according to which these various offices are always occupied in each country by the natives of that country . . .

With this remedial measure taken, the malcontents and the tepid will be won back, at the same time that a powerful impetus is given to our priests to exert themselves more and more in the ministry . . .[3]

We have the record of one more appeal which must have been made the latter part of 1901, just before Taft departed for Rome. Calderon, a conservative Catholic layman, whom we first met as a delegate to the Malolos Congress, writes in his memoirs:

Matters being this, I in agreement with several persons of acknowledged Catholic sentiments, and in conformity with the aspiration of the Filipino clergy, addressed in the name of the Filipino Catholics 2 cablegrams to his Holiness Leo XIII, representing the precarious situation in the Church and the imminence of a schism, and announcing at the same time that soon a memorial would be forwarded to His Holiness petitioning that Filipinos be appointed as auxiliary bishops with the right to succeed the bishops. This memorial drafted by myself and revised by Don Florentino Flores, was signed by a large number of persons in the several provinces of the Archipelago and forwarded to his Holiness.[4]

Realizing that the war was over after the surrender of Aglipay in May, 1901, Isabelo finally acknowledged American sovereignty, pledged allegiance, and made up his mind to leave Spain for the Philippines. He did this with something of the same sense of risk which Rizal had felt when returning home in June 1892. Isabelo had been a bitter enemy of the Americans. He had urged guerilla operations, not knowing but what he might be arrested and deported as a dangerous character, a fate which befell the irreconcilable Mabini. However, he was impelled by that same irresistible inclination which had driven Rizal into danger and death. Arriving in Manila in June or July, 1901, he plunged like a whirlwind into the midst of affairs and immediately began organizing the labor movement. Naturally he at once got into touch with Aglipay who had come down from the north.

Aglipay had said, when he laid down his arms, that "all beings need rest"; but it is doubtful how much he rested, for he soon came to Manila. He had much to decide about the fate of the Independent Catholic Church which had been organized at Paniqui, Tarlac, and of which he was still the head. All was confusion and the air was filled with many voices. The sheep had been scattered and it was difficult to know just what to do. He had not given up hope that his excommunication might be rescinded provided that he could secure the backing of all the Filipino clergy. With a united front there might come a change in the Papal attitude. Taft was undoubtedly interested in this hero of the Ilocos, and Isabelo de los Reyes, Jr. reports that he offered Aglipay the post of Governor of Ilocos Norte. Doubtless Taft felt that Aglipay might be of aid to him in holding that important area in line. We must remember that during that period the American authorities believed that the Revolution might break out afresh.

Aglipay, bruised, battered, but still unsubdued, was casting about for support from any quarter, and Stuntz reports that the former had a conference with the Protestants in August 1901. He gives the following report of the meeting in the minutes of the American Bible Society.

In August of 1901 he (Aglipay) sought a private conference with several Protestant ministers to discuss the religious situation in the Philippines, outline his own plans and seek some kind of cooperation if union of effort proved impracticable. He took the initiative. It was his first contact with the Protestants whom he had always denounced as the offscourings of the earth. The fact that he visited us was an indication of his intellectual hospitality.

The Conference was held in the office of the American Bible Society in the walled city, Manila. Those present were: Reverend J. C. Goodrich, agent of the Bible Society; Rev. James B. Rodgers, senior missionary of the Presbyterian Church; Rev. J. L. McLaughlin and myself of the Methodist Episcopal Church; and Sr. Isabelo de los Reyes, a Filipino gentleman of good education and an inveterate fondness for agitation. We spent several hours in hearing the first disclosure of a plan to rend the Roman Church in the Philippines in twain. Senor Aglipay, with great cleverness, set forth the situation as he saw it. He pictured the popular hatred of the friars as we had seen it. He pointed out the systematic ill-treatment of the native clergy by the foreign friar and the unrest which this caused in the entire native community. He showed us proofs of the passionate fervor of all Filipinos for their own islands. He then told us that he proposed to lead in the establishment of an Independent Catholic Church in the Philippines and that he wished us to make common cause with him. The first item on the program was separation from the Papacy and complete autonomy in the Philippines. His next step was to stand for the "Catholic doctrine in its purity." Other details were of less importance.

We pointed out to him the impossibility of any attempt to unite with a movement which did not make the Scriptures the rule and guide in doctrine and life, and urged him to study the situation more carefully and throw his strength into the Protestant movement. If he could not do that we all represented the certainty of failure if only a program of negation were entered upon, and secured a promise that he would carefully consider the question of the endorsement of the Word of God, marriage of the clergy and the abolition of Mariolatry.[5]

So the meeting came to an end and an opportunity was lost. The eyes of these good men were holden, and it may have been the Lord's doing. However, in later years, looking back to that historic conference when Aglipay came to the door and knocked, Protestants have regretted that the outcome was not different. Dr. Donald A. McGovran, Visiting Professor of Missions in the Divinity School of Drake University, writes as follows about this interview:

Why did not the Protestants welcome this church? The Iglesia Independiente was a massive revolt from Rome. Yet Protestant missions in the Philippines never considered it their business. It went its way and they went theirs. It is clear that in the first years three or four million Filipinos could have been brought to Evangelical Christianity. They were, in fact, steered past Evangelical Christianity into the extreme Unitarian position . . . Why did not Protestants at once recognize in the I.F.I. millions their own chief work? Here was the potential Reformation in the Islands. Why was it not recognized? Why, between May 1901 when Father Aglipay took the oath of allegiance to the USA and August 1901 when "of his own initiative" he secured a meeting with the Evangelical missionaries, was he not continuously befriended, aided, instructed, taken on a visit to America to see Protestantism, given missionaries and money to translate into Spanish the tremendously pertinent facts of the Reformation?

If this is expecting too much of missionaries just arrived in the Islands in the midst of a War of Independence, why then, during the year following August, 1901, when acquaintance had been made and the potentialities of the movement were clear, was this Philippine Reformation not given the services of several missionaries and considerable grants of money to help it form an Independent Church along as sound lines as possible. We suggest four answers.

First, because the movement of populations to Evangelical faith was not "Missions" to Evangelical leadership. They were immersed in the individualistic process. Stuntz says he urged Aglipay to "throw his strength into the Protestant Movement." Had Aglipay done so, accepting the missionaries as leaders, he would have found them insisting on standards of individual conduct *before* accession which would have embarrassed Luther and the Church of England when they broke with Rome. Father Aglipay was leading a peoples' movement. The Evangelicals were establishing gathered churches.

Second, each American Church was reproducing its denominational pattern rather than creating a free Biblical Philippine Church. The extent to which this was true in 1900 is difficult to realize in 1956.

Third, between Filipinos and Americans there was a maximum degree of mutual suspicion. Negotiations were in Spanish, which the Americans spoke as a foreign tongue. They looked on these Filipino ultra-nationalists, these ex-insurrectos, with many misgivings. The Filipinos, too, who had escaped Spanish control to fall into an American imperialism, who knew nothing of America save what they had heard incidentally, and who saw the excesses of our soldiery, must have approached the Evangelicals through a haze of misunderstanding.

Fourth, the IFI was substantially an Asian revolt against European domination. It was a nationalistic movement tinged with religious fervor but lacking in Biblical conviction. Protestant leaders did not appreciate at all the degree to which it was able to be guided, not by superiors but by friendly equals." [6]

In spite of his declarations before the Protestant Committee, Aglipay had not made the final decision. Various considerations still made him hold his hand, much to his friend Isabelo's annoyance. Taft had doubtless urged him to do nothing radical until the former had seen what he could do with the Pope. His case would be strengthened if the schism were a threat rather than an accomplished fact. A potent influence making Aglipay hesitate was doubtless his hope that he could unite all the clergy under his banner. At one time he had been the most powerful ecclesiastical force in the country. It was hard to realize that he no longer commanded a great national following. Foreman, the historian, declares that Aglipay had made up his mind to the break by December 1901, but this does not seem likely and it is well to recall that LeRoy states that Foreman is notoriously unreliable.

What is sure is that Aglipay was back in the north by the beginning of 1902 to meet with his clergy following there. Here he was at home and among loyal friends. Two meetings of the Ilocano clergy are recorded, the first one occurring in January. The record reveals that at the time the sentiment of this group was strong for secession, but the door was left open for favorable action by the Pope. Another meeting was held at Kullabeng, Badok, on May 8th. Achútegui quotes Santiago Fonacier who describes the meeting as follows:

Aglipay celebrated his 42nd birthday in Kullabeng, Badok, Ilocos Norte, now the site of the municipality of Pinili. Several priests and laymen attended the affair and then and there they resolved to declare their independence from the Church of Rome and establish a Filipino Independent Church. Father Aglipay, however, requested the Assembly to postpone the formal launching of the Church to give him time to contact all Filipino priests and laymen leaders, so that the movement would count on the unanimous support of the Filipino people and clergy. In that same meeting, some of the priests and laymen, led by Pedro Brillantes, Farolan and Bonoan, advocated for reforms of doctrines and religious practices. Padre Pio Romero led the conservatives who were of the opinion that the Church should follow the same doctrines, dogmas and tenets of the Roman Catholic Church, except obedience to the Pope, for the time being.[7]

Here, for the first time there was a division among the priests as to whether separation from the Pope might also include a change of doctrine.

Again, as we see, Aglipay hesitates. He may have felt under some obligation to Taft to wait for a personal report about his conference with the Pope. It is also probable that a complete break with the Pope seemed to him to be a very painful thing. That underlying loyalty—reinforced by all his early training—still made him play for time, hoping perhaps, that some miracle from heaven would relieve him of the heavy burden he was carrying. To him, this was much more than a political decision:

it was religious, and perhaps more than others of his following, he realized the seriousness of it. His apparent indecision at this moment reveals his depth of character.

But he reckoned without Isabelo de los Reyes. The latter had long since gone beyond the point of no return. With Don Pascual Poblete, editor of *The Cry of the People* and head of the radical Nationalista Party, he planned a public meeting to protest against the friars. This was to be held the end of July, and preparations were made for a monster rally. On July 26, or a couple of days before the time set, Taft cabled the result of his negotiations with the Pope which made possible the sale of the friar lands. The cable also indicated that the friars would remain. There was a tremendous storm of protest. It seemed as if the war had been fought in vain; all its letting of blood and suffering were useless, all attempts to touch the heart of the Vicar of Christ so much effort thrown away. In view of the tension, the American authorities thought it wise to cancel the permit for the meeting fearing that an anti-friar demonstration might turn into an anti-American riot.

Isabelo, however, was not to be gainsaid. He called for a meeting of his Labor Union at the Centro de Bellas Artes for August 3, 1902. It was not a large meeting but it was an important one in the history of the Philippines, for in it Isabelo exploded a bombshell. He said, in part:

Consulting the General Council of the Democratic Labor Union, I am authorized to give our humble cooperation to Mr. Poblete upon whose initiative this demonstration against the friars is held and at the same time to declare, without vacillation, that from now on we definitely separate ourselves from the Vatican, forming a Filipino Independent Church.

We shall follow all the lofty inspirations of God but not the injustices and caprices of men. We respect devotion to the Virgin and to the saints, but above all we shall place the worship of the only one God.

As a tribute of fealty to the sovereign will of the Filipino people, solemnly manifested at the Council of Tarlac (Paniqui) in 1899, we propose as the supreme head of the Filipino Independent Church the most virtuous and greatest patriot, Father Aglipay.[8]

The announcement rated banner headlines in the papers the next day and caused a sensation. If Isabelo had wanted to put his friend on the spot and force a decision, he was eminently successful. Aglipay, as surprised as anyone, disclaimed any connection with Isabelo and his meeting. But he was at once subjected to heavy pressure on every side and he had to get away somewhere and think. At this juncture the Jesuits invited him to go to their country house in Santa Ana for a retreat. All this was natural enough as retreats were often made by both clergy and laity. He could visit with the Jesuits without much comment as they were regarded in a somewhat different light from the other orders. They had no great landed estates, they were devoting themselves to education and doing a good job of it (in comparison with such institutions as Santo Tomás), and what parish positions they had were few and far away. Aglipay was on good terms with them as he had saved the lives of two of them during the war. So he went to make a retreat with the Jesuits.

Achútegui and Bernad give the impression that no pressure was brought to bear upon Aglipay during his four or five day stay at Santa Ana. This is hard to believe. The country was in a turmoil; a schism in the Church was threatened. Right in their midst was the man who might stop the whole thing; the right word from his lips would put confusion into the hearts of the schismatics. A retraction would be the ideal solution. The fact was that Aglipay was subjected to tremendous pressure. The report of what happened is given by the Rev. (now Rt. Rev.) Manuel Lagasca who says that when he was pressed to retract, Aglipay asked if his retraction would mean that the rights of the native priests would be recognized. Would they be given charge of parishes, made bishops and archbishops? In response to this he was told that the Filipino priests were too inefficient to be considered for such positions. But he, Aglipay, was of different caliber. Let him make his peace with Rome, disavowing all that he had said against the friars and very wonderful things would happen to him. Finally he was presented with a document which he was to study and sign. Following is Lagasca's description of the incident:

The conference lasted four days in the house of the Jesuits in Santa Ana, Manila, between the ex-Vicario General Castrense of the Philippine Republic and the Machiavellian Father Francisco Foradada. In the morning of the fifth day the Jesuit, believing that the Filipino priest had already been persuaded to submit himself to the Roman Catholic Church, presented to the latter a document which he was to sign after studying it carefully. The document was a degrading retraction that had been ably prepared, tending to despise liberalism and to discredit Mons. Aglipay in the eyes of his people and of his friends.[9]

Aglipay indignantly refused to sign and left the house forthwith. That this is substantially what happened the present writer has no doubt. Bishop Lagasca became an intimate friend of Bishop Aglipay in later years, and went with him on many of his travels. There he had ample opportunity to hear what happened from the Bishop's own lips. Bishop Lagasca is a man of honor, and he tells the truth. But in addition, the whole things fits beautifully. The technique was the usual one. These Jesuits were acting without doubt under the direction of the hierarchy; but the meeting was in no sense official and, if anything went wrong, could be quickly disowned. No promises made by the Jesuits had any validity, while on the other hand a signed and witnessed retraction which is what they were after, would be valid no matter how informal the circumstances under which it was secured. It would have been given the widest possible publicity.

There have been different ideas as to when the Philippine Independent Church actually began. In my own opinion it began when Aglipay, in anger, left the house at Santa Ana. At that moment he had left the Roman Catholic Church.

Chapter X

Religious Reformation
in the Philippines

Aglipay had left the retreat at Santa Ana about the first of September with his mind made up. The miracle he had hoped for had not come to pass. By his circular—advising clergy and people that he was not to be associated with the speech of de los Reyes at the labor meeting of August 2nd—he had kept faith with Governor Taft, but the latter had arrived in Manila on August 24 confirming his cable that the friars were not to be expelled. Taft's statement that a new Apostolic delegate was coming brought no conviction that there would be a change. Aglipay was in conscience free to act, but one thing restrained him. Isabelo was in jail! On August 17th he had been arrested in connection with some labor trouble. On August 29th he was sentenced to four months in prison for violating the Spanish Penal Code prohibiting the organization of workmen to force up wages. Judge Roxas gave him a special pardon, but Isabelo insisted on going back to jail as he claimed that he was innocent. His son and biographer, José, describes the episode as follows:

The ridiculous provincial jail was transformed into a happy hotel by the multitude who felicitated him and who continually offered him feasts with all manner of choice foods to the extent that they even brought him decent beds, blankets, towels, chairs and other equipment. In the evening he was allowed by the town authorities to leave the prison confidentially until the next morning, accompanied by some friends.[1]

While the trial was pending Aglipay felt that the moment was not an auspicious one for joining forces with the happy warrior. With his acquittal matters were different, and although Isabelo was keeping open house in the provincial jail, the issue was settled. Incidentally, Isabelo did accept a pardon from Taft after serving two months of his sentence.

Soon after the first of September, 1902, Aglipay decided to accept the nomination made at the meeting of the labor union. Though not as yet formally inaugurated or consecrated, he assumed the mantle of the Supreme Bishop of the Philippine Independent Church. He was *not* the founder of the Church and neither was Isabelo de los Reyes, although the latter was undoubtedly the catalyst. The first form of the Church was outlined at the Paniqui conference in the fall of 1899 while the war was still going on. Paniqui, however, did not start the Church on its way so much as it gathered up the history of the preceding centuries. This Church grew out of the heart of the Filipino desire for liberty, for the opportunity to express its own self-consciousness. For centuries this self-consciousness, this manhood, had been steadily and deliberately repressed, both politically and religiously. Finally, the smoking flax caught fire. Of course, many did not lend their aid; it is always the few who see the issues and bear the brunt of the struggle. We must remember that many Americans did not see the issues in 1776: they either kept well to the background or emigrated to Canada.

So this Church was the end product of many antecedent causes, but Aglipay was the man of the hour. The times demanded a leader. It is significant that the call to lead came from the labor movement, from that strata of society which had always been at the bottom of the heap. Today, while this Church represents a cross section of the Filipino people, it is firmly planted in the ground soil of the common man—rooted in the spot where the basic problems of the Philippines wait for solution.

The religious reformation of this nation came to life with Aglipay's acceptance of the call to responsible leadership. Protestant missionaries, arriving after Dewey's victory, represented the

Reformation of the 16th century in Europe, but this was the reformation from within the life of the Philippines itself. It had had to battle for its existence against every conceivable obstacle. Its strength today, after half a century, is a miracle and gives sure evidence that its mission is a true one. During years of trial, God has guided it through a physical and a theological wilderness.

At the moment we have been describing it was impossible to foresee the future and Aglipay, once his mind was made up, plunged into the thick of a very complicated situation. The strong and steady hand of America had brought a peace and security which were welcomed by the tortured nation. There was a devolution of political power to the municipalities and provinces. The constabulary, led by American officers, replaced the hated Guardia Civil. Justice was obtainable, and along with this the rights to which the Filipinos had aspired for so many years. There was freedom of the press, freedom of speech, freedom of association, freedom of conscience, freedom from censorship. This was a new experience to a land where these things had been so long denied. Only complete political independence remained to be gained, and the first Filipino Assembly called in 1907 was a great step in that direction.

But when Aglipay took hold of the helm of the Philippine Independent Church, the religious question still remained. Was there to be political independence but religious colonization? The outlook was dark indeed. Rome was bereft of political power but it had legal status. Many of the Filipino clergy remained loyal to the Roman Catholic Church, although they hoped that they might remain as pastors of parishes and that some of them might be appointed bishops. When Aglipay came to power many were waiting for Rome's final disposition which was to be brought by the new Apostolic Delegate Guidi in November.

Aglipay had to think of many things. On the political side he had to convince Taft that he was firmly opposed to further resistance to American sovereignty. Taft, for his part, felt that Aglipay, a revolutionary leader, might be very useful in consolidating the American position. It was reported that Taft offered him the position of Governor of Ilocos Norte, counting on him to use his influence in that region where he was so immensely popular. While this never happened, he did accompany the Governor on his trips through the country in order to show his allegiance and to influence the people. Aglipay would have nothing to do with the unreconciled remnant of the Katipunan. In 1904 he even formed the Republican party which was dedicated to carrying out Taft's program. As a result Taft came to believe in him and was convinced that the Independent Church was not a political party in disguise. He even became the Honorary President of the Philippine Independent Church. Taft may well have thought that, apart from immediate political considerations, this Church offered the best guarantee that religious freedom would really take root in the Philippines. Perhaps, like many others, he believed that the Roman Catholic Church is at its best only when it has strong competition.

But the fate of the Philippine Independent Church was Aglipay's first concern. A Supreme Council was formed, and it immediately began to study a Constitution for the Church which had been prepared by Pio Romero about whom we have already heard.

One of the key questions facing Aglipay and his advisers was the matter of Church property. Who owned the great parish churches which stood like cathedrals in so many of the towns of the Philippines? In Aglipay's opinion they belonged to the people who had built them, or at least to the municipalities which had shared in the expense. He felt that he represented the people and for a time he signed his proclamations as "Bishop of the Philippines." He was always a man of action. On September 27, in the name of the Filipino clergy and people, he informed the Governor and the Archbishop that the existing Roman Catholic Church Government could not be recognized. The cathedral in Manila belonged to the Filipino people and not to the Holy See, and for that reason he asked the Governor to determine the title thereto. Implicitly this meant a claim on the part of the new Church to

all the property hitherto owned by Rome. A judgment in Aglipay's favor would have wide significance. So began a struggle
which was not terminated until 1906. Aglipay had taken the of-
fensive.

Other significant events occurred during these early days, and
one of the most important was the solution of the question of the
episcopate. This was a knotty problem indeed for how could this
be solved with any appearance of validity? It was quite evident
that the Gordian knot had to be cut. Father Pedro Brillantes was
appointed to the Diocese of Ilocos Norte and made Bacarra his
See city. He took possession on October 1, occupying the old
Roman Church of St. James the Greater together with its com-
modious rectory. On October 19 he was consecrated bishop by
more than twenty priests, and it was claimed that there was
ancient ecclesiastical precedent for such an act. Achútegui and
Bernad refer to a "report" that Brillantes arrived with bolo in
hand and threatened with instant death any clergy who would
not take part.[2] As a matter of fact Brillantes needed no such
method in order to secure a quorum as Ilocos Norte was almost
solidly Independent. Apparently unsubstantiated rumors have a
value even for the best scholars, when they serve one's cause.
Brillantes, therefore, has a place in history as the first Independent
bishop to be consecrated.

On Saturday and Sunday, October 25 and 26, Aglipay was
inaugurated in the Tondo district of Manila with much rejoicing
and excitement. Sunday morning Aglipay celebrated his first
mass as Supreme Bishop and afterward delivered a sermon. This
he did in the open air of the street as there was not room for the
crowd upstairs in the building. Afterwards the editor of the
newspaper *El Grito del Pueblo* read the third "Fundamental
Epistle" which is quoted later in this chapter. A letter from
Aguinaldo was read which ended with the words, "Long live the
Philippine Church."

An important event took place soon afterward. In November
the second Apostolic Delegate, Giovanni Baptista Guidi, arrived
in Manila. He came bearing the final answer of the Pope to all

the issues raised by the Revolution, and in reply to all the appeals which had been made by the Filipino people and clergy. It was in the form of a "Constitution" and, as was the custom, it took its title from the first three words *Quae mari Sinico*. As usual in such matters, its contents had "leaked" in one manner or another so that Aglipay was able to answer it in his "Fifth Fundamental Epistle" on the same day that it was officially promulgated from the Manila Cathedral on December 8, 1902.

The Constitution which had been so eagerly awaited by all classes of the people, may be summarized as follows:

Introduction

The Philippines were scarcely opened up at the beginning of the 16th century before the Holy Cross was placed on its shores and it was consecrated to God and offered as a first fruit of the Catholic religion.

From that time every effort has been made to convert the inhabitants, who were idol worshippers, to the faith in Christ. This was done with great success with the aid of different religious orders so that Gregory XIII appointed a bishop and constituted Manila as an Episcopal See.

Growth followed in every way. Slavery was abolished, the inhabitants were trained in the ways of civilization by the study of the arts and letters so that the people and Church in the Philippines were distinguished by the renown of the nation and their zeal for religion.

But the fortunes of war, which effected changes in civil matters, affected religion also. When the Spanish yoke was removed, the patronage of the King ceased and the Church has attained a larger share of liberty, ensuring for everyone rights which are safe and unassailable.

It was necessary to restore ecclesiastical discipline promptly. For this purpose we sent Placide Louis Chapelle, Bishop of New Orleans, as our delegate. He was to study the situation, take what immediate measures were necessary and report to us. This he did to our great satisfaction.

The Government of the United States sent a legation to adjust certain questions, and this effort we encouraged so that a settlement is to be effected on the ground.

We decree this Constitution for the best interests of the Philippine Islands, trusting that with the aid of the Civil Government it may be zealously observed.

(I) *On the new boundaries of dioceses.* This article prescribes the creation of certain new dioceses.

(II) *The Metropolitan and his Suffragan Bishops.* The Archbishop of Manila is to have the title of Metropolitan. His duties and his relations to his suffragans are to be in accord with existing ecclesiastical law.

(III) *The Metropolitan and Suffragan Chapters.* The Metropolitan should have a College of Canons. As the Spanish Government no longer pays salaries, the Delegate must see that provision is made.

Other cathedral churches should form such colleges. Until this can be done the bishop shall choose as consultors priests, both regular and secular, who are distinguished for their piety, learning and experience.

(IV) *Vacant Suffragan Sees.* Provision is made for their administration in case there is a vacancy.

(V) *The Secular Clergy.* As a native clergy is needed everywhere their number must be increased in such manner, however, as to form them thoroughly in piety and character and to make sure that they are worthy to be entrusted with ecclesiastical charges.

Let the bishop gradually appoint native priests to more responsible positions.

The clergy must not be mixed up in party strife nor should they engage in worldly pursuits. All priests, both secular and religious, must cultivate religion. Synods should be called from time to time.

(VI) *The Seminaries.* There should be a seminary in each diocese. The candidates shall remain until, if deserving, they shall have been ordained priests, and never permitted, except for grave reason, to return to their homes.

The administration of the seminary shall be entrusted to one of the clergy, whether secular or religious, who is distinguished for his prudence and experience in governing, and for his holiness of life.

Since the halls of Rome are open to young students who may wish to pursue the higher studies in this very center of truth, the Holy See will do its share to advance the secular clergy in higher learning so that in good time it may be worthy to assume the pastoral charges now administered by the religious priests.

(VII) *The Religious Education of Youth and the Manila University.* Bishops must look after the young who are instructed in the public schools. They must see and insist that teachers are fitted for their task and that the books in use contain no errors.

Then follows praise for the University of Santo Tomás, and it was declared to be a Pontifical University.

(VIII) *The Regulars.* The Holy See has decided to make suitable provision for the members of the regular clergy. Instructions for the religious follow, including the admonition that they must reverence and honor their bishops. They must also live in concord with the secular clergy.

(IX) *The Parishes.* The bishops are to determine what parishes are to be entrusted to pastors from the religious orders.

(X) *Missions.* Mission work is to be done in areas where the people are still buried in monstrous idolatry.

(XI) *Ecclesiastical Discipline.* To restore ecclesiastical discipline we have sent John Baptist Guidi, Archbishop of Stauropolis as Apostolic Delegate with full authority. He is to hold a provincial synod as soon as possible.

(XII) *On peace and reverence for those in authority.* The appeal is made to all the inhabitants of the Philippines to maintain union in the bond of peace. This is necessary for the good of religion and for the welfare of the country which can gain nothing by public demonstrations. Let them reverence those who exercise authority, for all power is of God. The Holy See will never fail to protect their interests.

(Follows the usual affirmation of the validity of the Constitution and the penalties for disobeying or opposing it).[3]

If anything were needed to make Aglipay take the irrevocable step of being consecrated bishop without the aid of Rome, this pronouncement by the Pope would have settled the matter. It was a bitter disappointment to all Filipinos whether or not they remained loyal to the Roman Catholic Church. The Constitution showed that lack of apprehension of the intense desire of all Filipinos for recognition. Aglipay's own reaction is revealed in his "Fifth Fundamental Epistle" which is summarized later in the chapter.

In the midst of popular indignation, therefore, he was consecrated bishop on January 18, 1903 in a temporary chapel on Calle Lemery in Manila. From the Roman Catholic point of view the consecration was invalid, and no one was more conscious of this than Aglipay himself. The break with Rome was in reality one of a series of steps, and this consecration was one of the most important. There must have been an ache in his heart no matter how justified and in fact inevitable the action. Reformation does not come without pain.

It is necessary, if one desires to know Aglipay's inner motivations and attitudes at this critical time, to read the six "Fundamental Epistles" which he issued to the clergy and people of the Philippines. They are important. Here was a man who shared the aspirations and the dangers of the greatest of his predecessors. He was carrying a torch handed on by that small group of prophetic figures who had gone before. His detractors may ransack the libraries, and explore the archives from Washington to Manila, in order to blur this figure in the minds of men and to cast discredit on the religious reformation in the Philippines; but the fact remains that here was a *man*. He was not afraid to speak his mind and to take decisive action "against wind and wave." With this in mind, we read a summary of the first official statements with which he addressed his countrymen. The first of these was dated September 22, 1902.

First Fundamental Epistle
THE EPISCOPATE

This is in the form of a letter to a priest of the Independent Church who has been elected bishop.

After informing the priest of his election, he goes on to urge that all loyal Christians everywhere, and in the diocese in question, should recognize and obey him in his new capacity.

He urges the bishop-elect to act worthy of his office, devoting himself night and day to the welfare of his flock and conforming himself to St. Paul's instructions to Timothy.

He recommends that twelve brother priests of the province be formed into a Council, or at least three if twelve are not available.

After consulting with many authorities including impartial

Romanists, he is convinced that the consecration will be valid. The reasons for this are:

A. The apostles themselves have not prescribed any formula for a consecration, the will of the congregations being sufficient.

B. He agrees that Jesus Christ, who consecrated the Apostles, was a Bishop—but priests are true representatives of the blessed Redeemer.

C. Many authors assert that bishop and priest mean the same thing. The bishops merely represent a hierarchy which many in democratic lands consider to be non-essential.

D. If a layman, in emergency, can administer Holy Baptism, why cannot a priest administer Holy Orders in case of necessity? St. Thomas Aquinas has the opinion that necessity makes licit that which is illicit by law.

E. St. Paul said that old things are passing away. We now have all things new.

In the Philippines, therefore, all should be new except the divine. If we now seek for Greek, Russian, Anglican or Protestant (ministers) to ordain us we are not willing to escape from our slavery . . .

> President of the Executive Committee
> Isabelo de los Reyes

El Obispo Maximo
Gregorio Aglipay

Second Fundamental Epistle (Manila October 2, 1902)
No Schism—Further Instructions to Bishops

Not a sparrow falls to the ground without God. In the divine Providence good comes out of evil, and the Revolution through which we have passed has castigated the errors of the friarocracy.

Bishop Alcocer[4] blasphemes in denouncing that which is evidently the design of Providence. He controverts what Jesus said about giving to Caesar the things that are Caesar's, and also he denies the encyclical of Leo XIII which orders that the clergy should not meddle in politics. Bishop Alcocer also excites the Filipinos against the Americans. This is seditious. He says that this "new people" came with the desire to proselytize, to proclaim false liberties, and to encourage immorality, superstition, impiety, scandals, and hatred of Catholicism. The promises of the Americans have not been kept. We should not be astonished that such a bishop treats us with so little Christian charity, defying even Providence and the Americans to whom we owe protection.

If we defend ourselves against the Pope who treats our poor Filipino priests unjustly, they call it a "schism." We do not grant that there has been a schism because we have only obeyed a natural necessity to defend our rights. We leave the Romanists in silence and shall follow our road with our spirits fixed on God.

We charge the (Independent) bishops that they should make their rectories and parish houses into seminaries and that they ordain as large a number of new priests as possible. They should teach the minor orders no more than Christian doctrine as the Council of Trent orders.

Later they will study theology in order that they may receive the order of priesthood within one or two years at most. These shall complete their instructions afterwards. The scarcity of priests is the pretext used by Rome to bring in foreign priests. We must do this before the Spanish friars, after training in the United States, come back to take possession.[5]

Unless we do this, the municipalities who have claimed ownership of the church buildings, in order to return them to the priests of our Church, will undoubtedly bow to the foreign prelates and give the churches to them.

In any event, the Executive Committee urges that the towns and parishes should construct our own churches, rectories and cemeteries.

President of the Executive Committee

El Obispo Maximo
Gregorio Aglipay

Third Fundamental Epistle (Manila, October 17, 1902)
THE FAITH OF THE INDEPENDENT CHURCH

Greetings, Sons of Jesus Christ.

May the spirit of eternal wisdom descend upon you and make you understand that we have separated ourselves not because we are thinking of our own dignity but because we wish to re-establish in all its splendor the worship of the one true God and the purity of his Holy Word which have been lost under the reign of obscurantism.[6]

The Roman Church has been guilty of simony and exploitation, at the same time deceiving the credulous with the most daring fairy tales and absurd miracles which it attributes to the saints in order to deify them and depreciate the worship of the one true God. The greed of the imposters is so great that they have relegated to oblivion the idea of God symbolized in the august Trinity.

The creation itself is the great miracle. It is the duty of the Christian priest to enrich his intelligence in many fields of knowledge in order to communicate to the faithful the progress of science, explaining and pondering on the prodigious grandeur of the universe . . . and the exact and surprising laws of nature. All this proves the existence of a Supreme Being who has created all things, at the same time awakening in our hearts admiration, gratitude, and love for the Providence which guides and protects us as well as ministering to our necessities. Behold the lilies of the field.

Compare this sublime conception with the absurd heroics attributed to the sacred miracles credited to the saints. This is pagan, not Christian. The Romanists have invented the miracles to get money from us at the cost of serious religion.

You must make known the sacred Scriptures, suppressing absurd commentaries. God does not need daring interpreters in order to make himself known to his creatures. It is sufficient for the priest to explain and emphasize the application of biblical teachings; but never let us dare to change the genuine sense. Read and savor the Bible without fanciful commentaries.

In the place of idolatrous prayers, put the Psalms into the hands of the people. They teach us to glorify him from the intimate recesses of our hearts. They make us say, "Praise the Lord, O my soul," who made the heaven and the earth, the sea and all that in them is, who guards the truth, does justice to the aggrieved, gives bread to the hungry, opens the eyes of the blind, loves the just, pardons sinners. He is the father of all without distinction of peoples or religions.

Read to our brethren *The Book of Job* where God shows his eternity, majestic power, and wisdom by the consideration of natural things.

God exists in the measureless heavens and in the wonders of a drop of water. This cannot be the work of chance.

God fills all the universe with his marvellous essence. He is goodness itself, the supreme power, infinite omniscience, greater than our tongue can define or our intelligence conceive.

Jesus taught that God is One, but there are three who bear witness in heaven: the Father, the Word and the Holy Spirit, and these three are One.

There are diversities of gifts but the same Spirit, the same Lord, the same God and Father who is over all things and through all things, and in you.

In the Trinity we see the Omnipotence which created the universe, the supreme abnegation of Jesus who dies to redeem man and the whole creation, and the Holy Spirit who sustains and guides us with love ineffable.

God became man to redeem us and to teach us to love all creatures. In him we confess our failures, implore his pardon, and pray that he may continue to plead for us before the tribunal of his justice, putting into the balance the immensity of his own mercy.

It is holy and praiseworthy that we preserve our simple customs and a profound veneration of the saints of the Lord, and especially for the ideal Virgin; but we must not diminish the majesty of our religion with heretical exaggerations. We condemn the deification of the saints that causes almost complete forgetfulness of the one true God. We must not pray ten *Ave Marias* to one *Pater Noster*.

Let us shake off the obscurantism of four centuries and have the strength to think with the reason God has given to us.

We recommend to our venerable bishops and priests that they always reserve the central place on the altars for the symbols of the divine Trinity, allocating the sides for the sweet Virgin Mary and the servants of God.

We urge our brethren to exercise charity and to lead holy lives, especially in this epoch of trial through which we are passing, so that no one can say that we have separated from Rome only to indulge our own weaknesses.

El Obispo Maximo
Gregorio Aglipay

Fourth Fundamental Epistle[7] (Manila, October 29, 1902)
ORGANIZATION—THEOLOGICAL TRAINING

Here you have, my friends in Jesus Christ, in the brilliant inauguration of our Philippine Independent Church, the unhoped for culmination with which our Lord has crowned the forces of our compatriot Catholics who, zealous of the true glory of the only God and of our national dignity "against wind and wave" (according to our detractors), have carried forward the great enterprise of religious redemption.

In spite of my absolute lack of merit they have designated me as your pilot to carry the ship of Jesus to a secure haven. Therefore, my most loved and courageous mariners, I accept with resignation that difficult and thorny mission—although I consider it superior to my feeble strength—in the hope and on the condition that each one of you will give me the effectiveness of your indomitable will and your titanic forces.

The first step of separation came from a *cumulo* of forces pent up for many centuries; but the second step, the creation of new organizations, needs greater inner strength, constancy, intelligence, and good will.

Let us therefore create diocesan communities, and sub-committees in parishes, in order to divide the work. (Follows a statement as to just how the organization shall be completed. It includes a direction that there are to be committees of women paralleling those of the men.)

These committees shall demonstrate to the faithful that this is not a schismatic body. Rather, the Pope is schismatic because he has separated himself from the justice of God and from the purity of his Word. He teaches false doctrine about the saints, beclouds the Bible and denigrates our priests claiming that they are inefficient.

The committees must make plain that before taking this radical step we have drunk the dregs of humiliation. We have refused, to the last moment, to sanction the separation declared three months ago in the Centro de Bellas Artes. But because even the just American Government has had to send our wise Governor General to give impartial testimony about the religious question in these Islands . . . and because the Jesuit priests told me, when I was defending the rights of the clergy and the faithful Filipinos, that we must not think about clerical dignities because our Filipino priests are unfit to be bishops, the cup of indignation overflowed.[8]

The committees must convince the parochial, and other priests, of the propriety and the necessity of transferring to our national Church as it is not in harmony with their dignity nor with patriotic sentiment not to do so.

The committees must induce the municipalities to give to our Church the church buildings, parish houses and cemeteries of which they are the legitimate owners, having been constructed by municipal workers and municipal funds for the spiritual service of the towns. The municipalities have never ceded these properties to the Roman Church.

The committees must speedily create seminaries to provide parishes with young and instructed priests. The scarcity of priests is the principal pretext which the Romanists have for introducing foreign clergy. They shall attract students, assuring them that in two years only they will be given instruction which is complete, precise, and more nutritious than the interminable years of unnecessary dissertations and unfruitful discussions . . .

It is recommended to the committees that they build chapels, or modest churches, according to the resources of each community.

Do not be afraid of the excommunications with which the intrusive Bishop Alcocer threatens those who will not listen to the friars. (Then follows an allusion to St. Peter who said "Truly I find that God is no respecter of persons," and similar references from the New Testament).

We have the same beliefs as the Roman Christians, except that we do not obey the Pope. This is not unusual as we find the same thing in Europe, England, Russia, Germany, and the United States.

The friars may fulminate excommunications, but they avoid reason and calm discussion. We appeal to the inexorable tribunal of God.

We are the ones who have given proofs of our love of our country, risking our lives on the field of battle. It is the friars who have assassinated Rizal, Burgos Gómez, Zamora, Herrera, Prieto, Diaz, and other poor brothers of ours.

But let us forget the past and pray for those who so greatly persecute us.

El Obispo Maximo
Gregorio Aglipay

Approved by the Supreme Council.

Fifth Fundamental Epistle (Manila December 8, 1902)
REACTION TO THE POPE'S CONSTITUTION

Pope Leo XIII has just sent his awaited Constitution by his delegate Monsignor Guidi. This has brought terrible disillusionment to the Filipino people.

The Filipino people, having engaged in a vigorous Revolution and winning the admiration of the whole world, have demonstrated their worth. This has also been proclaimed by the Congress of the United States. There is also the evidence of such writers as José Rizal, Isabelo de los Reyes, Pardo de Tavera, and others who have made plain that the Filipinos at the time of the arrival of the Spaniards were a cultured people, having their own religion, legislation, writing, armament, shipping for foreign trade, and populous cities. The Spaniards actually hindered the growth of the Islands. In spite of this the Pope in this Constitution, casting aspersions upon our ancestors, states that the friars rescued us from idolatrous worship and introduced us to human culture.

The idolatry of the people was not so bad as that introduced by the friars with their images.

The Pope also praises Chapelle who showed that he was in favor of the friars. Mr. Taft, the Governor of the Philippines, no whit inferior to the Pope, wished to expel the friars if they would not go voluntarily. Yet the Pope establishes this "Constitution."

Filipino priests are told that, while they must go to Rome—the very "center of truth"—their places will be occupied by the friars who will refuse to be removed. The friars, in the meantime, will have all the ecclesiastical honors.

The Pope would not disinherit the indigenous clergy completely; but only those candidates will be accepted for a seminary who can give assurances of their meekness and servility. This they describe as "discipline."

The seminaries are to be directed by outstanding men, and this means the friars. The Pope gives the title of "Pontifical University" to Santo Tomás, yet it was here, according to report, that the assassination of Burgos, Zamora and Gómez was contrived. Here is printed a periodical which daily insults our priests.

The Pope proclaims *Urbi et Orbi* that he "agrees to give providential opportunities for the return of the friars."

In regard to the parishes, the Pontiff does not remember the

Filipinos and only remembers the friars. Nor does he remember that in accordance with the Council of Trent the parishes should be provided with secular clergy.

The Pope says that "the parishes must commend themselves to the ministers of the religious orders." And the Pope will not even keep the friars from their former curacies, considering them as founders and proprietors.

The Pope tells the Filipino clergy to "regulate their lives and customs," with the implication that the friars were blessed saints.

The last paragraph of the Constitution treats of the pacification of minds and the reverence which is owed to them that govern. We believe that instead of pacifying us, this Constitution will make the Filipino clergy shake off the Roman yoke.

"To no one," terminates the Pope, as if dealing with savages, "shall it be licit to infringe on, or with reckless audacity to contradict, this letter. And if anyone does so, let him know that he will incur the indignation of the omnipotent God and of his blessed apostles St. Peter and St. Paul."

If later the Pope shall come to modify this Constitution, in the sense of nominating Filipino bishops and parochial priests, it will be due, no doubt, to the rapid progress of the Philippine Independent Church.

By the Supreme Council of the Philippine Independent Church
Gregorio Aglipay
Supreme Bishop

Sixth Fundamental Epistle (Manila, August 17, 1903)
LIBERTY

This epistle treats of the Independent clergy of Jaro who declare that they will not obey the Pope in discipline but they will obey him in dogma. Aglipay says that no compromise like this is possible. Either the clergy must return to Rome or remain loyal to the Independent Church. He speaks also of some clergy in Luzon who seem to have come over into the Independent Church with the object of "boring from within" and thus creating dissension within the ranks. These are false brethren secretly entered in like those mentioned by St. Paul, in order to destroy the liberty which we have in Christ Jesus. They do not understand the true spirit of the Philippine Independent Church.

He then concludes with the ode to liberty which has been quoted in chapter one. Its last paragraph reads:

"Holy, Holy, Holy, Thou art the eternal Trinity to whom we owe our religious liberty. Heaven and earth are full of thy glory." [9]

El Obispo Maximo
Gregorio Aglipay

From the theological point of view, these epistles are orthodox, unless one confounds orthodoxy with the claims of the Papacy and considers that the Holy Catholic Church is to be identified with the Vatican. They are in conformity with the great Creeds of historic Christianity. Except in one respect this reformation most resembles that of the Church of England, in that while maintaining the historic faith and much of the liturgy and ceremonial, it discards certain accretions, distortions, and superstition of the centuries. It feels that the importance and function given to the saints and to their images, obscure the worship of the Trinity. It emphasizes that these heroic figures should have our veneration in the Communion of Saints, and it magnifies Mary as the mother of our Lord; but it says that the saints should not be worshipped nor have such a part in the cultus that the vision of God is clouded.[10] So these epistles conceive that the great mass of the people would find themselves at home in a Church purged of certain of these emphases.

There would be, however, a new feeling of emancipation. There would come a conception of that true "Christian liberty" which does not repress the creative spirit of God leading the individual to a more abundant life. The emphasis here is on that second part of St. Augustine's doctrine in the *City of God* which maintains that we are "saved by faith." This means personal religion. It means the grace of God working in the heart leading to personal self-realization and even to prophecy. This emancipation is still within the framework of revelation.

Revelation is also made through nature. With the Hebrew psalmist, Aglipay says that the heavens declare the glory of God and the firmament shows his handiwork. The mind of man must be free to explore the mysteries of nature—as it does in scientific investigations—not denying fact as fact, but believing that every fact rightly interpreted adds to our appreciation of the majesty of God.

In only one respect does this statement of faith differ essentially from that of the Anglican Reformation. In England the historic continuity of the Apostolic succession had been maintained without a break. In the Philippine Independent Church it had been abandoned under the force of necessity. This, of course, was the weakest part of the armor, and Rome did not fail to take advantage of it.

Chapter XI

Popular Success and Legal Failure

The Apostolic Delegate, Guidi, was greatly disturbed by the claim which Aglipay made to the Manila Cathedral in September 1902. His concern was not lessened when the latter had replied to the Pope's Constitution on the same day that it was officially issued. In the midst of all the excitement, an incident occured at a public reception given by Governor Taft which Mrs. Taft recorded in her book.[1] It reveals something of the temper of the times.

"At one of my first receptions that season quite a dramatic scene occurred in the ballroom. A thousand or more people, perhaps, had passed in the receiving line. Monsignor Guidi came in all his stately regalia, and shortly afterwards Aglipay put in his appearance. The people wandered all over the place, circulating through the spacious gardens and around the verandas; so there was a possibility that these two would not meet, even though they were both very conspicuous figures. But it was not long before the Papal Delegate hurried up to Mr. Taft and, in a state of visible excitement, asked who the stranger in striking religious garb might be.

'That,' said Mr. Taft, 'is Aglipay.'

'But you know,' said the Monsignor, 'it is impossible for you to receive him here when I am present!'

Then Mr. Taft once more laboriously explained the standpoint of the American Government, saying that Aglipay was in his house as a citizen and that it would not be possible to ask him to leave as long as he conducted himself as a guest should.

'Then I shall have to go,' said Monsignor Guidi.

'I am very sorry,' said Mr. Taft. 'I understand your position perfectly and I trust that you understand mine as well.'

So the highest of the insular Church dignitaries got his hat and hastened away while the 'renegade and impious imposter' remained in serene unconsciousness of the disturbance he had created. Perhaps not. At least he was serene." [1]

This episode was, of course, headlined in the Manila press. The present Supreme Bishop of the Independent Church, Isabelo de los Reyes, says in a letter to the writer, "This incident greatly increased the faith of the people in America's devotion to freedom of worship and fair treatment to all, and also explains Aglipay's leaning toward Unitarianism."

Many causes, however, led to the landslide to the Independent Church which began in 1903. The Pope's Constitution seemed to be a denial of Filipino dignity and the people as a whole were offended. It appeared that they were still considered as incompetent children not mature enough to do a man's work. At the time that the Constitution appeared, Filipino priests of all persuasions were occupying the parishes no longer as assistants but as pastors. Now it was evident that they were to be reduced, in most cases at least, to their former inferior positions. It was humiliating. On the other hand, the Supreme Bishop of the Independent Church had fought in the wars and both he and all his bishops and priests were Filipinos. Transferring to this Church was one way to express a sense of outrage.

Guidi's announcement that American bishops would replace the Spanish prelates added fuel to the flames. The war against America was still fresh in men's minds and many remembered what Archbishop Nozaleda had said about that barbaric country in his earlier manifestos. The mass of the people had no conception of the separation of Church and State, and it appeared to many that these American bishops might prove to be even worse that the Spanish friars. One foreign sovereignty which they knew was being exchanged for another which might be even more objectionable.

The movement toward the Independent Church was looked upon with great sympathy by the Protestant leaders. These men, as had been shown, were not willing to assume any responsibility for the movement but they welcomed it because the break with the Papacy would make their evangelistic work easier. There was the not altogether admirable feeling that many Independents might come to them—in other words that the Independent Church would prove to be a half-way house to a Protestantism of their own pattern. As one said, "Aglipay shakes the tree and we gather the fruit." For whatever reason, the Protestant bodies looked with favor on the movement and had their influence upon public opinion.

Masonry had become strong in the Islands. Emanating from Spain, it was of the Latin variety and therefore strongly anti-Roman Catholic. It had played its part in revolutionary days and now it helped to create a climate of opinion helpful to the Church which was independent of Rome.

The Labor movement was another source of strength. While it is doubtless true, as Achútegui states, that the number attending the historic labor meeting on August 3 has been exaggerated, it cannot be denied that the spirit of organized labor was anti-Roman Catholic. That particular meeting, it should be remembered, was hastily organized when the great anti-friar rally was forbidden by the American authorities. It is not strange, therefore, if the number was comparatively small. The speech of Isabelo de los Reyes, in which he proclaimed an Independent Filipino Church, struck a responsive chord. Organized labor was interested in the new Church and helped it on its way.

There can be no doubt, moreover, that Taft's doctrine of "peaceable possession," described later in the chapter, gave the Church great impetus.

For all these reasons the Philippine Independent Church provided a rallying point for the national feeling at a time when it needed some outlet for expression. From the end of 1903 until the Supreme Court decision of 1906 the Independent Church spread rapidly. Thousands, one could say hundreds of thousands, allied themselves with it. More than this, it was organized on a national scale from one end of the Philippines to the other, and to this day it is the only Church beside the Roman Catholic which has such a wide distribution.

The defection from Rome was greatest, of course, in those regions where the friars had had great land holdings and where consequently the anti-friar feeling was at its height. It was not, however, confined to those areas, for the universal sentiment was that Filipino priests and bishops should be given due recognition. Achútegui and Bernad, who may be expected to give the most conservative estimate, say that the Church spread most rapidly and extensively in Ilocos Norte where whole populations went over. The spread was slower in Ilocos Sur. Three towns in Abra Province were strongholds. The Church, they say, made but little headway in Manila but it was organized in Victoria, Tarlac, in Lingayen, Dagupan, and in the provinces of Zambales and Cavite. One Roman priest reported that in Marinduque one Independent priest had partially failed in his "satanic work." In the Visayas, Negros, both Occidental and Oriental, the Independent Church obtained a strong hold and it was particularly successful on the north coast of Mindanao. Achútegui's list might have been a good deal longer. For instance, the classic case before the Supreme Court in 1906 was in reference to a parish in the Camarines which was claimed both by the Independent Church and Rome.

When we come to consider the actual number of people who belonged to this Church during the period we are considering, the estimates vary so much that it is impossible to get at the exact truth. In 1903 there were some 7,000,000 Filipinos, more or less. Aglipay told Taft in 1905 that the number of his adherents was 3,500,000; this would represent about one half of the population. Stuntz reckoned that in 1904 the number of Independents was 2,000,000 which would be about one fourth of the population, and Cameron Forbes agrees with this estimate. Blair and Robertson say that in 1904 the number was about 1,500,000. The official census of 1918 gives the figure of 1,417,418 members out of a total population of about 10,000,000. This would indicate that more conservative estimates about the years 1903-1905 were nearer the truth. The Church records tell us little or nothing.

One must remember to take all of these figures, whether large or small, official or unofficial, with a certain amount of salt. The Filipinos of the period were not used to exact statistics. In Spanish days the people were not prone to admit any belief save that of Roman Catholicism, and the tendency to say as little in response to inquiry was one of long standing. For years the Independent Church was popularly known as "The Filipino Catholic Church," and we may well imagine that people in many cases simply said "Catholic" when asked their religious affiliation. This would put it up to the census taker to decide whether this meant Roman Catholic or not. In this same election of 1918 there were over 600,000 unregistered voters, and no one knew what their affiliation was. Many of the figures given were estimates, and we may as well settle for the figure of 2,000,000 as representing the high point in the years before 1906.

However, Achútegui and Bernad admit that the emergence of this Church was highly important and that its religious significance cannot be minimized. It claimed a fourth of the population and was in truth a major religious revolution.[2]

The rapid spread of the Independent Church was not accomplished without pain. In many cases it divided towns into factions and in families it was often brother against brother. In some towns where there was no great Roman Catholic Church building, it was quite simple. The Independent priest would arrive, win converts and start a parish. In places where the Roman Church has been well established for many years, one of two things happened. Either the priest and the whole town population went over, or there would be two groups claiming the property. Aglipay claimed that all Church property belonged to the Filipinos, and thus the Independent faction believed that it was simply fighting for its own. This could and did lead to trouble and even to violence. The events in Pandacan, Manila, soon after Aglipay's inauguration illustrate the temper of the times. Wise quotes Laubach and Stuntz as follows:

"The spread of the new Church from this point was most dramatic. A Filipino priest, Father Serrondo, at Pandacan, Manila, made some insulting reference to Bishop Aglipay. When Father Serrondo came out of the Church he was assaulted by a mob of women. They tore his cassock in shreds, rolled him in the dirt and let him go, glad to escape with his life. Members of the congregation sent for the new Archbishop Aglipay to come and say mass in the Pandacan church. This he did "before a vast crowd." Two hundred irate women took their bedding and cooking utensils and slept in the churchyard to prevent the regular priest from entering the building. Other churches invited Aglipay to use their buildings and the city was in a furor." [3]

One can really feel sorry for Mr. Taft in those days. This is what he writes about this same incident:

"In the case of a church in Pandacan, the women of the parish in the temporary absence of the priest, took possession of the church, obtaining the keys, and Father Aglipay celebrated mass in the church. I sent for him and for his counsel, and advised them on the unlawful character of the action of the women and directed them to see that possession was restored. They promised to do so, but I found the women so obdurate that I called in the women and told them that I must have the keys. The leader of the women delivered the keys to me with the statement that they would deliver the keys to the governor but not to the 'fraile.' The new priest who had been appointed was not a fraile but a Paulist Father. They announced to me that they had separated from the Roman Catholic Church and were standing with Aglipay. I turned the keys over to the chief of police and put the regularly appointed priest in possession of the church and quiet now reigns there. Yesterday (Sunday) I am informed that Father Aglipay assumed the robes and functions of an archbishop holding services in the town of Cavite and in the neighborhood." [4]

During these early years Aglipay endeavored to restrain his followers and urged them to keep within the directives of the Commission about such matters and later to abide by court decisions. But feelings were aroused and it was extremely difficult to control matters all over the Islands. Some charges made against his followers are unsubstantiated. Other incidents undoubtedly occurred for which the leaders of the movement could not be blamed. All that one can say is that things of this sort were inevitable in the heat of passion. To put it mildly, many unfortunate things happened in connection with the Protestant Reformation in Europe. This does not mean that the first great Reformation was unjustified.

As was to be expected, there were many passionate utterances from the pulpits of both Churches, and the press was full of vilification. All that one can say is that such things are a part of the frailty of our human nature and are not without precedent. This is not an absolution, but the pot need not call the kettle black.

Taft, at first, tried to settle the controversy about church property by executive action. The Pandacan incident had revealed to him how serious the whole matter was and so, in 1903, he issued a proclamation confirming the actual occupants of church property who were in peaceful possession, provided that in the future there was to be no acquisition of property by violent means. This was known as the doctrine of "peaceable possession" and it did a great deal to strengthen the growth of the Independent Church, as did the fact that many municipalities had claimed the church properties in the towns and then had handed them over to Aglipay. Among other things they claimed that the churches stood on public ground and so belonged to the towns.

However, Taft's attempt at solution only made matters worse as many difficult questions arose. One Roman Catholic bishop sent a priest to take possession of a parish which had been claimed by the Independents but was untenanted. Could this be called "peaceable possession?" Mr. Taft, probably in some desperation, appealed to his attorney general who answered that each case must be settled in the courts, not by the executive. The result was that the lower courts were flooded with cases, and while these were generally settled in favor of the Roman Church there was always the opportunity for an appeal.

On July 24, 1905 the Philippine Commission enacted a special law to settle such disputes which was worded as follows:

An act for the speedy disposition of controversies to the right of administration or possession of churches, convents, cemeteries, and other church properties and as to the ownership and title thereto, by vesting in the Supreme Court of the Philippines original jurisdiction to decide such controversies and for other purposes.[5]

The primary case in the Supreme Court which became a precedent for all succeeding cases was that of Father Jorge Barlin, a Filipino Roman priest, against Bishop Vincente Ramirez representing the Philippine Independent Church. Bishop Ramirez had been a Roman priest and had taken possession of the parish of Lagonoy, Camarines Sur, in July 1901 under the regular Roman Catholic authorities. In November 1902 he and the whole town went over to the Independent Church with the approval of the town authorities who passed a resolution to that effect. The Roman Church now claimed the parish.

The main argument in favor of Ramirez, the defendant, was as follows:

(1) The people built the churches by their forced labor; and if they belonged to anyone, they should belong to them that built them or their successors; the people having gone to the Independent Church the property should belong to it.

(2) That Pope Alexander VI by his Papal Bull of May 3, 1493 gave to the Catholic King of Spain supreme control over all matters in the Roman Catholic Church in the colonies, surrendering also titles to Church properties. This, together with the fact that the Church and the State were then identical, made the United States the rightful successor of Spain over these properties and hence these properties should be employed for public (religious) purposes thus maintaining the status quo at the time of the proclamation of the Peaceable Possession.[6]

It should be noted that at this juncture the Independent Church was claiming only that property of which it was in "peaceable possession." It was not seeking to oust the Roman Church from buildings and institutions over which the latter had not lost actual authority. The Independents wanted to retain the status of the moment. This was, of course, a recession from the position that it owned all the property in the name of the people and sought to oust the Roman Catholics where they, too, were in peaceable possession.

On November 24, 1906 the Supreme Court decided the case in favor of the plaintiff, Jorge Barlin and the Roman Catholic Church, and ordered the Philippine Independent Church to return the property. Wise quotes a portion of the decree as follows:

(1) (The Court held) That the Spanish Government at the time the treaty of peace was signed was not the owner of the property nor of any other property like it situated in the Philippines and that the Spanish Sovereign was a mere "patron."

(2) That in 1898 and prior to the treaty of Paris, the Roman Catholic Church had by law, the exclusive right to the possession of this church, etc. as article 8 of the Treaty of Paris definitely states: "And it is hereby declared that the relinquishment or cession as the case may be to which the preceding paragraph refers, cannot in any respect impair the property or rights which by law belong to the peaceful possession of property of all kinds, of provinces, municipalities, public or private establishments, ecclesiastical or civic bodies or any other associations having legal capacity to acquire and possess property in the aforesaid territories renounced or ceded, or of private individuals of whatsoever nationality such individuals may be."

(3) That the Government of the Philippines never transferred the property to the municipalities.[7]

It is worthy of mention that Justice Carson, while agreeing with the decision of the Court, took exception to the statement that prior to the Treaty of Paris, the Church property did not belong to the King. He felt that the Spanish "Law of the Indies" settled the matter. By this law the churches etc. were to be built at the cost of the royal treasury though a part of the expense was to be laid on the "Indians." No new church could be built without the royal permission, doubtless because the King had to pay the salaries of the friar incumbents. A man who pays for the cost of building construction, has the power to decide on new construction, and pays the salaries of the operatives is much more than a "patron" in the usual sense of the term. While other provisions of the "Law" seemed to indicate that the churches belonged to no man but, by implication, to God, the Justice must have felt that in the adjudication of affairs concerning them the King had the final say. He was, in the human sense, the owner and he had to act as such. It is worth while once again to call attention to the fact that at the Paris Conference the Roman Catholic Church must have been well represented, while no Filipino was allowed to plead the cause of his people. Justice Carson did not press his objection, being moved doubtless by the consideration that these buildings were built for the Roman Catholic Church and, no matter what the circumstances, to that Church they must return.

On the same day that the Supreme Court handed down its decision in the case we have just described, it made a similar decision in the case of The Roman Catholic Church versus Santos. An appeal was made by the Independent Church to the Supreme Court of the United States which in 1909 upheld the decision of the Supreme Court of the Philippines. While this ended the great controversy, it cannot be denied that the Independent Church had a "case." Its legal arguments were not absurd.

In equity the case was much stronger. These people believed that the Roman Catholic Church had never been on their side in the struggle for political and religious liberty. It had never shown sympathy with their national aspirations, any expression of which being ascribed to the spirit of schism or of treason to Spain. Any approach to the Spanish Government or to Rome had fallen upon deaf ears. Evidence of individual initiative had been crushed. These church buildings had been built by them or by their fathers by forced labor and under the lash. These people were patriots, not the scum of the earth as had been claimed, and they believed that Rome had lost all claim on their souls as well as any further jurisdiction over the churches which they themselves had built by the sweat of their brows. In equity, heart, sympathy, and insight have something to say. But equity played no part in this transaction, although men like Taft and Brent felt sympathy with the independent cause. Taft, during these days, may have felt his kinship with some of the good Governors General of Spanish times!

We may sum this up by saying that as the Treaty of Paris was a cold-blooded affair, so this decision of the Supreme Court was cold-blooded and calculating. In the background was the enormous pressure of the Roman Catholic Church in the United States.

The decision of the Court was, of course, a tremendous blow, and many thought that it meant the end of the Philippine Independent Church as a significant element in the national life. Gone forever was the dream that this Church would dominate the Islands. It was only too evident that the Roman Catholic Church was there to stay. It was humiliating to abandon these great churches where they and their parents had worshipped, and the wonder is not that so many abandoned the Independent Church but that so many stayed in it. We might imagine how any of us in the United States would feel if, by some fiat from above, we had to give up our church homes and go forth without a place to lay our heads. To get the picture further we must imagine that all about us we can hear voices saying, "Ah, thus would we have it." We would, I think, feel that we had been driven into the night and that no man cared for our souls—the worst kind of loneliness. So these people tasted the gall and bitterness of defeat and humiliation.

But they did not give up, whether because of native courage or of something deeper. My own theory is that they felt, as no other group, *identified* with the Philippines and carried an ark of the covenant with them into the wilderness. That covenant was with the heroes of the past who had seen visions of a fairer Philippines—and had suffered. They could not see the future but they knew that something precious had been entrusted to them. Like Abraham, they ventured forth into the unknown. Confused and homeless, they started in to rethink and to rebuild.

Chapter XII

Theological Pains

Great as the shock of being expelled from their Church homes was, no physical hardships were involved. This is a tropical country, and the visitor from the north is always intrigued to see how construction problems are simplified by not having to think about central heating. The damage done by the decision of the Supreme Court was more to the pride of the new independent Church than to anything else, because the great old buildings meant prestige. But the faithful swallowed their pride: in the larger cities they put up temporary structures, and in the smaller towns there was bamboo and nipa in abundance. There was even a spiritual value in this because the building was all on a voluntary basis. The old buildings, impressive as they were, were built under the lash. The new ones were built with a glad and willing heart; the priests were paid from their own pocket books; and as for prestige—well, that is a frail reed to lean upon.

From the beginning the minds of the great mass of the people were not much concerned with theology. They knew that they were no longer under the pope and they had a sense of emancipation. All the clergy were Filipinos and that gratified something deep within them. The Fundamental Epistles were quite orthodox in the sense of conformity to the great creeds; and the clergy, for the most part, went on using the old Roman Missal. It was all that they had. This was in Latin and it passed over the peoples' heads. They were not even alert to the new doctrinal emphases of the *Oficio Divino* when it appeared later, for they worshipped before altars as usual, the vestments of the

priest were the same as were the ceremonial and general movement in the great act of worship. People called it "The Filipino
Catholic Church" and the priests celebrated mass, baptized, and
administered all the sacraments in the name of the Trinity.

In the top echelons of the Independent Church hierarchy it
was different; but before we attempt to trace the theological
development from 1906 on, we must turn back to one aspect of
it prior to that period. One of Aglipay's first impulses after the
break with Rome was to make an approach to the Episcopal
Church, and in fact he is quoted as having said at that time that
he would like the new Church to resemble that of the Anglican
Communion. In 1904 he visited Bishop Brent more to sound
him out however, than to make a definite application for the
Anglican Episcopate. The two men did not get very far. Aglipay was wary about making a definite petition in writing and
the whole thing came to nothing. Achútegui and Bernad, in
their book *Religious Revolution in the Philippines*, make much
of these exchanges and the episode will be discussed in greater
length in another chapter. Suffice it to say now that the matter
was dropped.

During this same year Bishop Aglipay was corresponding with
Bishop Herzog of the Swiss National Church, a part of the Old
Catholic Church, which, like the Anglican had the apostolic
succession of bishops. Herzog was interested, and finally told
Bishop Aglipay that he and two others could be consecrated if
they would forward detailed information about the Independent
Church and subscribe to the Declaration of Utrecht. This would
have presented no difficulty as the Declaration was agreeable
to the Church of England. Bishop Aglipay was urged by Morayta, a prominent Mason in Spain, to go ahead as only a Church
with the apostolic succession, he wrote, could cope with Rome.
However, the Bishop hesitated, giving various excuses, and the
moment passed.

Why he took this attitude is anyone's guess. Roman critics of
Aglipay suggest that his conscience was still troubling him about
the break with the Vatican, and they endeavor to show that he

had a continual psychic disturbance about it. The implication was that he was conscious of sin. This, of course, is pure conjecture and, from a psychological point of view, does not seem in accord with his resolute character. He may have been "astute," but that is no criticism. The dictionary gives the word "astute" the following fundamental meanings: "Keen in discernment, acute, shrewd, sagacious, cunning." Certain it is that he had both the inclination and the power to feel the full force of every argument. Until he was ready, he could, like a good military strategist, conceal his main objective. He was faced at this time, even in the midst of marked success, with a very complicated situation. He recognized, even at a time when multitudes were flocking to his banner, that his Church was in a very lonely position. Rome was attacking his theory of the episcopate and claiming that he and his colleagues were bogus bishops. By accepting either Old Catholic consecration he would be able not only to meet the Roman criticism which weighed heavily with Filipinos, but would secure the friendship and possible financial aid of a great world body of Christians. His priests were no longer paid by the State and had only the fees of their parishioners to depend upon, while Rome was receiving substantial aid from the Catholics in the United States and, a little later, was to receive $7,000,000 from the sale of the friar lands.

On the other hand, he had committed himself to the Protestant theory of the episcopate in his Fundamental Epistles; and to accept consecration from some outside Christian body would invalidate all of his arguments. A strong nationalist, it may have been a point of pride not to acknowledge dependence upon any "foreign power." So far as the present writer can ascertain, these approaches both to the Anglican and Old Catholic Churches were purely individual and partook of an exploratory nature. Aglipay wanted to get the "lay of the land," but certainly he would not take definite steps without the approval of his Supreme Council. Certainly he was under no pressure from his colleagues, and he may have been conscious that some among them would not approve.

This same general attitude doubtless explains his courteous reception of well-meaning Catholics who made various attempts to win him back to the "true faith." If he seemed interested, it was from a desire to find out what people were thinking. We remember that at the retreat at Santa Ana with the Jesuits he temporized until he found out what they really had in mind. As any real leader would be bound to do, he explored the whole situation—Anglican, Old Catholic, and Roman. This is conjecture, but it is in accord with the character of the man as we know him. The certainty is that he hewed to the line he had set, and in that "line" the values of the Reformation were implicitly contained.

One must never reckon without Isabelo de los Reyes in attempting to understand the theological development of the Philippine Independent Church. More than almost any other Filipino, with the exception of José Rizal, he had been affected by modern thought. It was a heady draught to one who had suffered both physically and intellectually from the strait jacket imposed by the friars. When this obstacle to the free exercise of the mind was removed, there was an explosion. Foreman speaks of it as "a natural reaction following the suppression of sacerdotal tyranny—an extravagant sense of untrammelled thought which time may modify by sober reflection."[1]

Isabelo, after his release from Montjuich prison in Barcelona in 1897, had remained in Spain for a number of years. During this period he read and wrote prodigiously. Anxious like Rizal to justify his people in the eyes of the world and also to instil self-confidence in the hearts of his countrymen who were fighting and dying on the battlefield, he wrote *The Religion of the Katipunan*. Here he endeavored to show that, prior to the arrival of the Spaniards, the Filipinos had developed an advanced religion. He believed that all religions were at heart the same and that God, the same God of the Christians, had not left himself without witness among his remote peoples. There was the light that lighteth every man that cometh into the world. He sums up the teaching of the ancient religion in one of his letters as follows:

"Let us repeat that God has written in our conscience these three rights.

(1) Always love and do not injure anybody. Let us be all love, as is the pure essence of the Creator.

(2) Be just always and do not commit excesses.

(3) Work eagerly in one's own and another's perfection because God created us for this. There is nothing more worthy of pity than the man who does not care to perfect his intelligence and improve his fate and that of his children by honest work.

If we fulfill these three duties, we shall not have great disappointments and we shall be happy in the life here and in the next.

For the rest, love one another and you will be happy. Everybody, without exception is a child of God. Heaven and earth are common to all of you, and my greatest aspiration would be that all frontiers disappear; that all men without distinction of nationality or of class, love one another; and all the good sacrifices as well as the good actions belong equally to all, like brothers that we are." [2]

Years later, after the establishment of the Philippine Independent Church, it was evident that the Fundamental Epistles were not sufficient and that a prayer book was needed to take the place of the Roman Missal. Isabelo, therefore, as the chief theologian of the Church, undertook the task and composed the *Oficio Divino* which was published in 1906. In the preface it was made plain that it was to supersede any statements in the Fundamental Epistles which might be in conflict. However, recognizing the background of the people it was necessary, so the apology ran, to use the Christian forms to which they were accustomed. Christianity, therefore, had to be the vehicle for the *Religion of the Katipunan;* the new wine had to be poured into old bottles.

The first part of the book was called "The New Evangel" and consisted mainly of a harmony of the Gospels. The second part was the "Eucharistic Cultus," plus other offices for morning and evening prayer and observances of the Church's year. The third part, not mentioned in the Preface, was "The Ceremonial for Bishops and Presbyters" with forms for the celebration of the remaining seven sacraments.

In the harmony of the Gospels Isabelo out-did Marcion.

In it he harmonized or deleted all accounts in the original Gospels which appeared to be in contradiction. Only the miracles of healing were retained, although he made one great exception. Original sin was thought to be absurd. He did believe in life after death, although he based his faith on what he considered to be scientific evidence. Quite inconsistently he retained the supreme miracle of the Incarnation. Jesus, born of the Virgin Mary, was God; his manhood was an appearance only. God cannot suffer upon the cross, therefore there was no sacrificial atonement. God cannot err, and so de los Reyes omitted all accounts which emphasized Jesus' humanity. We are saved by God's perfect teachings which are enunciated by Jesus. Naturally the Trinity of Persons is not allowed, although there is a Trinity of attributes—God as Omnipotent Creator; God as Eternal Love and God as Omniscient Providence.

The fundamental tenets of this new theology may be discerned in the passages and prayers in the "Eucharistic Cultus" and in the Ordinal. As they allowed of different interpretations, especially as regards the Trinity, both the conservatives and the radicals were content—at least they did not raise any objection. The essential thing to be emphasized about the *Oficio Divino* is its deeply religious spirit as revealed by the sayings of Jesus quoted in the progress of the service, the frequent use of the Psalms and in the content of the prayers, many of which are beautiful. As we look through the book with a sympathetic eye, we are impressed not so much by its doctrinal deficiencies (this point does not need to be labored) but by its spirit. Just as the fundamental theology of a Church may be judged more by its hymns than by its official statements, so the prayers of the *Oficio* reveal deep, though hidden doctrinal foundations. Many examples may be given; we quote only a few:

Prayer of Isabelo as he writes the Oficio Divino
Oh celestial Father: All is yours and we can offer nothing except what is thine. Inspire us to perform something that is agreeable to your divine eyes in order that we may be able to offer to the most good of all fathers and benefactors a Eucharist which may not

be completely unworthy of your immense charity toward your creatures.

In your divine Word and in the spiritual worship of love which you have taught us, inspire us to form our *Oficio Divino*. There is no Master more faithful than you, Oh Jesus our Master. Help us, Oh Lord, to open our lips, and our mouths shall proclaim your glory. You know, Oh God of all good, that we, like the poor widow, would offer from our extremity all that you have given us.

Satisfy these good desires, Oh Lord, and extend your loving right hand over us while with our eyes fixed on the ground, we say with all the fervor of our souls, "Blessed be the sweet name of our Father-Jesus."

Gradual

Oh God, thou art my God; in the morning I lift up my soul to thee; in a barren and famished land where no water is, my soul thirsteth for thee, to see thy power and thy glory as I have seen them in the sanctuary. For thy mercy is better than life. My lips praise thee. Thus I bless thee in my life; in thy name I will lift up my hands . . . With my joyful lips my mouth shall praise thee. I will meditate on thee in the watches of the night. For thou hast been my succor, and in the shadow of thy wings I shall rejoice. My soul waits on thee, thy right hand has sustained me. (Psalm 63).

Offering of the Mystical Bread

We have heard, Oh Lord, your divine word which is the true bread of heaven and the perpetual food of our souls; and now desiring to comply and to commemorate your charge that we act always as true brothers we offer to you this immaculate bread as a mystical symbol of your sweet universal fatherhood which unites us in your sacred love. Accept it, Oh our God, and inspire in us a living and profound sentiment of brotherhood, in order that, seeing in it the figure of your sacred body, we may all participate in this spiritual union and feel ourselves as beloved children of one merciful Father.

The Cup

Bless, Oh Lord, this wine in which you have symbolized your precious blood in order that this spiritual drink may make our parched souls a fountain of virtue and of charity which will calm our passions and wash away our faults.

Prayer of Humble Access

Oh Lord, we are not worthy to partake of your divine body and precious blood because of our sins. But, Father, what would become of us without you. We are weak and so helpless against our bad inclinations that without your hand to aid us we are eternally lost. Aid us, Oh God of our salvation, for the glory of your name.

Once more, sweet Jesus, we beg for pardon. Come, Oh God, to deck our poor souls with virtues more agreeable to your divine eyes in order that we may be less unworthy of your perfect community with us. Sanctify to us your divine teachings; give us that food of eternal life which you have promised and finally (grant that) we may comprehend that celestial food consists in doing the will of God in order that planting the (seed of) charity and good works, we may receive our recompense and bear fruit for the life eternal.

Prayer for the Dead

Oh Lord, even though it may offend your wisdom and justice, and above all your infinite mercy, give to our sad spirits the liberty to pray for our dear departed and especially for the soul of your servant (X). Behold with favor, Oh God, the tears of your poor family and do not forget your consoling promise to resurrect not only the just but also those who had a sadder fate, making the splendid sun of your mercy to shine forth.

It is evident, however, that still another stage in the theological evolution of this Church was in course of preparation. William Howard Taft, as Governor of the Philippines, was greatly interested in this new non-Roman Church. It is reported that when he came back to the Philippines as Secretary of State to open the new Assembly in 1907, he brought with him much literature from the headquarters of the American Unitarian Association in Boston. This he undoubtedly delivered to Aglipay. His exalted position as President of the United States soon afterward lent prestige to the form of religion he espoused and all this made an impression on Aglipay and de los Reyes. The *Calendarios* of the Independent Church, edited by de los Reyes, began to reveal that this omnivorous reader was really studying the Protestant Reformation for the first time. He mentions the names of Wyclif, John Huss, Luther, and George Fox, among others, and this reading was affecting his Christology.

In 1912 it was evident that the Unitarian Church in the United States was considering the growth of Unitarianism throughout the world. In that year the Rev. Charles W. Wendte, under the auspices of the American Unitarian Association, published a book entitled *The Promotion of Unitarian Christianity in Foreign Lands*. In the course of his preparations for this book, he stopped at the Philippines and made a brief survey of the Independent Church. As a result he decided that this Church presented a unique opportunity to the liberal Christian Churches. It was obviously not Roman; it was just as obvious that it was not in accord with orthodox Protestantism, and for both reasons might be open to Unitarian influence. His analysis was brief and necessarily superficial, but it undoubtedly served to focus attention on this unusual religious phenomenon in a distant country.

But other developments were taking place within the Church itself. After 1920 Bishop Aglipay to an increasing extent became the theologian of the Church. He convinced himself, in the process, that the future of the Church lay with the liberal Christian movement throughout the world. Mentally, he was growing farther and farther from Rome and also from orthodox Protestantism. The Malolos Congress during the war years had showed surprising, liberal strength. There were many liberals in the Islands like the Masons (whom he joined), and in these groups he believed that he could find support for a modern, "scientific," and up-to-date Church. A new "reform" was in order and this was embodied in a series of official books published during this decade.[3]

In these new manifestos Aglipay really did away with the *Oficio Divino*, just as the latter had superseded the Fundamental Epistles. Jesus was now just a man, a very good man to be sure, but that was all. The last and greatest miracle, the Incarnation, had disappeared. The Mass became just a brotherly meal. The official creed reads as follows:

I believe in one God, we praise his Holy Name, the Force which fills the universe, as said the prophet Jeremiah; which fills the heavens and the earth; intelligent, eternal, supreme and mysterious; which gives life, directs, moves and sustains all beings; which is the great soul of the universe, the beginning of all life and movement. Although his nature has not yet been completely manifested unto us, we try to apprehend it and to see in his marvellous works his power and his admirable wisdom. We hear in the depths of our conscience his most holy voice, we experience his diligent and loving fatherhood in the providential satisfaction of our daily needs. I believe that as God is the Supreme Being, He is also the Supreme Perfection. I believe that God made man to contribute with his virtues and activities to the general well-being and progress; and for this reason we ought to be useful always, and with our work we should seek for the satisfaction of our needs, think and work well for God will recompense the good in this world and will punish in this world bad intentions and deeds, but not with the absurd Hell. The inexorable justice of God is perfected through his infinite compassion. I believe that the eternal as my most loving father, protects me now and will recognize me at my death as a good father, full of pity, would recognize his son. As it has been proved by modern science, I shall not disappear forever, but only be transformed. Amen.[4]

One can trace the change in Aglipay's thought by comparing this creed with that of the *Oficio Divino* which states that God became flesh in Jesus in order to save us by the truth of his doctrine and by the example of his holy life. In the creed of the later period Jesus is not mentioned, although the name of Jeremiah appears. God is revealed through the glories of nature. It is quite evident, however, that it is the Christian God who is being described, and the belief in eternal life also betrays its Christian origin. While on the surface the leaders were struggling with the problem of the relationship between science and religion, the great body of the Church was quietly going on its accustomed way, administering the sacraments in the name of the Father, Son, and Holy Spirit.

In 1929 Mr. John B. Lathrop and Mr. Curtis W. Reese, two dignitaries of the Unitarian Church, came to the Philippines to consult with Aglipay and to study the situation, their object being to bring about closer relations between the Independent Church and Unitarians in the United States, Canada, and

Europe. Following this, Mr. Earl M. Wilbur, President of the Unitarian Churches of the Pacific Coast, invited Bishop Aglipay to visit America, all expenses paid. The latter, pleased by the recognition thus accorded, then informed the Rev. Dr. Louis C. Cornish, President of the American Unitarian Association, that the Philippine Independent Church had bestowed upon him the degree of "Doctor of Religious Sciences" in recognition of his work for freedom and science. Dr. Cornish responded by seconding the invitation previously given by Mr. Wilbur. With these preliminaries the trip was decided on, and on March 28, 1931 Bishop Aglipay, accompanied by Bishops Isabelo de los Reyes Jr. and Santiago Fonacier left for America.

An interesting experience in connection with this trip occurred soon after the party arrived in the United States. It seems that President Manuel L. Queson, one of the greatest leaders the Filipino people ever had, was then in this country negotiating with Congress in behalf of Philippine independence. He became ill, and at the time Aglipay arrived was recuperating at the Monrovia Sanitarium near Los Angeles. It was only courtesy for the latter to call upon him. Bishop de los Reyes, now the Supreme Bishop, gives the following account of the conversation which ensued.

Queson: What has brought you to America?

Aglipay: We are here as guests of the American Unitarian Association to attend the May meetings in Boston.

Queson: That is absurd. You should be here as guests of the American Episcopal Church, not the Unitarians. Our people are faithful to the Catholic Faith and have no inclination towards Unitarianism. Your Church is the equivalent of the Episcopal Church here and is the one that can really understand it. As for me I shall never favor any move to de-catholicize our people. The Catholic faith is one of the sources of national cohesion in our nation and of its strength.

Aglipay: I am sorry, but my efforts for better relations with the Episcopalians have failed in the past.

However, the trip turned out to be a triumphal procession.

The time was propitious as the agitation for independence had brought the Philippines anew to public attention. Aglipay, in his robes of office was a striking and glamorous figure and he appealed both to his audiences and to the press. He was good copy. In Chicago he attended a banquet given in his honor at one of the hotels. Lagasca, in describing the occasion, says that one of the speakers was the Honorable Mr. Hall then a member of Congress. The Congressman was enthusiastic in his praise and it is quite evident that Aglipay had created a most favorable impression by his appearance, his masculinity, and the vigor of his address. He was a good spokesman for the Philippines at a time when independence was being debated by the United States Government.[5]

Aglipay's appearance at the annual convention of the Unitarian Association in Boston was one of the great moments of the trip. The meeting ended with a banquet at the Statler Hotel where he was reported as having "stolen the show" by presenting a bolo to Dr. Cornish—explaining that Filipinos give bolos only to friends whom they trust, as symbols of life, liberty, and honor.

The call upon President Hoover was another high point in the trip. Excitement about granting independence to the Filipinos was at its height at the time and, true to his convictions, Aglipay lost no opportunity to press the matter upon his hearers. He did not change President Hoover's views, however, but his reception by the head of the United States Government reveals that even at the age of seventy he was still regarded as a powerful figure in the life of the Philippines.

In 1934, Bishop Aglipay, accompanied by Bishop de los Reyes, visited the Triennial Congress of the International Association for Liberal Christianity in Copenhagen. The Boston triumph was repeated and again he was presented to the head of the State. The King of Denmark received him graciously and gave him words of praise. To these men he represented what was in truth a striking phenomenon—the emergence of a great body of oriental Christians who had cast off subservience to Rome.

This, to them, was "Liberalism," and details of theology and custom seemed quite irrelevant. Unitarianism had made Aglipay into a world figure and confirmed his resolution to reform the Philippine Independent Church.

A climactic moment in the association with the Unitarian Church came with the visit to the Islands of Dr. Louis C. Cornish, President of the American Unitarian Association in 1939. Dr. Cornish was a great and distinguished man, and a record of his visit was made in a book published after his return.[6] He was given an enthusiastic welcome and travelled widely in the Islands. He must have wondered a bit just how a Unitarian Church could still be using forms of worship so closely akin to those of the Roman Catholic Church and so alien to the simpler cultus to which he had been accustomed. Every effort was made, however, by Aglipay and others, to assure him that the Unitarian philosophy could permeate these colorful ceremonies, and he allowed himself to become convinced.

He writes as follows on this subject:

Lack of liturgical form and color were characteristic of the Reformation in western continental Europe and Great Britain, and the same simplicity, or bareness if you will, continues among the Churches of many names in the United States which descend from the great protest, including the more liberal groups . . . All these Churches . . . repudiate formalism, no matter how colorfully alluring, even as they repudiate the medieval doctrines of the Mother Church.

The Independent Church of the Philippines just as firmly refuses to be separated from the ancient forms, although in retaining them the Church has given them a modern content. More thoroughly than many a Church which never builds an altar or lights a candle, the Independent Church has laid aside the older teachings. How did it come about that form and color were kept?

During more than three centuries these forms have been part of the warp and woof of Filipino life. A deeper reason is that the Filipino people are artistic. Boxes of flowers hang in the windows. Orchids are everywhere. The brass studded harness on the pony is polished brightly and flashes in the sun. They love color, and they are musical . . .

The tropics, outdoor life, the nipa houses, bring ways of life and also ways of conducting public worship which could not be followed in colder lands. Different ways of worshipful procedure may be right enough, each in its own environment. The important fact is that men, using two widely varying procedures in public worship, which even appear to be antagonistic the one to the other, may yet be equally abreast of modern religious thought, each just as "liberal" as the other.

Failure to grasp this fact has caused much misunderstanding about the Philippine Independent Churches.[7]

At the conclusion of Dr. Cornish' visit he was made Honorary President of the Philippine Independent Church and must have departed feeling that the bond between the two bodies was close indeed. In the light of history there is a touch of sadness about all this when one thinks of his obvious sincerity, his love for the Filipinos, and his deep feeling that the Independent Church had a great part to play in the life of the nation. What he did not realize was that the old Bishop did not speak for the Church.

Human nature runs true to form, and there had been a conservative as well as a radical group among bishops and clergy from its very first days. In the discussions at Kullabeng, as far back as May, 1902, the tension between the two groups was evident. Fr. Brillantes at that time led the party which wanted to make changes of doctrine, and Fr. Pio Romero was at the head of the group which wished to retain the doctrines and dogmas of the Roman Catholic Church—adhesion to the pope alone excepted.

In the early days both groups were able to use the *Oficio Divino* as it allowed different interpretations to the doctrine of the Trinity. When, after 1920 Bishop Aglipay published his reform doctrines, abrogating the *Oficio Divino*, the alarm of the conservative group grew. Their numbers grew as well, for only a few were convinced Unitarians. By 1930 the discontent with Aglipay's teachings began to manifest itself openly. Bishop Servando Castro, Bishop of the Ilocos and one of the elder statesmen, was the spokesman. He believed that the Church had gone

far astray and should return to its original position. Still affirm-
ing independence of the Papacy he was alarmed because the
Church no longer affirmed the divinity of Christ. He had no
sympathy with the so-called "reform" of the mass which made
of it simply a "brotherly meal." He made his opposition known
in the public press saying that the rank and file of the Independents were opposed to the new changes in doctrine.

Aglipay's powerful personality and the reverence which
people had for him prevented a possible split. This movement,
however, should be borne in mind in view of later events. The
sincerity and conviction of its leaders were proved by the fact
that it took courage to oppose Aglipay. At the time the conservative movement came to a head the latter's association with
the Unitarians was becoming intimate, and it is not to Aglipay's
discredit if he were looking for financial as well as moral support. Every prudential consideration was in favor of keeping
silent. In the emergence of Bishop Castro we see the spirit of
conviction which, after the death of Isabelo de los Reyes and of
Aglipay, was to result in the return to orthodoxy as interpreted
by Anglicanism and to the petition to the Episcopal Church for
Anglican Orders in 1947.

It took forty odd years in the wilderness for the Philippine
Independent Church to find itself theologically, and it was a
process which could not be hastened. We need not blame the
Protestants in 1902, or Bishop Brent in 1904, because they did
not open their arms to the Church. The Old Catholics, while
willing to grant the episcopate, really knew very little about the
Church and were too weak to have furnished material assistance. God, in various ways, refused to open the door. The leaders of the Church were dazzled by the new freedom and the
new learning. There had to be time for that "sober reflection"
after an exciting period of untrammeled thought of which
Foreman spoke.

The Church was Unitarian only in the sense that it was anti-
Roman and seemed to be open to new ideas. From the very beginning the Unitarians failed to realize the gulf between the few

intellectuals and the body of the Church. The old forms which were retained preached silent sermons on the great Christian verities, and belief that the stream of Unitarian thought could flow through those old channels was an illusion. Moreover there were other essential differences beside form and ceremony. The Unitarians would never suffer a figure like that of Gregorio Aglipay. Their Church has no priesthood, no sacraments, no fixed creeds. At the same time distinguished and devoted men of the Unitarian Church did much to give the Independent Church the moral support and a sense of belonging to the greater Christian community which were greatly needed. It was a lonely Church and it needed a friend. The Unitarian contribution was along this line, and the Christian world should always be grateful.

Looking at the theological contribution of Isabelo de los Reyes and of Bishop Aglipay in broad perspective, we can recognize its essential validity if there were to be a true Reformation in the Philippines. It guaranteed that the conservative movement would not eventuate in a poor and even pathetic replica of the Roman Catholic Church in the Philippines. Something new had been added which was never lost.

That something new was a recapture of that other side of St. Augustine's teaching which puts stress on the work of God in the individual soul. Salvation comes from faith and faith includes faith in one's self as a son of God. It includes the freedom to think, and to initiate, and even to make mistakes. Authority has its place, but in the last analysis it is the authority of God speaking directly to the human heart. It says, "Son of Man, stand upon thy feet."

This was the true message of these two great men. It was a message which the Philippines greatly needed. It needs the same message today.

Chapter XIII

The End of an Era

There has not been space in this short volume to deal adequately with the national background of the Philippine Independent Church after the American occupation. However, certain major events should be reviewed. From 1900 to 1907 the Philippine Commission had ruled the Islands, having both legislative and judicial power. At first the Commission was composed of five American members; but within a short time three distinguished Filipinos were added, the number being subsequently increased to four. In 1907 the First Philippine Assembly was organized, the Commission remaining as an upper house or senate. In 1916, through the passage of the Jones Act by the American Congress, the Commission was abolished and an all Filipino Congress composed of a Senate and a House of Representatives was inaugurated. The American Governor, appointed by the President of the United States represented continuing American sovereignty. The Tydings-McDuffie Act passed in March, 1934, authorized the Filipinos to draw up a constitution which was to be validated by a popular plebiscite. The act stated that the commonwealth thus to be formed should become an independent nation in ten years after the constitution should be adopted. This would mean independence in 1945. During the commonwealth period the United States was to be represented by a High Commissioner.

Work was immediately begun on the new constitution by an extremely able body of Filipinos who were well acquainted with governmental systems in other countries. The approaching plebiscite, of course, opened the gates to public discussion and the result was revealing. Osmena and Queson, between them, had governed the Philippines for nearly three decades through what was virtually a single party. The great issue of independence had so dominated the political situation that secondary issues, however important, had been submerged. This had made it difficult to develop a healthy two-party system. The work of the two men had been of vital importance, but there was what Hayden calls "The Unrepresented Minority." [1] This was a minority only in name as it consisted of the major part of the Philippines population—the laborers, the small and tenant farmers, the poor people, in a word, the "have-nots" as against the "haves." Under American tutelage great progress had been made but there was still no large, responsible and well-educated middle class.

The friars no longer held their old sway over the lives of the poor, but the *cacique* did. The caciques were the wealthy Filipinos in each town; we would call them political bosses. The municipal governments were largely controlled by these men and that gave them judicial and police influence. Under them there was a kind of debt slavery so that many men were in perpetual bondage. This condition was of long standing and while there had been a certain improvement under American rule, things were not as they should be. The most explosive section was in the great plains north of Manila, but caciquism still held sway in all parts of the archipelago. These bosses held up reforms and in general managed things to their own advantage.

Under the surface there was much resentment and these good, family-loving, but poor and ignorant people found men who both led and exploited them. In 1930 one Benigno Ramos had started a paper called *The Sakdal*. "Sakdal," in Tagalog, means to accuse or to strike; and the paper contained such virulent attacks on prominent Filipino leaders that it had to be suppressed. But it had been widely read even in the north and helped to inspire an uprising in that area in 1931. Of this Tamgulan rebellion, which was easily suppressed, Governor John C. Early speaks as follows:

"Take away a man's land and he is desperate. Other parts of Pangasinan, Tarlac and Nueva Ecija are just as bad. The whole of Central Luzon is ready for an uprising. It needs leadership only. Sandiko (General Geodoro Sandiko, an officer in the Revolution of 1899, leader of the tenant farmers of Bulacan, Vice-President of the Constitutional Convention) has said that land troubles in Central Luzon would not be settled so long as the Americans remain but will soon be dealt with after they leave. The Americans, General Sandiko says, have too much respect for property and property rights. Let the United States get out and the oppressed will soon right things with the bolo." [2]

Some time prior to 1930 Benigno Ramos, mentioned above, an employee of the Philippine Senate, was discharged for insubordination and for having fomented a strike in a Manila school. Hating Osmena, the leader of the Senate, he organized what was called the Sakdal Movement which sought to exploit the real grievances of the masses. In 1933 this group was organized into a political party. In the elections of 1934 it actually elected three members of the House of Representatives and the Governor of a Province. It planned to fight the implementation of the Tydings-McDuffie Act and stated that it wanted immediate independence. The basic platform of this party was as follows:

(1) The people are being exploited by the selfish politicians.

(2) The leaders have abandoned the cause of independence.

(3) The Commonwealth plan would kill independence forever, as the "oligarchs" would surrender to foreign influence and capital.

(4) The Sakdal party would obtain independence not later than December 31st, 1935. (It should be noted that American rule was equated with caciquism.)

While a few *Sakdalistas* were elected in 1934, the firm hold that Queson and Osmena had on the archipelago was amply demonstrated. So, incredible as it seems, the decision was made for direct action.

Ramos went to Japan to direct the movement from there and the people were led to believe that when they struck, Japanese warships would suddenly appear to assist them and that the skies would be dark with Japanese warplanes. The plan was to capture the *presidencias* in as many towns as possible with the expectation that in the confusion the flames of revolt would spread.

On May 2-3, 1935, just before the plebiscite was to take place, the uprising occurred. A few municipal buildings were taken, but the poor dupes scanned the skies in vain for the supporting planes and the whole uprising was snuffed out with ridiculous ease by the Constabulary.

Easily quelled as it was, the pathetic little rebellion was disquieting. It was estimated by the Constabulary that the Sakdalistas numbered about 68,000; but this body, supposedly close to the people, only got wind of what was impending a few hours before the attack came. There was no "leak," no low whisper in the confessional from somebody's wife. No Fr. Gil reported as in 1896. Hayden sums up this small but significant paragraph in Philippine history by saying, "Nothing could more clearly suggest the chasm between the classes in the Philippines, or the danger of revolt that is faced by the minority of the "haves" that rule the majority of the "have-nots." [3]

The plebiscite which had not been interrupted by the Sakdal uprising as had been planned, gave an emphatic endorsement to the new Constitution and was followed by the elections of 1935. Queson and Osmena had made up their differences and they ran for President and Vice-President respectively; it looked as if nothing could stop such a coalition. But, to the surprise of the Philippines, two great war leaders stepped out of the pages of history and ran as candidates. They were Aguinaldo and Aglipay.

Aglipay was then 75 years old but still apparently as vigorous as ever. Loyal and law-abiding, he was as nationalistic as of old and just as sure that the Filipinos could run their own affairs. He wanted independence as soon as it could be obtained, and he wanted to do something for the masses of the people. It seemed to him that their poverty was the main issue facing the country. His Church, for the most part, had its base among the masses and was identified with their interests. It was also, as we know, intensely nationalistic, and that would help. The defunct Republican party was therefore revived and the old warrior waged a vigorous campaign throughout the length and breadth of the archipelago.

Aguinaldo ran separately and his main reliance was upon the Veterans of the Philippine Revolution, an organization corresponding to our American Legion. Both of these old men, authentic national heroes as they were, were inexperienced in politics and were fighting a political machine which dominated the Islands from one end to the other. Without a real party organization behind them their cause was hopeless from the start. It was the old case of the amateur against the professional.

When the votes were counted, the result was as follows:

> Queson and Osmena, 694,104, or 69%
> Aguinaldo, 179,390, or 17.5%
> Aglipay, 147,951, or 14%

Achútegui and Bernad, in their recent book, quote Hayden out of context making him seem to agree that the vote for these two men was insignificant. What Hayden really thought may be found on page 427 where in analyzing the returns he says ". . . one elector out of six voted for General Aguinaldo and one out of seven for Bishop Aglipay, which means that one out of 3.2 voted for one or the other of these obviously hopeless candidates. This is a substantial minority—too large a one to be safely left without direct representation in the national government—especially as the majority of these voters are from a fairly definite class which feels that it is being exploited by the groups in power. And on page 407 Hayden makes this observation,

"That these two relics of the past should have entered upon such an undertaking, and have commanded the support of a substantial portion of the nation in it, is a remarkable demonstration of the vitality of their personalities and the hold that what they stood for has upon the hearts and minds of the Filipino people."

The Filipino people showed the maturity of their judgment in giving Queson and Osmena a large majority. These great men represented the only way in which there could be orderly progress toward independence. They were not unconscious of the needs of the great masses of the people. At the same time Aguinaldo and Aglipay accomplished two definite things. Acting as opposition parties before the law, they pointed to a great national problem and they made a protest vote possible. That makes for democracy and stability.

The problem of raising the living standards of the Philippines is still one of the most pressing in the nation. Hundreds of thousands, if not millions, of people are living close to the edge. The Huk uprising of recent years shows how receptive the people are to foreign ideologies which promise a quick solution to their wants. The Independent Church, with its base firmly planted in this group, has an unrivalled opportunity to show its traditional devotion to the nation by giving the masses a conception of religion in which freedom and authority are reconciled and by making them feel that the Church is on their side in the struggle toward a more abundant life. This Church is of, for, and by the people—and its potential is beyond calculation.

Aglipay was 75 years old when he was defeated for President, but he remained as active as ever. He had a national reputation, sincere conviction, and the idea of a graceful retirement never entered his mind. The decision of the Supreme Court about church properties made in 1906 still rankled in his mind and in July, 1937 he sent a petition to the President of the United States, and to Congress, asking that these church buildings should be returned to the "people." They were the true owners.

In 1938 he violently opposed the Religious Education Bill,

and this episode is worthy of somewhat extended comment. In the early days of the American occupation, the Philippine Commission found that some people wanted the teaching of the Roman Catholic religion to be made compulsory in the public schools. Others wanted no religious teaching in the public schools whatever. William Howard Taft, with his gift for conciliation, secured the adoption of the following legislation which was later embodied in the new Constitution of 1935:

Sec. 927 . . . No teacher or other person engaged in any public school, whether maintained from Insular, provincial or municipal funds shall teach or criticize the doctrines of any Church, religious sect or denomination, or shall attempt to influence the pupils for or against any church or religious sect. If any teacher shall intentionally violate this section, he or she shall, after due hearing, be dismissed from the public service.

Sec. 929 . . . It shall be lawful, however, for the priest or minister of any church established in a town where a public school is situated, either in person or by a designated teacher of religion, to teach religion for one half hour three times a week in the school building, to those public school pupils whose parents or guardians desire it and express their desire therefor in writing filed with the principal teacher of the school, to be forwarded to the division superintendent, who shall fix the hours and rooms for such teaching. But no public school teachers shall either conduct religious exercises or teach religion or act as a designated religious teacher in the school building under the foregoing authority, and no pupils shall be required by any public school teacher to attend and receive the religious instruction herein permitted.[4]

The Roman Catholic Church had never been satisfied with this arrangement. Basically it would have liked to have had complete control of religious education in the public schools; but of course this was impossible. It did think that certain steps might be taken as the hierarchy believed that the public school superintendents were not implementing the present law as well as they could. They were giving other subjects precedence during regular school hours, and extra curricular activities were allowed to interfere with religious instruction even after school was dismissed. The Archbishop's Committee on Education for the Diocese of Manila approached the Secretary for Public Instruction asking him to remedy the situation by executive order. The latter refused to comply with the request as it was contrary to the Constitution.

Various bills were introduced into the legislature and these, as might be expected, caused heated debate. The one finally voted upon read as follows:

Sec. 1. There shall be included in the curriculum of all the public schools of the Philippines from the lowest grade to the highest year of the high or vocational school, inclusive, under the direct supervision of the school authorities, a course in character building and good manners and right conduct. This course shall be a required subject scheduled during regular school hours and instruction therein shall be given for one half hour three times a week throughout the academic year . . .

Sec. 2. Where any religious organization or organizations are in a position to offer religious instruction with their own instructors and at no cost to the government, parents or guardians of minor children under parental authority in public schools, upon written request filed with the principal teacher of the school, shall have the right to have their children excused from the instruction in character building and good manners and right conduct as provided in Sec. 1 hereof and on the condition that said children attend the religious instruction offered by the religious organization, or organizations, chosen by the parents, all in accordance with the law.[5]

After prolonged discussion, the bill was passed and sent to President Queson for his signature. On June 4, 1938 he vetoed the bill for reasons which may be summarized as follows:

(1) This bill does more than implement the existing law as claimed; it actually amends it and, in addition, is quite contrary to its spirit.

(2) It deprives school superintendents of the authority over the schools and the school curriculum which is constitutionally theirs. It prescribes the curriculum in ordering that there shall be a course in character building and it places religious instruction in a category it does not possess.

The Roman Catholic Church was not content to let the President's veto settle the matter. Subsequent to the veto the Metropolitan Archbishop and Suffragan Bishops of the Ecclesiastical Province of Cebu issued a pastoral letter on the subject. To this the President made a reply in a release to the press on June 24. It follows in part:

"I am amazed at the boldness of the Metropolitan Archbishop and Suffragan Bishops of the Ecclesiastical Province of Cebu at taking up at an episcopal conference a matter concerning the constitutional duties and prerogatives of the officials and branches of the government of the Commonwealth.

I had so far ignored charges made to the effect that the hierarchy of the Catholic Church in the Philippines had instigated and was behind the movement for the enactment of the bill regarding religious instruction in the Philippines. But the pastoral letter, signed by the Metropolitan Archbishop and Suffragan Bishops of that province is an incontrovertible evidence that we did face at the last session of the Assembly, and we do face now, one of the most menacing evils that can confront the government and the people of the Philippines; namely the interference of the Church in the affairs of the State. It seems that the Archbishop and the Bishops who have written this pastoral letter are blind to the lessons of history, including our own, during the Spanish regime. Being a Catholic myself, I am less interested in preserving the independence of the Church from the State than I am in preserving the independence of the Government from the church.

It should be unnecessary to remind the ecclesiastical authorities that the separation of the Church and State in this country is a reality, and not a mere theory, and that as far as our people are concerned it is forever settled that this separation shall be maintained as one of the cardinal tenets of our government. The ecclesiastical authorities should realize, therefore, that any attempt on their part to interfere with matters that are within the province of the government will not be tolerated . . ." [6]

It is true that the legislature had passed the bill. How many members in doing so were simply "passing the buck" to the President cannot be determined. But how the people felt was shown by a vast concourse of citizens gathered on the New Luneta on July 17, 1938 to express their enthusiastic support of Queson's policy in upholding the Constitution. It was a far cry from the days when the civil Governors stood in awe of the friars.

Aglipay's instinct about this matter was right, and while he could not prove that 3,000,000 pesos had been raised by the Roman Church to lobby for the bill, the action of the Archbishop of Cebu in attempting to overturn the President's veto showed that his charges were substantially correct. The Roman Church was attempting to move in, and Aglipay knew it.

In 1938 Aglipay lost his life-long friend and associate, that doughty champion of intellectual liberty, Isabelo de los Reyes. On June 5, 1929 he had suffered a paralytic stroke which affected the right side of his body. This was followed by a long series of strokes so that for nine years he was practically confined to his bed. Soon after his first stroke he wrote a letter to his son, Isabelo Jr., in which he asked him to make certain that he would not have a Roman Catholic funeral, as the whole country was aware that he did not belong to that Church. Isabelo Jr. hastened to see his father and assured him that his wishes would be respected. During this visit the son quotes him as saying, "My son, learn a cruel lesson from me. Never entrust your children to a Roman Catholic School—you will lose them." This was doubtless in reference to his daughters, three of whom had become Roman Catholic nuns. He then added that he wished to be buried by the side of his wife (Isabelo's mother) in his son's chapel.

As the years went by, following the first shock, Don Isabelo gradually lost ground and his mind began to fail. By 1936 he was almost totally paralyzed. Going to his house one morning, Isabelo Jr. found that he was not being well cared for, and in the presence of others the son declared that he would take him to his own home on the following morning.

The next morning he borrowed Bishop Aglipay's car and returned to get his father. The bed was empty and the servants told Isabelo Jr. that at six that morning a group of Roman Catholic nuns had arrived saying that they were going to take the patient for a drive on the Luneta to get the air. He waited for

their return until three o'clock in the afternoon by which time
it was evident that the old gentleman had been spirited from the
house. It was not long, however, before he learned that his father had been taken to the house of his sister, Isabel de Barredo,
a Roman Catholic nun. It was quite plain that by a strategem
he had been whisked off to a place where he could be subjected
to continuous and intense Roman Catholic pressure. Consulting
with Bishop Aglipay and with Mr. Vicente Sotto, an attorney,
it was decided to take action by applying for a writ of *habeas
corpus*.

The trials which ensued had to be held by the bedside of the
sick man, as he was unable to come to court. The petition that
he could be taken from this house to which he had been spirited
was refused both by the Court of First Instance and by the
Court of Appeals. In reading the transcript of the court record
in both cases the disintegration of Isabelo's mind is evident, and
one feels a sense of tragedy. Justice Horrilleno in his dissenting
opinion held that, in spite of the confusion of his testimony, Isabelo's desire to leave could be plainly discerned. The majority
disagreed and he remained where he was until his death. Isabelo
Jr. was barred from the house. In a recent letter to the writer
he states, "For the last two years of my father's life I was never
allowed to visit, see, or talk with my father."

Isabelo Sr. died on October 10, 1938. It was not until after
this happened that the son learned that there had been a "retraction" signed on September 14, 1936. A facsimile of it is
printed in the book by Achútegui and Bernad,[7] accompanied
by a wealth of detail. The retraction is signed by Isabelo and
witnessed by a number of people including Fr. Louis Morrow,
at the time an official at the Apostolic delegation at Manila.

The chronology of this brief period is revealing. Early in
September, 1936 Isabelo Jr. goes to his father's house and finds
him in a pitiful condition. He announces that he will return
the next day to take him to his own house. However, on the
morrow he discovers that he has been anticipated and that his
father is gone. Later he finds that he has been taken to the house
of his sister who is a nun.

The so-called retraction is dated September 14 of that same year which indicates that it was felt that no time was to be lost. The fact that Fr. Morrow's name appears on the document is clear evidence that the hierarchy was keenly interested in this whole matter. If Isabelo could be brought to recant, it would be a blow to the Philippine Independent Church. When Isabelo announced that he was going to take his father to his own home it caused alarm in high quarters—hence the instant and well-engineered effort to get him somewhere else. The determined nuns who took him off for an airing were doubtless acting under very competent direction.

The question of the "recantation" did not figure in the action of *habeas corpus* which took place soon after the document had been signed; but the court records have a bearing as they reveal, as has been stated, that Isabelo was in a serious mental condition. It was when he was in this state that he signed a document which begins "I, Isabelo de los Reyes, in full possession of my faculties" etc. That Isabelo was not in full possession of his faculties at the time of his removal to the nun's house is indisputable. The document was signed under the duress of mental incapacity and of intense pressure. It is not difficult to make a man in his condition sign anything. The document is worthless.

Of course, following the usual technique, this "retraction" was exploited to the full throughout the Philippines. There is no evidence however, that it damaged Isabelo's reputation as a great patriot or as a fighter for intellectual and religious liberty. Nor did it endanger the Philippine Independent Church.

Isabelo concludes his defense of his father's memory as follows:

"Where do the mortal remains of Isabelo de los Reyes rest at last? Sometime between the war years of 1943 and 1944 I removed them from the Manila Northern Cemetery where they had been buried in the family lot, and buried them in the same grave as my mother, Don Isabelo's second wife, his Spanish and adored wife, Gelinos, who had died in Tokyo, Japan, on February 10, 1910, and whose mortal remains had been brought to Manila by express orders of my father in 1923 to be buried at the Maria Clara Church in Manila. To-day, at long last, the will of a dying husband has been fulfilled . . ." [8]

In 1939 Bishop Aglipay entertained Dr. Louis C. Cornish, President of the American Unitarian Association. The reception given these two men throughout the Islands marked his last triumphant appearance before great crowds of his people.

In that same year died another of his old friends and colleagues, Bishop Pedro Lagasca, Bishop of Ilocos Norte, at the age of eighty. Most of the old companions were now gone. Aglipay went to Laoag to officiate at the funeral, not only for old times sake, but because Bishop Lagasca was a great figure in that region like his predecessor Bishop Brillantes who had died many years before. A great orator, Lagasca was known throughout the Islands. He was the father of the present Bishop Lagasca, Secretary General of the Philippine Independent Church.

In 1940 Aglipay paid what proved to be a last visit to his native province. Achútegui and Bernad report that he stayed three days in Laoag (the place of his surrender as a guerrilla General) visiting with Simeon Mandac, his life-long friend. At Batac, his birthplace, he went from house to house visiting his relatives and bidding them all farewell. He met with all the Independent priests of Ilocos Norte charging them to be true to the Church, to obey the commandments of God and to respect authority and the law of the land. He may have had a premonition that he was approaching the end of the journey.

Returning to Manila he suffered a stroke, and soon after he died on September 1, 1940. He lay in state for two weeks in the Cathedral of the Independent Church in Tondo. The press publicized the event widely and said much in praise of the man who had loved his country greatly and to the end had followed the admonition of José Rizal. He was compared to Luther as a religious reformer. The press mentioned the names, and printed the pictures, of the distinguished people who came to pay their last respects as he lay in state in his church. Aguinaldo, the man to whom he had been so loyal, came. President Manuel L. Queson and President Sergio Osmena were among the visitors, as were the Cabinet members Manuel Roxas and Elpido Quirino who afterward became presidents. A multitude of others, both small and great, paid honor to the dead hero. The sermon was delivered by the present Supreme Bishop, the Rt. Rev. Isabelo de los Reyes.

Aglipay had expressed the desire to be buried in his native town of Batac; but the hierarchy decided that he belonged to the nation and he was buried in his cathedral at Tondo. When the building was destroyed during the Japanese war, his remains were transferred to the Church of Maria Clara—named after the heroine in Rizal's first novel—and now the temporary cathedral of the Philippine Independent Church. In 1959, however, his body was taken to the cathedral in his native town. It is reported in the *Christian Register* that over thirty thousand people attended the three day services on that occasion. He was, at last, like Isabelo de los Reyes, where he wanted to be.

Bishop Aglipay never recanted, as is acknowledged by Achútegui and Bernad. It is interesting and also somewhat baffling to learn that in the *Catholic Concise Encyclopedia* published in New York in 1957, it is stated, on pages 23 and 24, in the section devoted to Aglipay, that he died reconciled to the Church! [9]

Chapter XIV

Port after the Storm

Bishop Aglipay, through the devotion which people had for him, had held the Church together until the time of his death. Underneath were the theological divisions which have been mentioned, but there was no great difficulty in electing Bishop Santiago Fonacier in 1940 to take Aglipay's place as Supreme Bishop. Fonacier had been an associate of Aglipay from the very beginning. Tutored for the priesthood by Bishop Brillantes, he had in due course become priest and then bishop. He had gone to America in 1931 with Bishop Aglipay and Isabelo de los Reyes Jr. But he had other interests as well, and had learned the newspaper business in his younger days. He was also interested in politics and was elected a member of the first Philippine Assembly which met in 1907. In 1925 he was elected Senator, but was defeated in a number of subsequent elections. Fonacier was eager to succeed his old friend for political as well as other reasons. However, things were not to be as in the past. At the same time that he was elected to the highest office in the Church, the Supreme Council and the General Assembly effected a constitutional change by which the term of office of the Supreme Bishop was limited to three years, with only one re-election permitted for a similar period. This change was undoubtedly due to the fact that, much as the clergy and people respected Bishop Aglipay, they felt that he had been in power too long. A younger group was gradually taking over control.

Fonacier had not been in office much more than a year before the Japanese captured the Islands and this, of course, changed everything. Space does not allow us to review this period except to say that the war aroused the old fighting spirit of this nationalistic Church and it refused to go under. Men left to fight the Japanese, buildings were burned, records destroyed; but the clergy ministered to the people as best they could. In other words the old spirit of independence flamed anew in the presence of the foreign invader; and when the war was over the Church, like the flag in the *Star Spangled Banner* "was still there." Myrick sums up these years by saying that the Church suffered during the war as did the other Churches; but when the war was over it still held its place on the national scene, setting forth to the nation its tenets of independent Catholicism, patriotic duty, Philippine heritage and independence.[1]

Because of war conditions, it was impossible to have the regular election of a Supreme Bishop in 1943. In 1945, however, an attempt was made to have a meeting of the Supreme Council and the General Assembly, but travel was difficult and a quorum was not present. However it became plain at this time that Fonacier was eager to have the Constitution changed so that he could be re-elected for life. This caused much uneasiness.

There were other things about Fonacier which the Supreme Council did not like. During the war he had removed the central headquarters of the Church to Mabini, a barrio of Urdeneta in the Province of Tarlac, taking all the funds, titles, and records of the Church with him. No accounting had been given. Another cause of friction was his controversy with Bishop Remollino. This need not be described at length; suffice it to say that it caused deep feeling.

Fonacier saw clearly at this meeting that there was trouble ahead, and so between September 1945 and the first of January, 1946 he proceeded, without the authorization of the Supreme Council required by canon, to consecrate seven of his friends as bishops. The objective, of course, was clear enough—he wanted to stack the next meeting.

This proved to be the last straw. On January 21, 1946, Bishop

Aguilar, President of the Supreme Council, called a meeting to try Santiago Fonacier on the following charges: (1) Violating the Constitution in consecrating bishops; (2) Removing the headquarters of the Church to another town; (3) Failure to give an accounting.

The Supreme Council proceeded to remove Bishop Fonacier from office and elected Bishop Gerado Bayaca in his place. This action was ratified by the General Assembly on the next day, January 22.

Fonacier, as might have been expected, refused to obey. He said that he would not accept the ouster nor would he give up the funds, titles, and other records of the Church.

On February 9, 1946 a suit was filed in the Court of First Instance by Bishop Bayaca (with Bishop de los Reyes as co-plaintiff somewhat later) in order to give legal sanction to the action of the Bishops and General Assembly.

The break of the Church into two factions came on September 1, 1946 when Fonacier, still claiming to be the Supreme Bishop, called a meeting of what he called the Supreme Council and General Assembly of the Church. This, of course, was attended only by his immediate henchmen, including, we may assume, the bishops upon whom he had laid his hands so suddenly. Fonacier resigned his position to this rebel assembly and a Bishop names Juan Jamias was elected Supreme Bishop. There was a method behind this move, as is revealed by his defense before the Court, which will be given later in this chapter.

There were now two Supreme Bishops and two factions, one led by Isabelo de los Reyes who had been elected Supreme Bishop after a brief tenure of office by Bishop Bayaca, and the other led nominally by Jamias but in reality by Fonacier. Each group claimed to be the true Philippine Independent Church. Fonacier's following was merely a small rebel party. The Court records reveal that on January 27, 1948, there were 293 bishops and priests with Bishop de los Reyes while Fonacier had only 64.[2]

The course of the law moves as slowly in the Philippines as

it does elsewhere. In 1947 while the case was still in process, the Philippine Independent Church made a new declaration of faith and petitioned the House of Bishops of the Protestant Episcopal Church of the United States for the Anglican Episcopate. Late in 1947 this petition was granted as will be described in more detail later in the chapter. Suffice it to say that this procedure gave Fonacier a new idea. He thought that he could strengthen his case before the Court of First Instance by claiming that the Philippine Independent Church had lost its identity through this "change of faith." He, and his faction, by holding to the Unitarianism of Aglipay, became in consequence the true Philippine Independent Church.

Bishop Fonacier's defense in this trial is thus described in the record of the Supreme Court in its review:

Mons. Fonacier claims as a defense that he has not been properly removed as Supreme Bishop; that his legal successor was Juan Jamias who had been elected in accordance with the Constitution of the Church; that he had already rendered an accounting of his administration to Bishop Jamias and turned over all the properties to the latter; that Bishop de los Reyes Jr. formally joined the Protestant Episcopal Church of America and for this reason he has ceased to be a member of the Iglesia Filipina Independiente; and that Bishop de los Reyes and Bayaca, having abandoned the faith, fundamental doctrines, and practices of the Iglesia Filipina Independiente, they ceased to be members thereof and, consequently have no personality to maintain the present action.[3]

The Supreme Court quotes the judgment of the Court of First Instance as follows:

On May 17, 1950 the Court rendered judgment declaring Isabelo de los Reyes Jr. as the sole and legitimate Supreme Bishop of the Iglesia Filipina Independiente and ordering Mons. Fonacier to render an accounting of his administration of the properties and funds of the Church "from the time he began occupying the position of Secretario de Economia Temporal thereof until the present time.[4]

An appeal was made by Fonacier to the Court of Appeals which confirmed the judgment of the Court of First Instance. He then appealed to the Supreme Court. This Court gave its decision on January 28, 1955. In doing so it confirmed the decision of the Court of Appeals. There is not space to quote this long and well reasoned decision in full as it answered the various charges of error which Fonacier said the lower Court had made. Briefly, it declared that the seven bishops consecrated by Bishop Fonacier had not been validly consecrated and that therefore they were not true bishops of the Philippine Independent Church when they formed a separate "rebel" group.[5] It confirmed that the election of Juan Jamias as Supreme Bishop was invalid because "it had not been conducted by a quorum of qualified and legitimate members of the Philippine Independent Church but by rebels thereof who were not authorized to organize the so-called *Asamblea Magna*." [6] It confirmed the judgment of the Court of Appeals which was that the consecration of Bishops de los Reyes, Aguilar, and Bayaca had not made them members of the Episcopal Church, but was only for the purpose of conferring the Apostolic Succession upon them, the two Churches remaining completely independent of each other.[7] Finally it confirmed the lower court in its statement that a change of doctrine was not mentioned in the original suit, and added the observation that (even if it had been) such matters were not within the jurisdiction of the Court. The final two paragraphs of the decision of the Supreme Court are worth reading.

. . . The alleged doctrinal changes and abjuration took place, therefore, after this case was filed in court and after the division of the Church into two groups had occurred, and consequently they could not have been the cause of the division. Under these circumstances it would seem clear that the allegation regarding the alleged changes in doctrinal matters or in matters of faith incorporated in the constitutions of the Church are entirely irrelevant in the present case. And, on this matter, this observation of the Court of Appeals comes in fittingly: "The Amendments of the Constitution, restatement of the articles of religion and abandonment of faith or abjuration alleged by appellant, having to do with faith, practice, doctrine, form of worship, ecclesiastical law, custom and rule of a church and having reference to the power of excluding from the Church

those allegedly unworthy of membership, are unquestionably ecclesiastical matters which are outside the province of the civil
courts." To this we agree. Wherefore, the decision appealed from
is affirmed without pronouncement as to costs.[8]

So the Philippine Independent Church came through trium-
phantly, but to this very date Fonacier has refused to give an
accounting and there has been trouble (legal and otherwise),
subsequent to the decision of the Supreme Court, about titles
to some properties and about the recovery of funds and records.
While in each case as it has come up the Independent Church
has won a favorable judgment, the whole legal process has imposed a heavy burden upon its slender finances. A few are pending at the present time and it is hoped that the cases will be settled promptly. Fonacier is still the leader of a small group of
"bishops" and not more than 10,000 people. Located for the
most part in the north of Luzon, in a region where Aglipay was
so immensely popular, they carry on a perpetual campaign
against the Philippine Independent Church. They claim that
they are the true Aglipayans and make the charge that the Episcopal Church is "swallowing up" the Independents. Just how
46,000 Episcopalians can assimilate over 1,500,000 Independents,
or how two bishops can dominate thirty-eight they do not attempt to explain. This is especially difficult of explanation as
the two bodies are completely autonomous and, as yet, not even
in intercommunion. Intercommunion itself implies no surrender
of autonomy! They call themselves The *Independent* Church
of Filipino Christians.

While the Supreme Court had affirmed that a change of doctrine did not affect the legal "personality" of the Philippine
Independent Church, the deeper truth is that there had been
no essential change of doctrine. The first "Fundamental Epistles" had proclaimed adherence to the Scriptures, the Incarnation and the Trinity. The *Oficio Divino* had been let down from
above and its teachings had never permeated the thought of the
great masses of the people. Only a few priests in the later twen-
ties had thoroughly adopted unitarian beliefs. As a whole, the

people were only cognizant of the fact that their Church had separated from Rome. Aglipay and Isabelo de los Reyes had gone far afield and had lost touch with their army as the protests of Servandro Castro show. The adoption of a position similar in its essentials to that of Anglicanism meant simply that it had made explicit a theological structure implicit in its history. The death of Bishop Aglipay and Isabelo de los Reyes made it possible for the Church to declare its true position which was not the religion of the Katipunan nor that of Unitarianism, but rather to be identified with the faith of the ages.

The new leader of the Church was Isabelo de los Reyes Jr. who became Supreme Bishop on September 1, 1946 succeeding Bishop Bayaca. He represented the younger group of bishops who were assuming leadership. Isabelo Jr. was born on February 14, 1900 in Madrid, Spain. We have already heard much about his father. His mother was Angeles Lopez Mantero, a Spanish woman. She was a journalist who had advocated reforms for the Philippines in the Madrid papers, and it was doubtless this common interest which had brought his father and her together.

At the age of two his mother took him and a sister, who was born after him, to her home town of Ferrol, Galicia (the home town of General Franco) where they lived with her parents in the absence of Isabelo Sr. who had returned to the Philippines. From 1904 to 1909 they lived in Barcelona. While there Isabelo was enrolled in a Roman Catholic School. In 1909 the family left for Manila, but the climate there proved too hard for the mother so that, after trying different health resorts in the Islands, including Baguio, Isabelo took her to Japan in the vain hope that she would improve. She died and was buried there in 1910. Back in Manila, young Isabelo, aged ten, was sent to the Jesuit's Seminary College in Vigan, Ilocos Sur, Isabelo's home town. Here he finished the elementary and intermediate classes and the second year of high school. In 1916 he was transferred to the Ateneo de Manila run by the Jesuits, the same school which had been attended by José Rizal. Here Isabelo finished the third year and a part of fourth year high school.

In 1917, without his father's consent, he attempted to enlist in the Philippine National Guard. He was rejected for physical reasons and had to submit to a minor operation. Trying again, he was accepted and became a private in an engineer's regiment in which role he remained until the regiment was mustered out in 1919. Life in the armed forces seemed to fascinate him and he immediately joined the United States Navy, remaining with it for four enjoyable years, sailing the Atlantic, Baltic, Mediterranean, and Black seas—a broadening experience for this intelligent and eager young man. Returning to Manila in 1923, he was asked by his father and Bishop Aglipay to become a priest of the Philippine Independent Church and to take charge of a chapel which was to be constructed in memory of his mother. When this was finished her remains were to be brought from Japan and buried there. Isabelo was tutored by Bishop Aglipay who ordained him in 1923. He is still in charge of the Church of Maria Clara, his first assignment.

In 1925 he was consecrated Bishop of Manila at the Tondo Cathedral by Bishops Aglipay, Isidoro Pérez, Felix de Léon, Sabino Rigor, and Servandro Castro—the last named, as we have learned, being the head of the conservative party in the Church. He married and has had ten children, two of his sons being enrolled at the present time in St. Andrew's Theological Seminary (Episcopal) in Queson City.

Isabelo had inherited great qualities both from his father and from his mother who must have been a brilliant woman. It is no wonder that Bishop Aglipay was greatly taken with this young man and at one time wanted to adopt him as his own son. Isabelo reports that the Bishop gave him his first bicycle and taught him to play chess. For some years they had their meals together and Aglipay played with Isabelo's children. It was for many reasons therefore, including the fact that he could speak English well, that Aglipay took him as a companion and interpreter on his great journeys to the United States and to Europe. In the writer's opinion, this close relationship explains how it was that Isabelo, who inherited his father's flair for writing, could write articles explaining Aglipay's theology, even though a gradual evolution was taking place deep within.

Isabelo had undoubtedly been influenced in a rationalistic direction both by his father and by Bishop Aglipay. Bound by ties of great affection, he naturally was led to read widely and he was able to feel the full force of rationalistic arguments. We must always remember that these older men were fighting for the freedom of the human soul, and the impact of the scientific empirical method made upon them had been enormous. They were wrestling with a problem that had to be faced by any Church which hoped to keep in touch with whatever was valid in modern thought. They had not had the time to do the work of St. Thomas Aquinas who, in an earlier century, found himself confronted with the scientific approach of Aristotle. Nor had they learned how other reformation groups in other parts of the world had grappled with the problem of reconciling intellectual freedom with authority.

Even when Isabelo was interpreting the unitarian position of his revered father and of Bishop Aglipay, there was a tension within his soul. He reports in his short autobiography that during the entire period of his ministry at Maria Clara chapel he has always, with Bishop Aglipay's knowledge and consent, administered the sacraments in the name of the Trinity. Even when closest to Aglipay he had been subjected to other influences. In his travels with the latter throughout the Islands he had had a different kind of contact with the masses of the people. The old leader, living in a world of his own was obsessed with his own theories and under the influence of world Unitarianism. In this connection Isabelo writes, "Unlike my father and Bishop Aglipay, who had not administered parishes for a long time, my daily contact with the masses of the faithful and my contacts with the clergy convinced me that our people in the Philippine Independent Church had been Catholic before 1902, when the Church was proclaimed, and after that they remained Independent Catholics." Again in this same autobiography he writes, "Deep in my soul I have always accepted the Apostolic and Catholic faith and have done my best to preach it to my people. On the other hand, since my early childhood, I have entertained a deep hostility to the superstitions and commercialism . . . that characterized Roman Catholicism in the Philippines. And I have always believed that those nations that have a purified, reformed Christianity are the nations that have become truly great and civilized."

Here we have, then, a picture of this younger man wrestling as best he could with great spiritual problems. There was no *volte-face* on his part, as has been claimed, but rather an integration of his deepest beliefs. His was not a unique experience. In 1930, long before the approach to the Episcopal Church was thought of, Servandro Castro had led a similar movement; and with the death of Isabelo de los Reyes and of Bishop Aglipay the fundamental convictions of the overwhelming majority of the clergy and people had a chance to express themselves. This is shown by a bit of history which has just come to the writer's notice. It seems that Bishop Servandro Castro was a candidate for election to the supreme office in 1940 after the death of Bishop Aglipay. He agreed to withdraw his candidacy in favor of Bishop Fonacier on condition that a full revision of the official books of the Church be adopted in order to restore its Catholic and Apostolic faith. To this Fonacier apparently agreed. Bishop Castro was elected Chairman of the Revision Committee and immediately started with his work. The war interrupted the work and the Bishop died immediately after the liberation with his task unfinished. It is interesting to note that, at the time, with the office of Supreme Bishop at stake, Fonacier agreed to the revision which he has since so bitterly attacked.

From 1946 on Isabelo de los Reyes Jr. became the leader as well as the titular head of the Philippine Independent Church. Brief as his theological training had been, he had the capacity to assimilate and to digest more than he would have learned in a theological school. In addition to his inherited ability to read rapidly he also had the capacity, perhaps inherited from his remarkable mother, to formulate his conclusions after "sober reflection." His wide experience in the army and navy had taught him both how to understand and to lead men. His travels with Aglipay had given him a world view. All of these influences, internal as well as external, made him develop rapidly into the man he has since become. In addition, he has within his make-up the precious ingredient of humor which gives him balance and a sense of proportion. Like many educated Filipinos he speaks Tagalog, Ilocano, English, and Spanish with the utmost facility and felicity.

Together with his bishops and clergy, Isabelo decided that the theology of the Anglican Communion represented, in all essentials, their own developed thought. The Caroline Divines, years before, had wrestled with all the problems involved in a separation from Rome. Their attitude about the Apostolic Succession which the Church of England had retained, appealed to the Filipino leaders who were anxious to make their Church one with the Church of the ages. So the work begun by Servandro Castro was brought to completion.

The Constitution which was adopted is too long to be printed in full in this chapter. However, the Declaration of Faith and several of the Articles of Religion, will show how, in essentials, the position is that of the Anglican Communion.

Declaration of The Faith
and
Articles of Religion
of the
Philippine Independent Church

We, the Bishops, Priests, and lay members, delegates to the General Assembly of the Philippine Independent Church (Iglesia Filipina Independiente) held in the City of Manila on the 5th day of August, A.D. 1947, do reiterate our faith and publicly declare that we believe in

(1) *The Holy Trinity:*
One God, true and living, of infinite power, wisdom and goodness; the Maker and Preserver of all things visible and invisible. And in

the unity of this Godhead there be three Persons, of one substance, power and eternity—the Father who is made of none, neither created nor begotten; the Son who is of the Father alone, not made nor created but begotten; the Holy Ghost who is of the Father and the Son, neither made nor created nor begotten, but proceeding.

(2) *Jesus Christ, the only-begotten Son of God:*

Jesus Christ, the only-begotten Son of God, the second Person of the Trinity, very and eternal God, of one substance with the Father, took man's nature in the womb of the Blessed Virgin, after she had conceived by the Holy Ghost. He suffered under Pontius Pilate, was crucified, died, and was buried. He descended into hell. The third day He rose again from the dead, He ascended into Heaven and sitteth on the right hand of God the Father Almighty; from thence he shall come to judge the living and the dead.

(3) *The Holy Ghost:*

The Holy Ghost, the Lord and the Giver of Life, Who proceedeth from the Father and the Son; Who with the Father and the Son together we worship and glorify.

(4) *One Catholic and Apostolic Church:*

The Church, Holy, Catholic, and Apostolic, which is the Body of Christ, founded by Christ for the redemption and sanctification of mankind, and to which Church he gave power and authority to preach His Gospel to the whole world under the guidance of the Holy Spirit.

We hold to the following Articles of Religion taught by this Church:

(1) *Salvation:*

Salvation is obtained only through a vital faith in Jesus Christ, the Son of God, as Lord and Saviour. This faith should manifest itself in good works.

(2) *Holy Scriptures:*

The Holy Scriptures contain all things necessary to salvation, and nothing which cannot be proved thereby should be required to be believed.

(3) *The Creeds:*

The articles of the Christian faith as contained in the ancient Creeds, known as the Apostles' and Nicene, are to be taught by this Church and accepted by the faithful.

(4) *The Sacraments:*

The sacraments are outward and visible signs of our faith and a means whereby God manifests His good will towards us and confers His grace upon us . . .

The next step was to approach the Rt. Rev. Norman S. Binsted, Bishop of the Philippine Episcopal Church; but before an account of this approach is made, it is revealing to learn of an interesting little episode. The Roman Church, cognizant of what was in the wind, was concerned about the prospect that the Independent Church might acquire the Anglican succession of Bishops. A letter from the present Supreme Bishop says that in 1945 or 1946 the Rev. Patrick O'Connor, a Columban who was a writer for an American Roman Catholic magazine, came repeatedly to his home with the apparent purpose of securing information about the Philippine Independent Church. One morning he came again to the Bishop's home accompanied by the Father Superior of the Columbans in the Philippines and by another Columban priest from the parish church of Malate. These brought with them an American who was introduced as a high official of the Knights of Columbus. In the conversation that ensued these people intimated that if the Independent Church would return to the obedience of the Roman Pontiff, the bishops thereof would be consecrated in the Roman succession and there would be such marginal benefits as the authority to use the vernacular, permission for the clergy to marry etc., such as had been granted to other Christian minorities in the Middle East. Bishop de los Reyes told them that the only way to persuade his people to return to Rome would be to elect a Filipino Pope! His visitors smiled indulgently and left never to return. The only witness was Bishop Remollino who has since died.

This will doubtless be disavowed by the Roman authorities, but apart from the writer's confidence in the integrity of Bishop de los Reyes, the whole thing is so much in character that he has no doubt that such a "feeler" was made. The Rev. Richard

L. Rising, Rector of St. John's Church, Williamstown, Massachusetts, and formerly Dean of the Episcopal Cathedral in
Manila, reports that "two Jesuits called upon Bishop Wilner who
was Suffragan Bishop at the time and in charge of the Diocese
during the temporary absence of Bishop Binsted. These clergy
went into extensive detail with him trying to discredit the Philippine Independent Church, with the obvious goal of attempting
to prevent the consecration service."

Preliminary conversation with Bishop Binsted had revealed
that Article III of the Constitution of the Episcopal Church, implemented by Canon 42, made it possible for the House of
Bishops to grant a petition for Anglican Orders if all of the conditions were met by a body which might make application.
Armed with this knowledge the Supreme Bishop and Council
of the Philippine Independent Church, meeting with the General Assembly, voted unanimously on August 4, 1947 to petition the House of Bishops for the historic episcopate. This petition accompanied by all the documents required by Canon 42
was to be conveyed to the House by Bishop Binsted.

Bishop Binsted, as one might expect from the foregoing, had
encouraged the move. He had immediately seen the significance of such an appeal and realized that conditions were very
different from those prevailing when Bishop Aglipay and
Bishop Brent had been in conference over forty years before.
The Revolution of 1898 was far in the past; the nationalism of
the Independent Church was now an asset rather than a liability.
In addition, the petition came from the supreme body of the
Church representing a great people. It had a national significance which the Bishop was not slow to recognize.

The Episcopal House of Bishops met in Winston-Salem,
North Carolina, on November 4-7, 1947. With the approval of
the Rt. Rev. Henry Knox Sherrill, Presiding Bishop of the
Church, Bishop Binsted presented the petition and in a moving
speech recommended that it be granted. The Presiding Bishop
appointed the following Committee to consider the petition,
examine the documents, and report back to the House: The

Rt. Rev. B.F.P. Ivins, Bishop of Milwaukee (Chairman); The Rt. Rev. Edmund P. Dandrige, Bishop of Tennessee; The Rt. Rev. Lewis Bliss Whittemore, Bishop of Western Michigan; The Rt. Rev. Norman B. Nash, Bishop of Massachusetts, and The Rt. Rev. Theodore R. Ludlow, Suffragan Bishop of Newark.

By unanimous vote the Committee reported favorably and the petition of the Philippine Independent Church for the Apostolic Succession was granted amid considerable enthusiasm (for the House), only one Bishop voting in the negative on the ground that more time should have been given for study. The decision was made quickly but, among other things, it showed the great confidence which the House had in Norman S. Binsted.

On April 7, 1948 a great service was held in the Pro-Cathedral Church of St. Luke in Manila. Three bishops of the Philippine Independent Church were to be consecrated in the Anglican succession. The Rt. Rev. Norman S. Binsted, Bishop of the Philippine Episcopal Church was the Consecrator. Co-consecrators were the Rt. Rev. Robert F. Wilner, Suffragan Bishop of the Philippine Episcopal Church, and the Rt. Rev. Harry S. Kennedy, Bishop of Honolulu.

The three Filipino bishops to be consecrated in the Anglican line, and thus forever to have a place of honor in the annals of their Church, were Monsignor Isabelo de los Reyes Jr., Supreme Bishop and Bishop of Manila, Monsignor Manuel N. Aguilar, Bishop of Laguna, and Monsignor Bayaca, Bishop of Tarlac and Zambales.

The impressive service was conducted before a large congregation and at its end the historic episcopate of the Church of God was in the possession of the Philippine Independent Church. The three bishops at once consecrated the other bishops of the Church and all priests and deacons were re-ordained.

On the program for the consecration on April 7, 1948, we find the following:

"While the Iglesia Filipina Independiente will always cherish and maintain its independence and take pride in the record of its people in laying the foundation of national as well as ecclesiastical independence, it rejoices that in this service of Consecration the validity of its Orders is secured and very close cooperation with the Episcopal Church made possible. It is expected that in the future, by action of the two Churches, a Concordat may be concluded between them authorizing inter-communion . . ."

Chapter XV

The Roman Catholic Church
in The Philippines Today

The Roman Catholic Church in the United States did much to rescue the Catholic Church in the Philippines from the slough of despond into which it had fallen during Revolutionary days. How desperate the situation was is reflected by a saying current in Manila during one of the worst periods: "There are no longer boatmen for the barges because the Archbishop has ordained them all." [1] But Rome is always resourceful; and while sending American bishops to replace the Spanish episcopate was unpopular with the masses at the time, it proved to be a very wise move. One problem was financial as the clergy were no longer paid by the state, but these bishops were quite accustomed to a like situation in America; they knew the technique of money raising under the separation of Church and State. This they taught to the Filipino clergy. Realizing that the Church could no longer "raid the barges," but still feeling the need for native clergy, they took steps to remedy the situation by advertising the plight of the Church throughout the United States. They induced the Archbishops of New York, Philadelphia, Cincinnati, and St. Louis, as well as the Bishops of Trenton, Raleigh, and other bishops to receive sixty Filipino students into their seminaries, all expenses paid. [2] It is well to emphasize that from the very beginning the Roman Catholic Church in America showed its missionary zeal by doing everything in its power to put the Roman Catholic Church in the Philippines on its feet, while at the same time the Reformation groups in America were shying away from the Reformation Church in the Philippines.

Busy with innumerable duties in a strange land, the new bishops did everything in their power to recover the lost properties of the Church, their efforts coming to a favorable conclusion in the Supreme Court decision of 1906. They were also helped in the early days by the comfortable acquisition of $7,000,000 from the sale of the friar lands. Progress was made in other directions as well. The Roman authorities began gradually to appoint Filipino bishops and archbishops, the process having culminated recently in the appointment of a Filipino Cardinal. At long last this Church had learned a lesson, and their "Counter Reformation" was due in no small measure to the staunch fight the Philippine Independent Church had made through the years for the recognition of Filipino capacity.

The Roman Church was back in business. Many returned to the ancient fold. Some could not follow the new theology of Bishop Aglipay; others were affected by the new prestige of this Church once it had acquired possession of its former buildings. Seminaries were reopened and there was a new sense of confidence everywhere.

The Provincial Council, called in 1907, did much to strengthen the Church. Attended by the canonically required, and thus a representative body of clergy, it was an impressive affair. It accepted the Constitution contained in Pope Leo's *Quae mari Sinico* and it passed many decrees of a constructive nature. While not summoned primarily to combat the Independent Church, the Council still gave considerable attention to that troublesome body. Archbishop Agius, the Apostolic Delegate, referred to these people as "ravening wolves" who had given scandal by their impious rebellion. The Council itself called the Philippine Independent Church "the synagogue of anti-Christ;" Aglipay and other priests, it was stated, had acted out of the "pretext of nationalism;" all the sacraments of that

Church were invalid and people were warned not to harbor such heretics. There was, of course, the unctuous invitation to repent and return to the fold like erring children.

While this was rather rough on Aglipay and his followers, there is no question but what this Council revealed that the Roman Catholic Church in the Philippines was pulling itself together again after a distressing period in its history. Certain it is that the Council gave the Church new hope and determination, as has been proved by its growth since that time. In 1937 the importance ascribed to the Philippines was shown by the fact that Manila was made the scene of the International Eucharistic Congress of that year. It is stated that over a million people were present on the Luneta for the colorful ceremonies at the end. It is no wonder that hearts swelled with pride and that it began to seem more and more distressing that other religious groups should claim a share in the rich Philippine heritage.

This feeling of "possession" was implemented by the fact that the orders were back in the Philippines. Senator Roseller T. Lim in 1958 or thereabouts, gave the entire list numbering over thirty. There were orders old and new so far as the Philippines was concerned. We find the Order of St. Benedict, the Order of the Friar Preachers, the Franciscan Order, the Augustinian Order, the Order of Recollects—all headed by Spaniards. Then appears a bewildering array of orders headed by Italians, Americans, Australians, Canadians, Dutch, and Germans. The orders were indeed back and in force.[3]

These regiments of priests, considering themselves superior to the seculars, have always controlled the Church in the Islands, and it is quite evident that they constitute the greatest power in the Church today. The nationality may vary, but these organizations, under more than military discipline, have the same spirit as of old. They adhere with iron persistence to the decrees of the Vatican Council of 1870 and to the Syllabus of Errors. They are, therefore, by definition, opposed to the modern "error" of separation of Church and State. It is psychologically impossible for them to sympathize with nationalistic aspirations except in terms of their own specialized vocabulary. What they want is the old Roman Catholic State. The following condensed table is worthy of study.

Catholic Directory of the Philippines 1960

Population

Inhabitants (*Catholic Directory 1960*)	23,082,597
Estimated, Bureau of Census and Statistics	23,562,900
Catholics 83.11%	19,185,384
Non-Catholics	3,897,213

The Philippine Hierarchy

Archdioceses	7
Dioceses	14
Prelature "Nullius"	7
Apostolic Vicariates	4
Military Vicariates	1
Archbishops*	11
Bishops	35

Priests Engaged in Pastoral Work

	3289
Parishes	1447
Diocesan priests	1595
Religious priests	1644
One priest for 7,162 souls; 5,923 Catholics; 1203 non-C.	

Priestly Vocations for Diocesan Clergy

Diocesan Minor Seminaries	22 **
Diocesan Major Seminaries	4
Minor Seminarians	1387
Major Seminarians	982

Religious Orders and Congregations (Men) 1950-60

Number of Religious Orders and congregations (men) in the P.I.	30
Professed members	2588
Novices	138

Religious Clergy

Bishops	20
Priests	1876
Filipino	229
Foreign	1647
Scholastics	427
Philosophy	192
Theology	235
Brothers	276
Filipino	117
Foreign	157

* Apostolic Nuncio and all resigned bishops included
** Minor and Major Seminaries

Novices			138
Clerical			95
Brother			32
Candidates			
for priesthood			494
for brotherhood			60
Institutions			
Parishes			446
Schools (Students 368,987)			310
Diocesan Seminaries			310

Catholic Schools:	Elem.	H.S.	Coll.	Students
	273	535	108	368,987

Remembering that the words "diocesan priest" refer to the "secular" priest and that the term "religious" refers to a priest who is a member of an order, it is quite evident from the above that the great majority of Roman Catholic parishes are ruled by foreign "religious" who have a double allegiance—one to the bishop and the other to the superior of the order. Thus the age-long tension between secular and religious is being repeated in the Philippines today. Only a few Filipinos have been admitted to the orders, as the record shows, and this reflects the old feeling that the Filipino is incapable or untrustworthy. To be sure, there are Filipino bishops and archbishops, but the Catholic Church in the Philippines today is controlled by foreigners who have no sympathy with the struggle for independence, and conceive that any attitude except that of submission is heresy in the guise of false patriotism. While there is even a Filipino Cardinal, he is ranked by the Papal Nuncio.

A few years ago Senator Roseller T. Lim introduced a bill in the Philippine Senate which reveals the strong sentiment existing in the Philippines about what the Senator calls "religious colonization." He felt that while the Philippines is independent politically, it is still a colony religiously. The bill was not passed; however, the first section stated that: "Hereafter, no person who is not a natural-born citizen of the Philippines shall be head of any school, college or university, or teacher, instructor or professor of any social science subject."[4]

Himself a Catholic, Senator Lim explains in the Foreword of his pamphlet that,

. . . in spite of almost four centuries of Catholicism in our country, our religious priests and nuns are only assistants of foreigners in our land. In our Catholic educational set-up our Filipino Bishops and Archbishops have very little or any control of our Catholic schools, colleges and universities. The heads of the foreign orders are lording it over us.

That at least 80% of our Catholic schools, colleges and universities (58% in number) ruled by foreigners is an insult to us, develops colonial mentality because this system continues to inculcate in the minds of our youth foreign schools of thought—thus causing our people to lose our national soul, our nationalistic spirit. That is why our legislature has often found itself compelled to legislate on nationalization. Spontaneous nationalistic spirit seems to be lacking in our people now, I am afraid . . .[5]

Senator Lim hastens to say that many Roman Catholics have proved to be real patriots, but he does quote the Memorial of the Religious Orders issued in April, 1898 which said, "It is well known that very few of the native officials who went through their course in our schools have taken part in the rebellion . . . and the proclaimers of "Freedom" are, for the most part, individuals who have failed in their career, and were the refuse of our classes." This was the judgment on men who fought and died for the independence the Philippines now enjoys.

While Senator Lim is fearful that the dominance of the orders is damaging the national soul, the Roman Catholic Church has an entirely different approach to the problem. This body does not hesitate to declare, or at least to imply, that non-Roman religious bodies are damaging the immortal souls of countless people. It really gets down to a very simple syllogism: There is no salvation outside the Church; and the Roman Catholic is the only true Church. Therefore the souls of all those who are not members of the Roman Catholic Church are either lost or in extreme danger. All non-Roman religious bodies are under attack in the Philippines, but the great enemy is the Philippine Independent

Church together with its ally, the Episcopal Church of the United States.

From 1902 on the Roman Church has looked upon the Philippine Independent Church, hewn out of its own body, with both antagonism and fear. It has reiterated the charge that its bishops are not true bishops and that its priests are not true priests. In addition to this, the doctrine of the Independent Church, prior to 1947, contained in its *Catequesis*, and in the *Oficio Divino*, offered a wonderful target and the Roman Church took full advantage of it. In 1925 Fr. Candido Fernandez García, a Dominican friar, published a book under the auspices of the University of Santo Tomás. This book examined critically and in detail the *Catequesis* of the Independent Church, the general ideas of which we have examined briefly in discussing the *Oficio Divino*. The book was scholarly and well done and was quite devastating. Of course it has no relevance at the present time.

In 1947, when the Independent Church reaffirmed the ancient faith of the Holy Catholic Church (which it had never really abandoned), and in addition received from the Episcopal Church valid Orders for its ministry, the battle front was changed to an entirely new theatre of operations. As an example of the kind of battle now being waged against both bodies we might refer to a pamphlet written by Fr. Nicolas L. Rosal, published in 1959 by the University of Santo Tomás Press, and entitled *Aglipay-anism, Yesterday and Today*. It is rather interesting to remark how these attacks continue on an institution which has been declared (by the Roman Catholics) to be almost defunct and of little importance.

The booklet begins by saying that the Iglesia Filipina Independiente is the fruit of misplaced patriotic and religious zeal. In other words the Revolution of 1896, and continued in 1899, was a terrible mistake. As one result, its leaders have allowed a "Babel" of Protestant religions to invade the Islands. The freedom and contentment they meant to give the people have only produced "spiritual ruin."

There follows a brief resumé of Filipino history, stating that the Revolution was against Spain and ended, unfortunately, against the Church. The intent of this perversion of history, which is doubtless being taught in Roman Catholic schools, is obvious. A brief biography of Bishop Aglipay follows; and this is more of a caricature than a history. Rosal does not neglect to assail Aglipay's moral character, although he does admit that the Aglipayan movement served to call attention to the needs of the Filipino clergy.

He gathers momentum as he criticizes the Faith of the Independent Church as stated in its present Constitution and Articles, attempting to show that it differs at various points from Roman Catholic doctrine, particularly in refusing obedience to the pope. However, he emphasizes that deficiency even in the smallest point is fatal—like a drop of poison. For example, he attacks the Independent Church for allowing its people to read what books they want, unless the books are subversive of good morals.

The main guns, however, are trained on Anglican Orders as these are now the possession of the Independent Church. He repeats the time-worn, often and easily refuted charge that these Orders are worthless—that the bishops in the Anglican line are not true bishops nor are the priests true priests. The old clichés are dragged out for inspection by people who are ignorant of the subject and are not inclined to look into the matter. For this reason it may be worth while to have a brief review.

The fundamental fact is that there are two kinds of Catholicism—one the Catholicism of the Holy Catholic Church of the ages and the other the limited and rigid Catholicism of Rome. In this question the paramount issue is concerned with the nature of the historic episcopate, commonly called "The Apostolic Succession." The Vatican has to deny the validity of the Anglican succession, because to admit it is to allow that there is room for Catholics outside the fold of Rome. By this denial it is occupying a position which is becoming increasingly untenable. The intellectual honesty of many Roman Catholics is strained about this matter because Leo XIII in his Bull *Apostolicae Curae* published in 1896, took an absolute stand in a so-called "infallible" utterance. Roman Catholics must accept this utterance by an act of faith, in spite of the abundant evidence which points in the opposite direction.

The fact that the Roman assault on Anglican Orders has shifted ground so often through the years is evidence of its weakness. Romanists teach that the Church of England was in a state of separation from Rome following the excommunication of Henry VIII, this period lasting from 1533 until 1553. Next there was a period of reconciliation during the reign of "Bloody Mary" from 1553 to 1558. While still remaining in communion with Rome relations were strained from 1558 until 1570 when Queen Elizabeth was excommunicated and there was a final break with the Papacy. During the whole period from 1533 to 1570 there was not the slightest question about English Orders, although there had been ample opportunity.

The old English Church went on as before after 1570, with its bishops, priests, and deacons; and it was not until some forty-five years later that an assault was made on the validity of Anglican Orders. When at last the attack began, it was concentrated on Matthew Parker who had become Archbishop of Canterbury under Elizabeth. It was all rather ludicrous. First it was charged that his consecration had never taken place at all—the records had been forged! Again it was rumored that there had only been a mock ceremony—the so-called Nag's Head fable. Finally, many years after this, doubt was cast upon the validity of Parker's consecrators. Catholic theologians have disposed of all of these charges, and informed Catholics know that they were false. However, the stories are still being repeated in the Roman Catholic world either through ignorance or malice. Elizabeth, as a matter of fact, was well aware of the issues involved and took meticulous care that Parker's consecration was performed in a regular manner and that exact records were kept.

A new and vicious method was resorted to in an attack on the moral character of the "apostates" Henry VIII, Elizabeth, and Archbishop Parker. The idea in this was to discredit the Church to which they belonged by the law of association. As Lewis[6] points out, if the orthodoxy of the English Church had been jeopardized by the apostasy of some of its members, then the validity of the Roman Church had been endangered by the atheism, heresy, and immorality of many of the popes. Henry VIII was a saint in comparison with some of them. Again, informed Roman Catholics know this, but the ignorant do not, and even now these stories are being repeated.

Mention might also be made of the statements made to this day, publicly and privately, that "Henry VIII founded the Church of England" or, somewhat less frequently, that "Elizabeth founded the Church of England." Neither of these claims has been made officially but they are repeated by ignorant or malicious priests, and by teachers in Roman Catholic schools who ought to know better. While the Vatican has not proclaimed this officially, it has shown itself to be very complacent about this practice of telling such tales.

Such things are vexatious but of secondary importance. The thing to remember is that, up to the time that Queen Elizabeth was excommunicated in 1570, the Roman Church was willing to accept all the English bishops without reconsecration, provided that the Queen would make her submission. No question was raised about the Ordinal which had been used and which has since been so violently attacked. During Elizabeth's period the Church of England had been in full communion with Rome. Elizabeth and her people could communicate freely at any altar on the Continent. Otherwise, the excommunication of the Queen would have been meaningless. For the Pope, in 1896, to condemn Anglican Orders because the Ordinal in Elizabeth's time was defective was to admit that the Vatican had winked at heresy for a considerable period in English history. No other argument is really necessary.

Rome has a tenacious memory, but it also has the power to

forget when expedient; and so, disregarding that period in history in which it had implicitly endorsed the Ordinal used in Queen Elizabeth's time, it shifted its ground and tried again. More than a century and a quarter after the death of Elizabeth, the Pope in 1685 declared that the wording of the Ordinal used during her reign was defective. It was not until 1896 that Pope Leo XIII, claiming that he had given meticulous attention to the matter, issued the Bull *Apostolicae Curae*, an "infallible" utterance, declaring that Anglican Orders were null and void because of defects in the Anglican rite as to both form and intention. To get a clear picture of this period in ecclesiastical history one should read about the labors of Lord Halifax, a layman of the Church of England, who led a movement for the recognition of the validity of English episcopal consecration. He had strong support for his contention in various parts of the Roman Church, particularly in France. The Vatican, swayed by opinion in such quarters, was finally moved by the English Cardinal to accept the theory that England could be conquered "one by one"—a theory which history has since disproved. The English Cardinal won his battle. Just how carefully Pope Leo had studied the question may be doubted, for scholars have unearthed the ancient fourth-century rite of St. Serapion and the Apostolic Tradition of St. Hippolytus which, together with the studies of Dom Gregory Dix and others, have revealed that in ancient times there was a great variety of rites which showed confusion about such technical matters as "form, matter, and intention." From them it was made clear that these essentials of a valid sacrament might be expressed in a variety of ways.

Pope Leo did avoid one rather ludicrous mistake. It seems that in 1439 Pope Eugenius IV had officially declared that the "tradition of the instruments" (i.e. placing the cup, paten, staff etc. in the hands of the priest to be ordained) was an essential part of the ceremony. It was discovered in the 19th century that this "tradition" had not been a part of the Roman rite until the tenth century!

Such matters are highly technical and if one cares to go into them he can read many books, some of which are mentioned in the notes.[7]

The question of defects in the English Ordinal has been summed up by Dr. Massey H. Shepherd Jr., the distinguished Anglican scholar, as follows:

"The condemnation of the Prayer Book Ordinal in 1896 by Pope Leo XIII in his Bull *Apostolicae Curae,* wherein the claim is made that the Ordinal is defective both in its form and in its intention of continuing the historic Orders of the Ministry, as they have been received and understood by the universal Church, and that therefore the Holy Orders of Anglicanism are invalid, rests upon no foundation whatsoever. Not only does the Preface of the Ordinal state "the intent" of our Church to be that the Orders of Bishops, Priests and Deacons "may be continued and reverently used and esteemed in this Church" but the recovery in recent times of the early third-century work of St. Hippolytus of Rome, the *Apostolic Tradition,* shows unmistakably that the "form and matter" of the several rites of our Ordinal are more consonant with the practice of the universal, undivided Church of ancient times, and not least that of the Church of Rome itself, than are the rituals of the Roman Pontifical presently in use.[8]

It is clear from the foregoing that the Holy Catholic Church of the great Creeds, while it includes the Church of Rome, is not monopolized by it. There are other legitimate and valid havens for the Catholic as is proved by the Church of England, the Orthodox Churches, the Old Catholic, the Polish National Churches, and now the Philippine Independent Church.

A full-dress attack upon the Philippine Independent Church has now been made by two Jesuit priests in a volume entitled *Religious Revolution in the Philippines* which covers the period from the inception of the Independent Church to the death of Aglipay in 1940. This book appeared in 1960 and is to be followed by another volume carrying the story up to the present moment. Fr. Pedro S. de Achútegui S.J., a Spaniard, is a Professor of Theology and Rector of St. Robert Bellarmine seminary of Shanghai. At the present time, in exile from China, he is conducting his classes in Baguio. Fr. Miguel Anselmo Bernad S.J., a Filipino, his associate in writing the book, has the degree of Ph.D. from Yale. At the Ateneo de Manila he is Professor of Literature and has been the editor of *Philippine Studies*.

The first volume is impressive both in its size and by the vast amount of scholarly research which it reveals. The researches have been made in libraries, monasteries, and archives on a worldwide scale. Many letters, written in the heat of controversy and conflict, have been found on dusty shelves by these indefatigable workers and their associates. The appendices, bibliography, and index show the vast scope of their study. It is the most complete history of the Philippine Independent Church which has as yet been written. Careful in its chronology, written in a readable style, and printed in large type, it has historical value and should be in the library of anyone who is interested in the subject.

Having said this, one has said about all that he can in praise. Written from the Jesuit point of view, it is heavily slanted while claiming to be impartial. It distorts history in claiming that the Revolution was started mainly against the Spanish Government, although it admits that there was considerable resentment against the friars. Its main intent, however, is to discredit the Philippine Independent Church in the eyes of the Filipino and American people by attacking the moral character of Aglipay. This has been done not so much by making direct statements as by quoting the writings and letters of contemporaries, thus allowing anyone to judge for himself. For good measure, hints of Aglipay's constant inner turmoil if not of mental instability, are included. There had to be a certain amount of care in that Aglipay is a national hero to millions outside as well as within the Independent Church. For this reason a bow toward national sentiment is made now and then by telling of good deeds he had done, his power of leadership, and his physical courage.

There is no direct attack upon the Episcopal Church in this volume, as it concludes with the death of Aglipay. Written, however, after the new Constitution of the Independent Church had been adopted and after the bestowal of Anglican Orders, the conclusion is inescapable that these two events had thoroughly alarmed the Roman hierarchy. One must also conclude that the book is seeking to drive a wedge between the Episcopal Church and the Independent Church so as to forestall the impending Concordat of full communion.

This is made apparent by the prominence which is given to Bishop Brent, the first Episcopal Bishop in the Philippines. The book gives considerable space to the history of that great man; it also quotes many of the letters in which he criticizes Bishop Aglipay. As a result it definitely raises the question of how Episcopalians can wish to associate themselves with a Church whose first leader was such a bad character.

One has to go back to the days prior to 1904 to get a balanced view. The Revolution was barely over. In Samar it was smouldering as late as 1907. The Filipinos had been defeated in war, but the decision to cooperate fully was not made until the first Assembly met in 1907. The American Army leaders had bitter memories of the fighting. The cry in the Army was, "The Little Brown Brother may be a friend of William H. Taft, but he ain't no friend of mine." Bishop Brent was in the closest possible touch with the Army high command. He confirmed no fewer than three generals while in the Philippines. From them he received very unflattering accounts of the Filipinos and shared their view, in all likelihood, that the Philippine Independent Church, born of the Revolution, its leaders Filipino patriots, might in reality be plotting mischief. From the Army Bishop Brent heard the worst that could be said about the Philippines in general and about the Independent Church and Aglipay in particular.

Bishop Brent became extremely good friends with the American Roman Catholic bishops who had arrived to take over, and even then he was filled with the idea of a united Christian Church, the chief apostle of which he was to become in later years. The Catholic bishops, for their part, had listened attentively and sympathetically to the friars who hated Aglipay and this was all relayed to Bishop Brent.

Eager to put his ideas into practice on the spot, if possible, the

Bishop made a grand gesture. Stating that he would not "raise altar against altar," he declared that he would devote the major part of his work—beside ministering to the Americans—to the non-Christian peoples in northern Luzon and to the Mohammedans in Mindanao. It will be readily understood that this commitment, so pleasing to the Roman Catholic bishops, made it morally difficult for him to enter into close relations with a Church which had so recently torn itself asunder from Rome.[9]

So far as this writer is aware—and he worked under Bishop Brent for two years and lived in his house for one summer in Manila—the latter did not have close and sympathetic contact with the leaders of the Revolution and therefore had little or no opportunity to get their side of the story. He was working with the Americans, the mountain people, and the Mohammedans—not with the rest of the Filipinos, except to a minor degree.

Those were tumultuous days and there were recriminations and counter recriminations on both sides. It was not an atmosphere conducive to a calm and impartial judgment. In addition, Bishop Brent and Bishop Aglipay did not get along. Bishop Brent did not speak Spanish and Bishop Aglipay did not know English. It was hard for the American Bishop to make allowance for the oriental manner of approaching a vital subject. He liked to call a spade a spade. Apart from everything else, they did not like each other.

St. John tells us that any man who thinks that he is without sin deceives himself. Henry VIII, Elizabeth, Parker, Luther and Aglipay, Brent, and the Roman bishops may have shared the common lot of man. They also may have repented and have been forgiven. It is not for us to judge or condemn. If God cannot use imperfect instruments, then none of us can "apprehend that for which we have been apprehended" and strive to reach the goal. Whatever Bishop Brent may have decided about Bishop Aglipay and his movement, something was operating in him which was deeper than his surface thought. Bishop Brent was a devout man and his great decisions came in illumined moments. As a child of God he was led by the Spirit, and the decision not to ally himself with Aglipay was not, fundamentally, because the latter was a certain kind of man, or because he felt that he had to keep faith with the Roman Catholic Church, or for any other similar reason. It was made because God spoke to him. St. Paul was not "suffered" to go into Bithynia, and Bishop Brent was not suffered to go to the lowlands in an alliance with Aglipay. The fulness of time had not yet come for a rapprochement between the two Churches. Bishop Brent, adventurer for God, was to go to the hills and prepare an intelligent, virile, and yet isolated people not merely to renounce paganism but to become an integral part of the nation that was to be. He had to go to the south to win the Mohammedans to a way of life that would bind them into unity with their fellow Filipinos to the north. No more heroic or rewarding missionary effort, nor one of more value to any nation, has ever been undertaken. The Independent Church, on the other hand, had to come to full self-consciousness through many years of physical, mental and spiritual trial. That was in 1904. Now, with the maturity and strength which almost sixty years have brought to both Churches in the Philippines, they are coming close together as though driven by the winds of God.

It is rather surprising that men like Achútegui and Bernad should have used a discredited method in attacking the Philippine Independent Church. In basing the attack on moral grounds they have followed the examples of all those who have attempted to discredit the Reformation by picturing its leaders both in England and on the Continent as moral lepers. Both sides can play that game if they are inclined to do so. Moreover, the onslaught is completely irrelevant. This is 1961, not 1904 or even 1940.

At the same time, it must be admitted that this book represents a massive drive on both the Independent and Episcopal Churches. The Roman Church would destroy us if it could, and along with our debacle every Reformation group in the Islands would find itself in danger. With our fall the hope for true religious liberty would be gone forever. The Philippine Republic, in the grasp of the great orders, would once more become a colonial nation, except, perhaps in name.[10]

The Philippine Independent Church and the Episcopal Church, by entering into a Concordat of full communion, while in no sense surrendering their own autonomy, will be bound closer together by new ties of friendship. By inaugurating a program of mutual aid, both bodies will increase in strength for each has what the other lacks. In all this there is no desire to injure the Roman Catholic Church which itself has a mighty mission to fulfill in the Islands. The two Churches accept this historic Church, but they resent its attitude of implacable hostility. This is greatly to be regretted, as there is more than enough work for all to do in peace and amity. However, recognizing that the Roman Church is only impressed by strength, these two Churches, Catholic but Reformed, Reformed but Catholic, are determined to press forward with all vigor for the cure of souls and for the welfare of the new Republic which needs their witness to the fundamental freedoms without which no democracy can long endure.

Chapter XVI

Struggle for Religious Freedom

The events which followed the decision to grant the historic episcopate to the Independent Church have given evidence of God's blessing on this daring venture. The possession of the Apostolic Succession sent a thrill of confidence and of new life through this body of Christians which has held its sense of mission so tenaciously through many years of trial. Its backbone was stiffened as it met the constant Roman attacks on the validity of its ministry. The admission of its seminarians into the Episcopal Theological School in Queson City has raised its level of theological education. The young graduates of this school are showing their worth, and in due time bishops will be elected from among their number. Churches and chapels have been rebuilt since the war, others have been repaired and improved. Laymen have been organized into local groups and there is a national layman's association. The Woman's Auxiliary has been formed both in local parishes and on the national level. Youth groups are springing up everywhere and are consolidating regional associations. Two clergy of the Independent Church are ministering to many Filipinos scattered through the new State of Hawaii. The Church has become a member of the World Council of Churches and the East Asia Conference of Churches. The long awaited prayer book has at last made its appearance. Sound in its essential doctrine, beautifully printed and bound, it is a worthy production. This book is a milestone in the history of the Church as it will serve to unify its worship and to give it national cohesion on this level. Best of all, there is a new sense of self-confidence and of eagerness as it faces the future side by side with the Episcopal Church. The attacks of Rome have only served to cement the relationship between the two Churches. Recent events have borne witness to this significant development.

On May 8, 1960, the Supreme Council and General Assembly of the Philippine Independent Church, after consultation with Bishop Ogilby, Bishop Lichtenberger the Presiding Bishop of the Episcopal Church, Bishop Bayne the Executive Officer of the Anglican Communion, and other leaders, voted unanimously to propose to the Episcopal Church that there should be a Concordat between the two bodies. This was in no sense a petition, it was a proposal as between equals and reads as follows:

"*Resolved* that the Supreme Council of Bishops of the Iglesia Filipina Independiente propose that a relationship of full communion be established between the two Churches and approve the following statement, based upon the Bonn Agreement between the Old Catholic and the Churches of the Anglican Communion, as a definition of this relationship and agree to the establishment of full communion on this basis:

(1) Each Communion recognizes the Catholicity and independence of the other and maintains its own;

(2) Each Communion agrees to admit members of the other Communion to participate in the Sacraments;

(3) Full Communion does not require from either Communion the acceptance of all doctrinal opinion, sacramental devotion, or liturgical practice characteristic of the other, but implies that each believes the other to hold all the essentials of the Christian faith." (See Appendix).

In November 1960, the House of Bishops of the Episcopal Church, meeting in Dallas, Texas, passed the resolution which follows:

"Whereas, in 1947 the House of Bishops of the Episcopal Church granted the petition of the Philippine Independent Church for the consecration of their bishops; and

Whereas, the relationship between the two Churches since that time has been increasingly close as evidenced in many ways, but especially by the fact that candidates for the ministry of the Philippine Independent Church are trained at St. Andrew's Theological Seminary in Queson City; and

Whereas, the development and growth of the Philippine Independent Church will have an important bearing on the future of our own Church in the Philippines so that in the long prospect this Church may be enabled to do as much for us as we for them; and

Whereas, the relationship between the two Churches makes possible on a national scale of a strong Catholic but reformed tradition which has long been the purpose of the work of the Episcopal Church in the Philippines; and

Whereas, the Philippine Independent Church has now proposed that there be a Concordat of full communion between the two Churches;

Therefore be it Resolved, that this House receive this proposal with deep thanksgiving in Christ and unanimously recommend that such a Concordat be entered into; and be it further

Resolved, that the members of our Church in the Philippines be encouraged to pursue with all earnestness and warmth the steps presently taken looking toward closer companionship between the two Churches; and be it further

Resolved, that a committee of this House be appointed by the Presiding Bishop of which the Bishop of the Missionary District of the Philippines shall be Chairman, which committee shall make a study of the present needs and opportunities of both Churches and report on a program of increased cooperation. Recognizing that financial problems of considerable magnitude would be involved in any major effort, the committee is asked to analyze this aspect of the matter and to report in detail about amounts needed for specific projects if the program is to be implemented.

The Chairman is to have the power to appoint to the committee additional members, episcopal, clerical, and lay, from both Churches as the basic study must, of necessity, be done in the Philippines. These persons shall function in an advisory capacity; and

Be it further *Resolved,* that this committee report both orally and in printed form to this House and to the General Convention in 1961; and

Be it further *Resolved,* that this House recommend to the National Council that the sum of $25,000 be set aside for the expense of this committee."

At the end of January, 1961, the annual Convocation of the Philippine Episcopal Church, under the fine leadership of

Bishop Ogilby, made one of the most momentous decisions in its history by passing the following Resolution:

> "*Resolved*, that this Convocation, while recognizing that problems of considerable magnitude may be involved in working out the principles of the Concordat in the local scene; and while recognizing the existence in both Churches of diversities of cultural interests and traditions; but also recognizing the claims of Christian charity upon us all growing out of our Lord's will and purpose for His Church; and recognizing the opportunity set before us and the obligation placed upon us now and in the future to strengthen the two Churches in their witness to the Gospel of Christ; recommends to the 60th General Convention of the Protestant Episcopal Church in the United States of America, to be held in Detroit, Michigan, that this Concordat be entered into."

The Christian world is now awaiting the action of the General Convention of the Episcopal Church. Rome has a lively stake in this matter. The Anglican Communion is interested in the ratification of the Concordat, as this would open the door to Concordats with all its independent national branches. It is worthy of mention that Bishop Bayne, who in a sense represented the Anglican Communion, had a share in framing the House of Bishops resolution. The non-Roman world, particularly in the Philippines, is concerned because a strong Reformed Catholic Church would serve as a protection of its own liberties.

Implementation of the Concordat itself should present no difficulties. For years the seminarians of both Churches have made their communions together at the altar of St. Andrew's Theological School. The two bishops, in special cases, have accorded the privilege to individuals as a matter of "economy." The Concordat would simply make universal what already has been practiced under certain circumstances locally. It would regularize a *de facto* situation (and save a lot of office work). The general situation invites the Concordat, for the Episcopal Church is working in one part of the Philippines while the Independent Church is working in another. Any overlapping on the fringes can be easily adjusted.

While the Concordat, technically, imposes no burdens on

either Church, it does carry with it a deeper moral commit-ment. It should be remembered that the Episcopal Church made such a commitment when it bestowed the gift of Orders on the Independent Church. There was an immediate recognition of this in the admission of Independent Church men into St. An-drew's Theological Seminary. Young women of the Indepen-dent Church are being trained at the school of nursing in con-nection with the Episcopal St. Luke's Hospital. Bishop Bin-sted, who is looked upon as a patron saint of the Independent Church, gave a great deal of his time to its affairs as has his worthy successor, Bishop Ogilby. The faculty of St. Andrew's have taken time to advise with the Independent Church Com-mission preparing the new prayer book. One member of the faculty has helped in planning the architecture of at least one of their new churches. All this has been the natural result of what happened in 1947 and it has been done, not grudgingly but with enthusiasm as in a great cause.

But the Concordat makes the Independent Church a sister Church in a fuller sense, and with it the moral obligation is deep-ened. In taking the steps toward a Concordat, leaders of both Churches have been fully aware that the real responsibility for cooperation will be felt when the Concordat is an accomplished fact. It was for this reason that the House of Bishops at Dallas authorized the formation of a Committee which would make a thorough study of the needs of both Churches in the Philip-pines and report to the General Convention in the fall of 1961. This Committee consists of the Rt. Rev. Lyman C. Ogilby, Bishop of the Philippine Episcopal Church, Chairman; The Rt. Rev. Robert Fisher Gibson, Bishop of Virginia, and the Rt. Rev. Harry Sherbourne Kennedy, Bishop of Honolulu. In the Phil-ippines this official Committee will be assisted by advisory mem-bers from both Churches including, of course, the Rt. Rev. Isa-belo de los Reyes, the Supreme Bishop of the Philippine Inde-pendent Church. While not anticipating the report of this com-mittee, it is well to consider what problems they will find in the course of their investigations. These may be thought of un-der several headings.

Shortage of Clergy

The Philippine Independent Church desperately needs more clergy. It has, at last accounts, between 1,500,000 and 2,000,000 members. There are 36 bishops and 580 clergy who minister to this great body of communicants. As many of the bishops, in order to live, have to be rectors of parishes in addition to their episcopal duties, let us take a round figure of 600 clergy who are doing parish work. This would make the ratio of lay members to clergy as 2,362 to 1. If we take the larger figure of total membership, we would have 3,333 to 1. In the Episcopal Church, by way of comparison, there are 3,444,265 baptized members and 9,079 clergy, or a ratio of 379 to 1;[1] and this ratio is thought to be insufficient.

But this does not tell the whole story. In the regions where the Independent Church is strongest, the disproportion is much greater. In the town of Villasis in Pangasinan Province, the Independent Church claims 19,800 members out of a total population of 27,000. There is one central Church building in the town with five chapels in the barrios (wards). There is one priest who ministers to the entire membership. Binaloan, in the Province of Tarlac, has a population of 40,000 and the Independent Church claims 16,000 members. Here there is only one priest, an able young man, who is a graduate of St. Andrew's Seminary. This means that pastoral work and vital touch with individual parishioners, in our sense of the word, is out of the question. It also means that missionary work is impossible, although the Church could be established in other barrios of the same town.

An interesting sidelight is thrown on this question by the foregoing condensed report of the Roman Catholic Church of the Philippines for 1960. This report states that there is one Roman priest for 5,923 Catholics. Figures for both Churches show that there is a desperate shortage of clergy in the Philippine Islands. It is quite evident that millions of people are truly unshepherded and that the fields are ripe for the harvest. There is work enough for all without mutual distrust.

Finances

One of the most encouraging signs of the times is that the leaders of the Philippine Independent Church, filled with new hope and enthusiasm, are in a mood to look critically at their own organization and methods. Cheered by the presence of a staunch ally, with questions of orders and doctrine settled, these men are willing to forget past issues and to modernize the Church organization to meet the imperative needs of the present. One of the greatest of these necessities is to take a hard look at financial methods.

The Philippine Independent Church, as a Church, is very poor. This does not mean that all of its members, or even a great majority of them, are poverty stricken; they are not. While it is true that a majority are in the lower income brackets, the Church still represents a cross section of the population. It has a financial potential which has never been realized. A study of the financial reports of the Central Headquarters shows how true this statement is.

Problems of Central Headquarters

The Central Office, corresponding to the Presiding Bishop and National Council of the Episcopal Church, has an annual income, for all purposes, of less than 15,000 pesos. In American money, with approximately three pesos to the dollar, this income is pathetically small. The fact that this minute support is received by taxing the clergy *with no lay help,* comes as a shock to the investigator. It is as if the tax on the clergy of the Episcopal Church for the support of General Convention should represent the entire national income of the Church. This yearly tax for licenses to officiate is assigned as follows:

(1) Diocesan and Suffragan Bishops	50.00	(pesos)
(2) Priests in first class parishes	50.00	"
(3) Priests in regular parishes	30.00	"
(4) Priests in missionary stations	10.00	"

Laid on all the bishops and priests this gives a theoretical total of 14,790 pesos. Unfortunately this small amount is not paid in regularly. Some bishops who do not also serve as rectors of parishes have difficulty in raising the money. Many clergy, hard put to it to keep body and soul together, find it difficult to remit their modest quota.

It is quite evident, therefore, that this weakness at the center constitutes one of the main problems of the Philippine Independent Church. The national income of the Church is not sufficient to pay the salaries of the Supreme Bishop and his small staff. The spiritual leadership of these able men leaves nothing to be desired, but their hands are tied in the attempt to create a national structure within a Church which prides itself on its national fervor. The quarters are quite inadequate for the purpose, and this would be the more apparent if full time executives for promotion, missions, education, and social relations were to be added. The Church faces some of the problems of the nation itself, for communication between islands stretching in a chain a thousand miles long is difficult and expensive. Only a strong national government can bind these scattered islands together into an effective unity. In the same manner there must be a strong national headquarters for the Independent Church, if it is to secure united and enthusiastic cooperation from all its far-flung dioceses. The Supreme Bishop must have financial as well as spiritual power.

While there is not space to give a full account of the financial posture of the Church as a whole, a recent letter from the Supreme Bishop which is quoted in part, will give an impression of the situation.

". . . Generally, a first class parish has a monthly income of around three to five hundred pesos; the second class parishes usually have a monthly income of one hundred to two hundred pesos; and the barrio or rural parishes receive an equivalent of from sixty to one hundred and fifty pesos, mostly in kind like rice, eggs, firewood, chickens, vegetables, and fruits. In many small rural parishes the laity are given a quota of a meal monthly per family of the faithful, as substantial aid to the priest. The rural areas are considered second-class parishes.

One of the most painful problems is when a barrio or small town needs and wants a parish but lacks the means to keep the priest alive, especially when he happens to have several children.

Another grave problem is that our bishops, in many instances, have no parish of their own and depend for their support on a yearly quota—from each of the parishes within the diocese—of about fifteen to twenty-five pesos. In these cases, and even among those with small parishes, the bishops lack the financial means to supervise duly the work of the diocese and to help expand the Church. With a modest monthly aid from the Central Office, these bishops could perform real wonders . . .

A missionary priest will cost approximately, according to location, from forty to one hundred pesos monthly. If he is single he will need much less than if married. Naturally he will receive modest financial aid from our faithful wherever he may start his missionary activities. In the Ilocano provinces a missionary may get along with forty to sixty pesos a month. In the Tagalog provinces he will require from fifty to one hundred pesos monthly. In Mindanao something like forty to fifty pesos will do and the same will be true in the Visayas. In the large cities all missionaries will need larger aid, something like from eighty to one hundred and twenty pesos. But everywhere a missionary will become self-supporting within five years."

The Bishop goes on to describe the imperative need for a pension system. At the present time there are five bishops and about twenty priests who are over seventy-five years of age!

A Suggested Approach to the Financial Problem

While it must be remembered that living conditions and standards are different in a tropical country, it is clearly evident that there must be a radical reform in its methods if the Independent Church is to realize its financial potential. The Filipino people are as generous and self-sacrificing as any people in the world, but this Church is endeavoring to do its work handicapped by a financial system centuries old so far as lay contributions are concerned. The situation is even worse than in Spanish days: then the clergy salaries were paid by the Crown. Now the Church is endeavoring to do its work without this resource, relying entirely on what we would call the perquisites of the clergy. The fee system (i.e. paying so much for baptisms, confirmations, marriages, funerals etc.) not only is entirely inadequate financially, but it also narrows the lay vision and helps to kill the missionary motive. It must be abolished.

It is no simple matter, however, to change established habits of giving. If any rector should suddenly discard what are called "stole fees," his parish would go out of business. With this in mind, the late Rt. Rev. Norman S. Binsted, former Bishop of the Philippine Episcopal Church, who had given much thought to this matter, suggested that the salary of a number of rectors of pilot parishes throughout the Islands be guaranteed for a period of some years, the number to be determined by certain conditions. These conditions would be that the fee system be abolished and that every member be asked to make a yearly pledge to be paid regularly. The objective would be to meet a carefully prepared but still daring budget which would include provision for quotas to be paid to the diocese and National Church. In addition the parish must install a modern financial record system with provision for an annual audit. The rector, aided by the vestry, should prepare the budget, and the finance committee of the vestry should handle all funds in order to increase lay participation in financial problems. There should, of course, be a thorough education in the whole meaning of stewardship before the change takes place. It is believed that the laity would respond and that the parish, in addition to giving a substantial and self-respecting amount to the diocese and National Church, would prosper as never before. It would surprise itself. Success in these representative parishes would make it easier to reform financial methods throughout the Church.

The Increase of the Ministry

It can easily be seen that if the Philippine Independent Church can put its financial household in order, many young men who may be hesitating about entering the ministry for financial reasons will feel encouraged to do so. The Supreme Bishop writes that already, due to the new enthusiasm in the Independent Church more young men are applying for admission to St. Andrew's Theological School than ever before. With the financial future secure the numbers will greatly increase. These young men are the hope of the future.

Opportunity for Religious Education in the Public Schools

Philippine Law allows any Church to send teachers, whether clerical or lay, to hold classes three times a week in the public school buildings, either during the regular session or after hours at the superintendent's discretion. This religious education must be at the written request of parent or guardian. (See Chapter XIII) This legal provision presents a wonderful opportunity of which the Independent Church should prepare to take advantage. As a typical example, the town of Santa Cruz in Laguna Province has a population of about 27,000, of whom 20,000 are Independents. Two fine, young graduates of St. Andrew's Theological Seminary have charge of the central parish and of the chapels in the surrounding barrios. The High School has 1700 students and 1000 of these are members of the Philippine Independent Church. A majority of the faculty are also members of the Church. No advantage is taken of the opportunity to give religious instruction in the school for the simple reason that with this huge parish on their hands, the two clergy have no time and there are no trained lay people to do the work. A Baptist minister, who has a small congregation in the town, teaches regularly in the school with about a hundred pupils in his classes. The Independent Church is losing glittering opportunities like this throughout the Islands.

While it is going to take considerable time to man the Independent Church with a sufficient number of graduates of St. Andrew's, it should be possible to establish training schools for lay religious teachers so that these can begin to function within a comparatively brief period. A trained professional group would have to be secured on a full-time basis to train the prospective teachers, but this could be done if money for salaries were available. Eventually, in each diocese there should be one professional director of religious education who would have training institutes throughout the area. Possibly the whole operation could be under the direction of St. Andrew's Theological School. However the work is planned, it should be a major effort to raise up a trained lay order to supplement the efforts of the hard-pressed clergy. The general and pervasive influence of such a body of lay people would reach out in many directions. The education of the great mass of the laity is too big a job for the clergy alone, no matter how numerous they may be.

Secondary Schools

The public schools of the Philippines are free for only six grades. The Government cannot afford to do more, and it must be confessed that many problems even in this elementary area remain to be solved. After the sixth grade a fee for tuition is charged. In other words, these schools must be self supporting. Roman Catholic and so-called "non-sectarian" schools abound, the latter, for the most part, run under Roman Catholic auspices. They are non-sectarian only in name. In these schools to which so many Independent Church boys and girls go, a definite effort is made to wean them from their own allegiance, with the result that many come out either Roman Catholics or indifferent to any Church—fair game for any ideology. The Independent Church is losing much of the cream of its youth in this manner, and it is almost a mortal wound. Everywhere the leaders of the Church express the greatest concern over this situation. One of the great needs of the country, as well as of the Church, is for secondary schools of high standards which would be joint ventures of the Independent and Episcopal Churches. It is thought that in the course of a few years each one would be self-support-ing. One could be begun in Manila to start with and, if this suc-ceeds, others could be started in the principal cities in the Islands.

A Liberal Arts College

One cannot visit Rikkyo (St. Paul's University) in Tokyo without realizing what a tremendous center of Christian influ-ence this great university is with its ten thousand students. Silli-man Institute, under Presbyterian auspices and located on Ne-gros in the Visayan area of the Philippines, has work on the college level and is very influential. A liberal arts college in Manila, as a joint enterprise of the Philippine Episcopal and the Philippine Independent Church, would be a logical develop-ment. At the present time young men go to Saint Andrew's Theological Seminary immediately after having finished their high school course. Taking the five year course at the Seminary they get a certain amount of supplementary education on a col-lege level before beginning their theological studies. This means that a part of the time in the Seminary has to be spent in making up for previous educational defects. The ideal for the two Churches is to provide a sound secondary education to be fol-lowed by four years in a liberal arts college. Those with a priestly vocation would then have three years in theological school. One of the great needs of both Churches is to have a ministry which can be just as much at home in academic circles as it is anywhere else. These men must capture the mind as well as the heart of the Philippines.

Scholarships

More scholarships for study at St. Andrew's should be made available for young men of both the Episcopal and Independent Churches. There should also be scholarships which would make it possible for well equipped Filipinos of both Churches to go to America or England to seek Master's and Doctor's degrees in theology, academic subjects, education, medicine, science, and agriculture. It should be possible to bring religious and other leaders from the United States and elsewhere to lecture, and even to take temporary positions. Contacts must be multiplied. No nation or Church can do without them.

Travel Expenses

If the Independent Church is to realize its potential, one of its biggest problems is that of communication. It is an expensive matter to have meetings of a national character. The service by boat between islands is poor and time-consuming. Air travel provides the only feasible way of getting around, but it is expensive. The Supreme Bishop and his colleagues of the national office should not have to hesitate about taking necessary trips because of the expense. It is a financial hardship for the bishops of the Supreme Council to have a meeting in Manila as they have to pay their own way. One of the great needs of the Church is to strengthen the National Layman's Association, and its Board of Trustees should be able to meet without imposing a severe financial burden on its individual members. The head of the National Woman's Auxiliary told me that it is practically impossible for her to get her Board together as the members could not afford to take the journey. One of the greatest needs of the Independent Church is contact of its own leaders with each other.

Missionary Expansion

A long-range program for the missionary expansion of both Churches is needed. As a part of extending the program of worship, education, and social relations, new buildings should be constructed in strategic locations. A carefully worked-out plan for providing proper tools for an increasing number of clergy should be made.

Needs of the Episcopal Church

The Philippine Episcopal Church, a missionary district of the Episcopal Church of the United States, records in the 1961 Annual that it has a membership of 46,065 souls, 152 parishes and missions and 62 clergy. This Church has devoted much of its work to the Mountain Province of northern Luzon the population of which numbers more than 400,000. It was one of the non-Christian areas to which Bishop Brent first directed his attention. It is an important region now dotted by Episcopal parishes, missions, schools, hospitals, and dispensaries. Brent School in Baguio is one of the great educational institutions of the Orient, and pupils come not only from all over the Philippines but from south-east Asia as well. The response of the people of the Mountain Province to this missionary effort has been one of the outstanding phenomena of the century. They are ministered to for the most part by Igorot clergy trained in the Episcopal Theological School in Queson City. These men constitute an outstanding group—virile, intelligent and devout. Bishop Ogilby, the present Bishop, says that he would compare them with any similar group anywhere.

In winning souls to Christ and his Church these men are helping to integrate this hitherto isolated area with the rest of the Philippines giving the people a common Christian culture. Nothing could be more important from a national point of view. But vast areas of this mountainous territory still remain to be touched by the Episcopal Church. The vision of Bishop Brent, as he trod those hills for the first time, must not be allowed to fail. No money for missionary endeavor has ever been more wisely spent.

In Mindanao, with its population of over 5,000,000 people, the Episcopal Church is working among the Mohammedans who number more than a million. The Church is dedicated to interpreting the Gospel of Christ to these proud people through Christian service in hospitals and schools. Progress is necessarily slow but this is the Episcopal task and it, too, has both a Christian and a political bearing. Only gradually can these followers of the Prophet whose ancestors preyed on their neighbors to the north, come to have a sense of complete integration with the new nation. Here, again, our missionary money has been spent in a heroic enterprise, one which is worthy of Bishop Brent the adventurer for God. And the door of opportunity is still wide open.

In Manila and nearby Queson City we have our great and new Cathedral, Holy Trinity Parish, two Chinese Episcopal churches, the great St. Stephen's Chinese School, St. Andrew's Theological School, and the splendid St. Luke's Hospital with its associated nurses' training school.

All this represents one of the most exciting and rewarding missionary tasks in the world, and it stands to reason that whatever the Episcopal Church in the United States may do for the Philippine Independent Church, it must not be at the expense of our work already established. But this work is vulnerable.

The truth is that in a different way, the Episcopal Church in the Philippines needs the Independent Church just as much as the latter needs the Episcopal Church. In the first place it needs it for the protection of its work. If this great missionary venture is to continue in peace, it is essential that there should be a powerful Reformation Church throughout the Philippines to balance the Roman strength. The Roman Church in that country does not accept the existence of any other religious bodies. If any one doubts how the Roman Church feels about the Independent Church he need only read the recent volume by the Jesuits Achútegui and Bernad. If there is any question about the attitude of Rome about the Episcopal Church in the Philippines the recent booklet by Fr. Rosal will make the matter plain enough. The menace is real, and the only thing which will keep Rome from harrassing and undercutting both Churches is the growth of the Independent Church in power and influence. Strength must be opposed to strength. The Supreme Bishop of the Independent Church told the writer that unless these Reformed Catholic Churches join forces, there will be neither an Independent nor an Episcopal Church in the Islands a hundred years hence. He might, with equal truth, have said fifty years. It is as simple as that. The Pope may receive the Archbishop of Canterbury in Rome—but this is the Philippines.

This, perhaps, is putting the argument on the lowest level. We must climb to higher ground and think not only of the fate of the two Churches but of that of the Philippine Republic. Both of these two Reformation Churches have a sense of national mission. The Independent Church embodies the national conscience and carried that ark with it through all of its vicissitudes. Independence once meant independence from foreign power. Now the spirit of freedom demands freedom *within* the nation, and it is to preserve that inner liberty that the Church now bends its efforts. The Episcopal Church also has a national background. It, too, grew out of a national struggle. It understands, sympathizes with, and believes in the nation. It, too, is dedicated to the liberty which ennobles free men.

Bishop Brent came in 1901 as Bishop of the Philippines. He may have concentrated his work in certain sections of the Islands, but he never forgot his national responsibility. He became the foremost citizen of the archipelago and his voice thundering from the Cathedral pulpit reached the ears of the American Government, the Army, the Navy, the Capitol in Washington, and the entire Filipino community. He spoke the community conscience and he defended the Filipino nation in stopping the entry of the opium traffic. In him the Episcopal Church had a national position.

But Bishop Brent's position was based on American sovereignty, and with each step toward Philippine Independence the national posture of the Episcopal Church faded. In 1946 the Episcopal Church lost its national influence almost completely. From the standpoint of the Philippine Government at the present time we are just one group out of many, and off in a corner at that. The Roman Church calls us a sect.

The late war called for a reappraisal of the whole situation. When peace was declared and Bishop Binsted, released from prison in Santo Tomás, was free to return home, he spoke his mind to the National Council of the Episcopal Church. He said that the Episcopal Church in the Philippines had just three alternatives: one was to continue the work as it was done before the war; one was to remain in the pre-war areas serving them more intensively; one was to accept a larger vision of the work of the Church, to expand it into new fields, to integrate it into the life of the nation, and to take definite steps looking to the establishment of an autonomous branch of the Anglican Communion.[2] His own choice was the last and with him the Council heartily agreed.

It is of great significance in interpreting the Bishop's mind about his real purpose that shortly afterward he brought the petition of the Philippine Independent Church for Anglican Orders to the Episcopal House of Bishops. A Concordat of full communion now proposed would be the logical outcome of an historic process.

The Episcopal Church, in joining forces with the Philippine Independent Church, while retaining its own independence, is fulfilling its destiny. Like David called from the sheep, it has been summoned to that wider field of action for which its history, its conscience, and its patient labors have prepared it. God, who kept these two Churches apart in the beginning, now is bringing them close together for their own weal and for that of the Republic upon whose success on the world stage so much depends.

Appendix

A Statement by the Rt. Reverend Arthur Lichtenberger, Presiding Bishop of the Episcopal Church in the United States.

In view of the fact that there has been some confusion in the minds of many people both in the United States and in the Philippines regarding the exact nature of the proposed Concordat between the Protestant Episcopal Church and the Philippine Independent Church upon which final action will be taken by the General Convention of the Episcopal Church in September 1961, a copy of the proposed agreement is printed herewith. It is based upon the so-called Bonn agreement between the Anglican Communion and the Old Catholic Church.

(1) Each communion recognizes the catholicity and independence of the other and maintains its own.

(2) Each communion agrees to admit members of the other communion to participate in the sacraments.

(3) Intercommunion does not require from either communion the acceptance of all doctrinal opinion, sacramental devotion, or liturgical practice characteristic of the other, but implies that each believes the other to hold all the essentials of the Christian faith.

It could not be stated more clearly that nothing in this agreement is said about a "merger" of the two bodies such as would be effected by an organic union. Each Church remains completely and absolutely independent of the other. The Concordat would be a seal of the mutual trust and friendship existing between the two bodies. Good friends sit at each other's tables, and in this case members of both Churches can do likewise at the Table of the Lord in the Holy Eucharist. This will make it possible for members of either Church in a town where their own Church is not in existence, to partake of the Sacrament at the altar of the other.

Any attempt to read more than this into the agreement is far from the truth.

Both Churches, however, will be strengthened by this Concordat in their effort to preserve religious freedom in the Philippines. Political independence is only one aspect of freedom. Upon religious freedom rest all of the other freedoms necessary for a full and vigorous national life such as freedom of the press, freedom of speech, and of association, freedom of conscience and freedom from censorship. The Episcopal Church believes that the Philippine Independent Church is the great national bulwark of this freedom. The friendship and cooperation of both Churches offer the best hope that the Philippines, independent politically, will have that religious freedom which is essential for a democracy.

Notes

CHAPTER I

1. Joseph Ralston Hayden, *The Philippines* (New York: Macmillan Co., 1942), p. 3. Used by permission.
2. Preliminary returns from the 1960 Census give a population of 27,473,000 (*Catholic Directory*, 1961).
3. Paul Tillich, *The Protestant Era* (Chicago: University of Chicago Press), p. 194. Used by permission.
4. Jaroslav Pelikan, *The Riddle of Roman Catholicism* (New York: Abingdon Press), p. 71. Used by permission.
5. The Reformation leaders emphasized the other side of St. Augustine's teaching, the doctrine of justification by faith.
6. The Encyclopaedia Britannica, XXVI, 282.
7. Pelikan, *op. cit.*, p. 71.
8. This refers to the charge that the only basis for the break with Rome was the desire to have Filipino priests in charge of parishes and to secure the appointment of Filipino bishops.
9. C. S. Lewis, *The World's Last Night* (New York: Harcourt Brace), p. 48. Used by permission.

CHAPTER II

1. Barrows, *History of the Philippines* (New York: Bobbs-Merrill, 1905), pp. 33-34.
2. James A. LeRoy, *Philippine Life in Town and Country* (New York & London: G. P. Putnam's Sons, 1907), p. 19.
3. Kroeber, The Peoples of the Philippines (The American Museum of Natural History), pp. 14 ff.
4. Barrows, *op. cit.*, p. 80.
5. Kroeber, *op. cit.*, p. 144.

CHAPTER III

1. Fray Gaspar de Augustin, *Conquistas de las Islas Filipinas*. See Barrows' *History of the Philippines*, p. 126.

2. See Introduction to Blair and Robertson, *The Philippines*.
3. Barrows, *op. cit.*, p. 237.
4. The original document is quoted in the History of the *Philippine Independent Church*, a thesis written by Francis H. Wise, pp. 6 ff. It is also quoted in *The Filipinos Fight for Freedom* by Austin Craig (Manila: Oriental Commercial Co.), pp. 218 ff.
5. Louis C. Cornish, *The Philippines Calling* (Philadelphia: Dorrance & Co.), p. 37. Used by permission.
6. Wise, *op. cit.*, p. 19.
7. LeRoy, *Philippine Life in Town and Country*, p. 150.

CHAPTER IV
1. Wise, *op. cit.*, p. 25.
2. *Ibid.*, p. 27.
3. *Ibid.*, p. 35.
4. A Spanish instrument for strangling.

CHAPTER V
1. See Rafael Palma, *The Pride of the Malay Race* (New York: Prentice-Hall), p. 7.
2. Palma, *op. cit.*, p. 94.
3. *Ibid.*, p. 95.
4. *Ibid.*, p. 117.
5. English translation of *El Filibusterismo* is entitled *The Reign of Greed*, and is published by the Philippine Education Co., Manila.
6. Rizal, *The Reign of Greed*, p. 360.
7. Palma, *op. cit.*, p. 193.
8. *Ibid.*, p. 213.
9. *Ibid.*, p. 230.

CHAPTER VI
1. Wise, *op. cit.*, p. 43.
2. See Teodoro M. Kalaw, *The Philippine Revolution* (Manila Book Co., Inc., 1925), pp. 55-57.
3. Wise, *op. cit.*, p. 60.
4. See Achútegui and Bernad, *Religious Revolution in the Philippines* (Ateneo de Manila, 1960), p. 168.

CHAPTER VII
1. Wise, *op. cit.*, p. 42.
2. Achútegui and Bernad, *op. cit.*, p. 12.
3. *Ibid.*, p. 14.
4. *Ibid.*, p. 17.
5. *Ibid.*, p. 22.
6. *Ibid.*, p. 42.
7. Wise, *op. cit.*, p. 90.
8. *Ibid.*, pp. 91-92.

CHAPTER VIII

1. See page 61.
2. Wise, *op. cit.*, p. 108.
3. *Ibid.*, p. 115.
4. *Ibid.*, p. 121.
5. From the northern diocese came Santiago Serafica, Adriano Garces, Antonio Maria Padilla, Tranquilino Fernandez, Manuel Bonifacio, Segundo Urbi, Miguel Mamuyac, Mariano Dakanay, Andres Cadiz, Eusebio David, Domingo Salinda, Leoncio Evangelista, Juan Paquing, Domingo de Vera, Lucilo Meris, Emigdio Albano, Ponciano Manuel, Isidoro Perez, Isidoro Montoya, Fructuoso Tolentino, Mariano Gaerlan, Silvestre López, and Justo Claudio. From the northern part of the archbishopric of Manila came Gregorio Dizon, Anselmo Fermo, and Cipriano Valenzuela.
6. Achútegui and Bernad, *op. cit.*, p. 112.
7. *Ibid.*, p. 33.

CHAPTER IX

1. Achútegui and Bernad, *op. cit.*, pp. 147-48.
2. *Ibid.*, p. 156.
3. Wise, *op. cit.*, p. 147.
4. *Ibid.*
5. Stuntz, *The Philippines and the Far East* (Cincinnati: Jennings and Pye, 1904), pp. 489-90. See Wise, *op. cit.*, p. 143.
6. See magazine *Encounter* (Indianapolis: Christian Theological Seminary, summer 1958), Vol. 19, No. 3, p. 299.
7. Achútegui and Bernad, *op. cit.*, p. 163.
8. Wise, *op. cit.*, p. 100.
9. Manuscript by the Rev. Manuel Lagasca, *The Philippine Independent Church*, p. 4.

CHAPTER X

1. Wise, *op. cit.*, p. 167.
2. Achútegui and Bernad, *Ibid.*, p. 195.
3. *The American Catholic Quarterly Review*, XXVIII, 372.
4. Martin Garcia Alcocer, Bishop of Cebu, had been made Apostolic Administrator of Manila.
5. It had been reported that Spanish friars would go to the United States not only to study but to become American citizens, and then return to the Philippines as such.
6. Some have thought that this epistle marks the rupture with Rome. The author agrees with Achútegui that the break had taken place some time before.
7. The Fourth Fundamental Epistle was written immediately after Aglipay had been formally inaugurated and had celebrated his first Mass on October 25 and 26.
8. He is probably referring here to his experience at the "retreat" at Santa Ana with the Jesuits.

9. These Fundamental Epistles were printed in their entirety in *La Iglesia Independiente,* a Catholic Review edited by Isabelo de los Reyes in Manila. The first issue was printed in 1903. The summaries here were taken from this periodical.

10. Of course, Roman Catholic theology is sound enough in this manner. The thing itself, however, is difficult to control and lends itself to abuse. This has happened in the Philippines.

CHAPTER XI

1. Pp. 261-2. Reprinted by permission of Dodd Mead and Company from *Recollections of Full Years* by Mrs. William Howard Taft.
2. Achútegui and Bernad, *op. cit.,* p. 227.
3. Wise, *op. cit.,* p. 178.
4. *Ibid.*
5. Wise, *ibid.,* p. 226.
6. Wise, *ibid.,* p. 227.
7. Wise, *ibid.,* p. 228.

CHAPTER XII

1. John Foreman, *The Philippine Islands* (New York, 1906), p. 607.
2. Wise, *op. cit.,* p. 209.
3. E.g., *Sensacionales Discursos, Evoluciones, La Libre Razón,* etc.
4. Wise, *op. cit.,* p. 225.
5. Manuel Lagasca, *The Philippine Independent Church,* p. 37.
6. Cornish, *op. cit.*
7. *Ibid.,* p. 97.

CHAPTER XIII

1. Hayden, *op. cit.,* p. 376.
2. *Ibid.,* p. 400.
3. *Ibid.,* p. 391.
4. *Ibid.,* p. 564.
5. *Ibid.,* pp. 565-66.
6. *The Separation of Church and State.* Pamphlet issued by the Religious Liberty Association, p. 13.
7. Achútegui and Bernad, *op. cit.,* p. 506.
8. Isabelo de los Reyes, Jr., *The Religious Retraction of Isabelo de los Reyes y Florentino,* p. 7.
9. As another example of this kind of writing in a responsible Roman Catholic encyclopedia, it is stated in *The Catholic Encyclopedia Dictionary* (1941), on page 18, that the Independent Movement was largely political and that "the schism soon disappeared"!

CHAPTER XIV

1. Conrad Myrick, *The Philippine Independent Church and The Philippine Nation.* An unpublished manuscript, p. 28.

2. *Official Gazette, Republic of The Philippines.* Vol. 51, No. 3; p. 1351.
3. *Ibid.*, p. 1333.
4. *Ibid.*
5. *Ibid.*, p. 1342.
6. *Ibid.*, p. 1347.
7. *Ibid.*
8. *Ibid.*, pp. 1352-1353.

CHAPTER XV

1. Yorke Allen, Jr., *A Seminary Survey* (New York: Harper & Bros.), p. 446.
2. *Ibid.*
3. Senator Roseller T. Lim, *Church Leadership in the Republic of The Philippines*, p. 4.
4. *Ibid.*, last page.
5. *Ibid.*, Foreword.
6. G. F. Lewis, *The Papacy and Anglican Orders* (London: Mowbray & Co.), p. 10.
7. The title above is an excellent short summary. See also: Dom Gregory Dix, *The Question of Anglican Orders* (London: Dacre Press); J. C. Whitebrook, *The Consecration of Matthew Parker* (London: Mowbray & Co.); Felix L. Cirlot, *Apostolic Succession and Anglicanism* (Lexington, Kentucky: Trafton Publishing Co.); Massey H. Shepherd, Jr., *The Oxford American Prayer Book Commentary* New York: Oxford University Press).
8. Massey H. Shepherd, Jr., *The Oxford American Prayer Book Commentary* (New York: Oxford University Press), pp. 527-529.
9. While the Roman Catholic bishops gladly welcomed Bishop Brent's decision not to encroach upon what they considered their territory, they did not reciprocate by leaving him a free hand in the Mountain Province. No sooner had he started work in that region, than they invaded this territory which their Church had neglected for three hundred years. Their policy ever since has been to match our work anywhere in a new field with a mission of their own. This happened, for example, later on at Upi in Mindanao.
10. Further evidence of the attempt being made by Rome to prevent the proposed Concordat is contained in a letter to the author from the Supreme Bishop of the Philippine Independent Church dated February 20, 1961. The pertinent part is quoted as follows: "Three days ago I delivered to Bishop Ogilby a letter in Spanish signed by Mons. Dom Luis F. Castillo Mendez, Diocesan Bishop of Brasilia of the Catholic and Apostolic Church of Brazil, claiming as line of succession: Mons. Carlos Duarte Costa, consecrated by Cardinal Sebastian Leme, Archbishop of Rio Janeiro; Mons. Sebastian Leme, consecrated by the first Cardinal Archbishop of Rio Janeiro, Mons. Arcoverde; and Mons. Arcoverde consecrated Bishop by the late Cardinal Rampolla, Secretary of State of the late Pope Leo XIII. Mons. Mendez in his letters, offers Apostolic Succession to our

Church claiming that their succession is valid at the Vatican, and offering free tuition etc. to our seminarians who may go to Rio Janeiro. He also strongly presses a protest against our coming intercommunion with the Episcopal Church, and claims that the Brazilian Episcopate is about to bestow Apostolic Succession and valid orders to the Episcopate of the Mexican Church established during the regime of President Calles, etc." It is interesting to note that at the same time that Fr. Achútegui is warning the Episcopal Church not to have a Concordat with the Philippine Independent Church because of the character of Bishop Aglipay, a bishop of a Catholic body in Brazil having valid succession according to Rome, is offering the Apostolic Succession to the Independent Church, apparently without any qualms whatever.

CHAPTER XVI

1. *The Episcopal Church Annual 1961* (New York: Morehouse-Barlow Co.).
2. See *A Half Century in the Philippines* by Constance White Wentzel (New York: National Council of the Episcopal Church).

Index

Achútequi and Bernad, 57, 64-66, 88, 90, 93, 103, 128, 129, 137, 156, 164, 165, 193, 194, 197, 214
Agius, Archbishop, 183
Aglipay, Mons. Gregorio, 8, 53, 63, 64f., 69-76, 80-85, 87, 89, 90, 97, 99, 100, 101-110, 112, 113, 126, 128, 130, 137ff., 143-151, 155-158, 164, 165, 166, 171, 172, 179, 189, 194, 196, 197
Aguilar, Mons. Manuel N., 170, 180
Aguinaldo, General Emilio, 60, 62, 67, 69, 70-73, 81, 82, 109, 155ff., 164
Alcocer, Mons. Martin Garcia, 114, 120
American Catholics, 7
American and French Revolutions, 33
American Roman Catholic Bishops, 126, 182
Anda y Salazar, Don Simon de, 28ff., 34
Anglican Communion, 202
Apolinario de la Cruz, 30ff.
Apostolicae Curae, 190, 192
Archbishops Authority, 27
Articles of Religion (Phil. Ind. Ch.), 176ff.
Augustinian Order, 23, 29
Asamblea Magna, 170

Bad Press, 13
Barrows, David P., 14, 15
Bayaca, Mons. Gerado, 168, 170, 180

Bayne, Rt. Rev. Stephen F., Anglican Executive Officer, 200
Biak-na-bato, Peace of, 61, 67
Binsted, Rt. Rev. Norman S., 178, 179, 180, 203, 215
Blair and Robertson, 128
Bonifacio, Andrés, 41, 48, 60ff.
Bontife, Nava di, 95
Brent, Rt. Rev. Charles Henry, 135, 137, 179, 195, 196, 215
Brillantes, Fr. Pedro, 109, 149, 166
Burgos, Fr. José, 37, 52, 65

Calderon, 61, 96
Calendarios, 143
Campomanes, Mons. Hevia, 69, 75, 80, 93
Caroline Divines, 176
Castro, Fr. Servando, 149, 175, 176
Catholic Directory, 185
Cavite Mutiny, 38
Central Headquarters, 205
Chapelle, Placido Louis, 89, 94, 120
Clergy, shortage of, 204, 209
College of Liberal Arts, 210
Committee of Reform, 37
Concordat (proposed), 199f., 202, 203
Constitution (Malolos), 72
Constitution of Philippine Independent Church, 107, 167
Constitution (new) of Philippine Republic, 152, 155, 194

Cornish, Louis C., 30, 146-148f., 164
Counter Reformation, 183
Court of Appeals, Philippine, 169
"Cry of Balintawak," 60

Dandridge, Rt. Rev. E. P., 180
Democratic Party in the U.S., 82
Despujol, Governor General, 46, 48
Dewey, Admiral George, 61, 62, 68
Dix, Dom Gregory, 192
Dominicans, 25, 46, 48

Early, John C., 154
East Asia Conference of Churches, 199
Echevarría, Fr. Gregorio, 66
El Filibusterismo, 45
Elizabeth, Queen of England, 190-192
England, Church of, 4, 123, 137-139, 189, 190, 193
Episcopal Church, 8, 169, 179, 188, 194, 195, 212ff.
Episcopate, theory of, 109, 113, 114
Eucharistic Congress, 184
Eugenius IV, 192

Financial Problems, 205, 207
Fonacier, 100, 146, 166-169, 171, 175
Forbes, Cameron, 128
Foreign Trading Houses, 33
Foreman, 100, 150
Fox, George, 143
Franciscans, 25, 29
Freedom of Worship, 8
Friars, 4, 13, 23, 34, 35, 37, 41, 56, 65, 71, 92, 121, 122, 127, 128, 153
Fundamental Epistles, 8, 110, 112ff., 136, 144, 171

Gallardo, Fr. Eustaquio, 70
General Assembly, 166, 167
Gibson, Rt. Rev. Robert F., 203
Golden Age, 24
Gómez, Father, 36-41, 52, 120
Guidi, Giovanni Baptista, Apostolic Delegate, 107, 109, 120, 125, 126

Halifax, Lord, 192
Hall, U.S. Congressman, 147
Hayden, 2, 155, 156
Henry VIII, 190, 191, 196
Herzog, Bishop (Old Catholic), 137
Hocking, 20
Holy Catholic Church, 89, 123, 189
Hoover, Herbert, 147
House of Bishops, Episcopal, 200ff., 216
"Huk" Uprising, 157
Huss, John, 143

Ide, Henry C., 93
Igorots, 3, 16
"Independent Church of Filipino Christians," 171
India, influence on Philippines, 17ff.
Ivins, Rt. Rev. B.F.P., 180
Izquierdo, General Rafael de, 37

Jamias, Juan, 168
Japanese War, 167
Jesuits, 29, 30, 50, 70, 103, 104
Jones Act, 152

Katipunan, 39, 55, 58, 60, 108
Kennedy, Rt. Rev. Harry S., 180, 203
Knights of Columbus, 178
Kroeber, 17
Kullabeng, 101, 149

Labor movement, 59, 97, 102, 106, 127
Lagasca, Mons. Manuel, 103, 104, 164
Lagasca, Mons. Pedro, 164
La Solidaridad, 46, 52
Lathrop, John, 145
Layman's Organization, 199
Legaspi, Miguel López de, 23, 24
Leo XIII, 190, 192
LeRoy, James A., 16, 32
Lewis, C. S., 11
Liberalism, 37
Liberal Governments in Spain, 33
Lichtenberger, Arthur, Presiding Bishop of Episcopal Church, 200
Liga Filipina, 47

Lim, Senator Roseller T., 184, 186, 187
Ludlow, Rt. Rev. Theodore R., 180
Luna, General, 82
Luther, 143, 164, 196

McGovran, Dr. Donald A., 99

Mabini, Don Apolinario, 60, 71ff., 84, 85
Macabulos, General, 61, 62, 67
Malayan race, 14
Malolos Congress, 70, 144
Martínez, Archbishop, 35, 36, 38
Mary, Queen of England, 190
Masonry, 127, 144
Missionary expansion, 212
Mohammedans, 3, 18
Monotheism, 21
Morayta, 137
Morga, Judge Antonio de, 45
Moses, Bernard, 93
Myrick, Conrad, 167

Nash, Rt. Rev. Norman B., 180
Noli Me Tangere, 42
Non-Roman Communions, 8
North Borneo, colony in, 47
Nozaleda, Archbishop, 69ff., 78ff., 82, 83, 93, 94, 126

O'Connor, Rev. Patrick, 178
Oficio Divino, 136, 140f., 144, 149, 171
Ogilby, Rt. Rev. Lyman C., 200, 203, 213
Ogilby, Rev. Dr. Remsen B., 44
Old Catholic Church, 137ff., 150, 193
Orders, Monastic, 4, 8, 88, 184, 187
Ordinal, English, 191
Orthodox Church, 89
Orthodox Faith, 123
Osmena, Sergio, 153-155, 157

Paleontology, 13
Pandacan, 130, 131
Paniqui Assembly, 85, 86, 89, 95, 97, 106

Parker, Matthew, Archbishop, 190, 191, 196
Pelikan, 5, 6
Perfecto, Justice Gregorio, 59
Philip II, 23, 24
Philippine Assembly of 1907, 152
Philippine Commission, 92, 131, 152
Philippine Commonwealth, 152
Philippine Independent Church, 4, 8, 9, 11, 14, 39f., 88, 97, 102, 106, 108, 109, 118, 124, 126, 127, 129, 148, 169f., 176, 178-180f., 183, 187, 189, 193, 197, 216
Philippine Republic, 91, 215, 216
Pilar, General Gregorio del, 60, 90
Pilar, Marcelo del, 37, 46, 52
Pius IX, 5
Polish National Church, 193
Pope, 4, 86, 88, 89, 94, 95, 101, 102, 115, 121, 122, 136, 178
Prayer Book, new, 199
Press, influence of, 34, 107
Primitive Religion, 19ff.
Property, church, 108ff., 119, 128, 129, 132ff.
Protestants, 98, 106, 127, 138

Quae mari Sinico, Constitution, 110ff., 120ff., 126, 183
Queson, Manuel L., 146, 153, 155, 157, 159, 165
Quirino, Elpido, 165

Ramos, Benigno, 153, 155
Reese, Curtis W., 145
Reformation Church, 4, 8, 113, 123, 139, 143
Religious Education, 209
Religious Education Bill, 157ff.
Republican Party, 108
Reyes, Isabelo de los, Jr., 9, 126, 146, 165, 166, 168, 170, 172f., 175, 178, 180, 214
Reyes, Isabelo de los, Sr., 14, 22, 52f., 55f., 58, 95f., 97, 100, 102, 105, 139ff., 150, 151, 161ff., 172
Reyes, José, 105

Rizal, 4, 8, 22, 26, 39, 41ff., 52, 60, 61, 64, 65, 69
Roman Catholic Church, 5-8, 58, 89, 116, 134, 135, 159, 161, 178, 182, 183, 192, 214
Roman Catholic Laymen, 6
Roman Catholic State, 5
Romero, Pio, 85, 101, 149
Rosal, Fr. Nicolas L., 188, 214
Roxas, Manuel, 165
Revolt of South American Nations, 33
Revolution of 1898, 39
Rivera, Primo de, 55, 57

Saints, worship of, 123
St. Andrew's Theological Seminary, 201
St. Augustine, 5, 123
St. Hippolytus, 192
St. Serapion, 192
Santa Justa, 30, 34
Santo Tomás University, 13, 53, 121, 188
Sakdal Movement, 153ff.
Scholarships, 211
Secondary schools, 210
Secularization issue, 27, 35
Seminaries, Roman, 121
Sensacional Memoria, 55ff.
Separation of Church and State, 69, 70, 73, 125
Shepherd, Rev. Dr. Massey H., 193
Sherrill, Rt. Rev. Henry Knox, 179
South East Asia, 1, 2
Spain, 4
Stuntz, Homer C., 97, 127
Suez Canal, 34
Supreme Council, Philippine Independent Church, 107, 166ff., 179, 200

Supreme Court, Philippines, 131, 133-136, 157, 169f., 183
Supreme Court, U.S., 134
Syllabus of Errors, 5, 6

Taft, William Howard, 93, 97, 107, 108, 127, 131, 134f., 143
Taft, Mrs. William Howard, 125
Tangulan Revolt, 153f.
Terrero, Governor, 43, 44
Tiago, Capitan, 41
Tillich, Paul, 5, 89
Tinio, General, 69
Toynbee, 3
Treaty of Paris, 79, 135
Tydings-McDuffie Act, 152, 154

Unitarian Church, 143-145f., 148, 150f.
Urdeneta, Andrés de, 23, 24

Vatican Council, 6, 8

Wealth of the Friars, 25f.
Wendte, Charles W., 144
Whittemore, Rt. Rev. Lewis Bliss, 180
Wilbur, Earl M., 145
Wilner, Rt. Rev. Robert F., 180
Wise, Rev. Francis H., 35, 129f.
Woman's Auxiliary, 199
Worcester, Dean C., 93
World Council of Churches, 199
Wright, Luke E., 93
Wyclif, 143

Youth Organizations, 199

Zamora, Father, 37, 52